Can This Marriage Be Saved?

Can This Marriage Be Saved?

by

Paul Popenoe, Sc.D.

President
The American Institute of Family Relations

and

Dorothy Cameron Disney

Staff Associate of the Ladies' Home Journal

The Macmillan Company   New York

First printing, 1960

Library of Congress catalog card number: 60–8124
The Macmillan Company, New York
Brett-Macmillan Ltd., Galt, Ontario

Printed in the United States of America

Acknowledgments

The authors wish to thank the editors of the *Ladies' Home Journal* for permission to reprint the parts of this book which first appeared in that magazine.

8023

Introduction:

Marriage Counseling at the American Institute of Family Relations

When the American Institute of Family Relations opened its doors in Los Angeles, California, on February 4, 1930, we were incorporated as a nonprofit organization dedicated to employing the resources of modern science to strengthen marriage and family life. At that time there was much talk about the rising divorce rate, but almost no concerted effort was made to check it. Our undertaking, with skilled services available to everybody at minimum cost, was the first of its kind in the world.

In the beginning we had a group of four nationally known psychological consultants and eight medical consultants on whom to call whenever necessary. I myself did all of the marriage counseling with the sole aid of a retired psychiatric social worker, who also acted as the receptionist in our offices. To a large section of the general public in that day the purpose of marriage counseling was a mystery.

Our first client, a woman, appeared at my desk with a poorly dressed, dejected man who she announced was penniless. Despite this liability, she wanted to marry him. She had been informed that our chief function was to promote successful marriages, and she suggested it was my responsibility to lend her companion enough money so they could marry and start a new home. Unfortunately, my assistant and I were unable to meet this challenge; thus we failed on our very first case!

Another client of those early days was an orange grower to whom I gave a personality test. He listened with interest as I explained the results and said, "That's just about right." Then he asked, "Do you believe in numerology?"

"Not at all," I replied. "It hasn't the slightest scientific standing."

"Well," he rejoined, "I consulted a numerologist before coming here, and he told me exactly what you have just told me—only he didn't charge me so much for it!"

Still another client reported to me that his wife complained he did not support the family adequately, but that their money troubles were really all her fault. She controlled the finances and would not let him have enough capital to carry on his business and make a living. "What is your business?" I asked, and he replied after a momentary pause, "I play the races."

Most of our clients, of course, were burdened by far more serious worries. At that time Los Angeles had no Family Service, and people appealed to us with a wide range of questions they could not get answered elsewhere. A breakdown of our first 1000 cases shows that we gave assistance in premarital and child welfare problems, and advised on matters of education, law, heredity, and sex. Only 245 of our first 1000 cases were concerned with marital maladjustment, a field which now represents the major part of our work.

In our initial weeks of operation we began an active search for counselors who could be trained to specialize in marital problems. Locating candidates with satisfactory personalities and backgrounds and then educating them in the techniques of marriage counseling proved to be a demanding task. The more so, since we were obliged to discover and develop our techniques as we went along. Within a couple of years, however, we had a staff of twenty unique in experience and competence.

Today the Institute has sixty-one counselors and associate counselors, while there are also eight members of the administrative staff who do some counseling. In addition we have eight internes, who handle simple cases under supervision, and eleven trainees studying to become counselors.

As a basic part of our work, we conduct an extensive training course for counselors. Participants are very carefully selected. They must have a graduate degree in a field related to counseling. In the case of clergymen, who now make up about half of our trainees, a degree of bachelor of divinity suffices. Trainees must be (or have been) happily married, must have a natural aptitude for counseling, and must meet exacting requirements in emotional, ethical, and social maturity.

During thirty years of operation, we have given intensive training to more than 300 marriage counselors. We have given shorter courses of training in colleges, universities, and elsewhere over the country to more than 1500 other persons. Most of these people are teachers, clergymen, probation officers, public health nurses, youth organization executives, and others in similar positions who must do counseling in the course of their work whether they want to or not and whether they know how or not. We feel that any assistance we are able to lend in this particular area is of far-reaching value. During the last quarter of a century we have worked steadily to raise the standards of marriage counseling. Many people who claim to be marriage counselors are well meaning but untrained; others have scholastic training but in fields unrelated to counseling.

We carry our interest in advancing education for marriage directly to the public by working through high schools and colleges. Our home-study course in sex education is popular with parent-teacher groups as well as with individual parents. We publish a monthly bulletin, *Family Life*, which circulates news of activities in our field and reviews of current literature on the subject. Our educational specialists speak in churches, Sunday schools, clubs, and community organizations of all kinds. We have put on nearly 300 conferences throughout the United States, sponsored for the most part by colleges, universities, or public-school systems. Our lecturers have appeared in approximately 200 colleges and universities and in innumerable high schools, churches, and women's and civic clubs.

In the past few years we have begun to educate young women for normal childbirth. By means of lectures on prenatal care and by training in childbirth which includes individual instruction in muscular conditioning and breathing exercises desirable for the different stages of labor, we provide intellectual, emotional, and physical preparation, primarily for expectant mothers, but we hold classes for husbands, too. We also conduct a lecture course for wives called, "Less Work, More Fun, for Homemakers." In this course we outline various short cuts and timesavers in housekeeping, but we lay our main stress upon teaching wholesome attitudes toward domestic duties, ways to win the cooperation of children and the collaboration of husbands.

We offer special assistance and emotional support to senior citizens, whose numbers are increasing so rapidly. At the other end of the scale we work in the sphere of child guidance. A recent expansion in this activity of ours was made possible by doubling the size of our office building and through the generosity of Mr. and Mrs. Lee B. Milbank of Pasadena. Assisting disturbed children demands a highly specialized staff and specialized equipment.

Children are counseled directly, through play therapy and other modern techniques. Necessarily much of our work with youngsters is done through their parents. Almost invariably the relationship between father and mother benefits when we help their children; quarrels over children loom large in many unsuccessful marriages. Husband and wife cannot be very happy if their children are in constant difficulties, nor can children develop normally if their parents are in continual conflict. Our ability to help the entire family is one of our great strengths.

We deal with problems of adolescence, with problems of choosing a mate, with courtship quandaries. Two sets of parents sometimes call on us accompanied by a high-school boy and girl who have "got into trouble." The whole group sits down with a counselor to figure out how the situation can best be faced.

With our premarital service we aim to assist engaged couples to enter marriage with as great a prospect of success as possible. We do not consider it our function to advise the young people whether they are qualified to marry or whether they should marry each other. Usually they come to us a few weeks before the wedding date, have planned the marriage, and we feel our task is to help them ensure its success. With this objective we try to teach them to understand themselves as well as to understand the personality and temperament of the other person. We aid them in setting up a budget. We help in preparing them for the sexual adjustment which will be the first major adjustment in their marriage.

So much research in our field has been published in the last ten years that it is hard to believe how little was available a generation ago. There were almost no statistics and definite information on the subject of love and marriage. From the outset we undertook numerous investigations and surveys of matters we needed to understand in order to work more effectively with clients.

Where did married couples first meet each other? Most frequently, we found, in school. Second in importance were introductions by friends and meetings at ordinary social affairs, followed closely by "business contacts." If young women did not find future husbands in the educational system and were short of friends, they were largely limited to marrying men with whom they worked.

How long did couples know each other before they became engaged? About two years in the educated (high school or better) part of the population; one year of acquaintance was usual with the less educated.

Where did couples become engaged? Most frequently in an automobile, the only place in a good many instances a young man could find sufficient privacy to propose.

How long did the average engagement last? A year among the educated, six months among those with less education.

How many times had the average girl been engaged? Once before the engagement that ended in marriage.

The Institute collected most of the detailed case material the late Lewis M. Terman of Stanford University used in his epoch-making book, *Psychological Factors in Marital Happiness;* but in recent years our research department has been largely concentrated upon studying our own procedures with a view to improving them in every possible way.

During the past decade we have placed increasing emphasis upon group counseling, which is less expensive and frequently has other marked advantages. We have been especially successful with group counseling for women (and men) who are overweight. Since the fundamental problem of the obese so often has an emotional basis, counseling is a necessary supplement of other treatments.

We have been equally successful in counseling groups in a skill we describe as "Social Effectiveness." These groups are composed of young women (or men) who have passed the average age of marriage. They are thirty years of age or beyond it. They want to marry but do not seem to know how to do so. We make no effort to introduce these young women to men—as a rule they are meeting men every day—but we endeavor to teach them how to reach a more satisfying relationship with other human beings. Through group counseling, lecture courses, and individual counseling we aid these young people to rid themselves of the feelings of inadequacy, the doubts and fears, and, perhaps, we help loosen excessive emotional ties to their own families that may hinder them from making a good adjustment socially. They learn how to face the world on even terms with a richer living experience and, in many instances, how to achieve a happy marriage. We have helped nearly 1000 women and a quarter as many men in this way.

During recent years, the Institute's case load has averaged about 15,000 consultations of one hour each, each year. We are open for business from Monday morning through Saturday evening with office hours from 9 A.M. to 9 P.M. Our latest weekly report, covering a six-day period, lists interviews with 347 clients.

Our most recent analysis of our work—we arrived at the results by removing numbers of cases at random from our files and then tabulating the information each contained—disclosed that 87 per cent of our counseling was done with married couples, 13 per cent with single persons. Among the unmarried were people who wanted to wed, people with problems of personality and temperament, questions about heredity, and the like. Women accounted for 65 per cent of the group, men for only 35 per cent. In our work with couples 57 per cent of the time was devoted to wives. Nearly half of our clients visited us on the recommendation of members of their family or of friends; others were referred to us by physicians, ministers, lawyers, teachers, employers.

A very large proportion of the unhappy couples who seek our help have been married from five to fourteen years, although we have counseled brides and grooms of one day and, on occasion, elderly couples who have been married half a century. A tabulation of 961 cases in our records showed the following distribution:

	Cases	Per Cent
First year of marriage	106	11
Second year	96	10
Third year	54	5.5
Fourth year	55	5.5
Fifth year to ninth	266	28
Tenth to fourteenth	180	19
Fifteenth to nineteenth	108	11
Twentieth to twenty-ninth	75	8
Thirtieth and up	21	2
	961	100

In a tabulation of 1000 cases (including a few where the client failed to state), we established the median age of the unhappily married men at thirty-five, the women at thirty-three. The distribution was as follows:

Age	993 Men		942 Women	
	(number)	(per cent)	(number)	(per cent)
19 and under	4	0.5	21	2
20-24	68	7	136	14
25-29	181	17	198	21
30-34	215	22	191	20
35-39	193	20	166	19
40-44	129	13	113	12
45-49	97	10	57	6
50-59	77	7.5	49	5
60 and over	29	3	11	1
	993	100	942	100

An examination of 1130 cases showed that the couples averaged two children per family, the figures being:

Number of Couples	Per Cent of Total	Number of Children in the Family
137	12	Had no children
115	10	Did not state
266	24	Had one child
370	33	Had two children
166	15	Had three children
55	5	Had four children
15	1	Had five children
4		Had six children
2		Had eight children
1130	100	Total children, 1839

If excessive childbearing is a factor in family disharmony, it is not revealed by our records. Large families rarely appear as a cause of dissension in the unhappy marriages we treat, which possibly may be explained by the fact that we draw upon the better educated part of the population. Most of our clients are business or professional people or skilled workmen. A research project we carried out some years ago seems to indicate that the happiness of a marriage is favorably associated with the number of children. By studying 5260 completed marriages in which it was certain no more children would be born, we found the following:

	0 or 1 Child		*4, 5, or More*	
Happy	2259	58%	1115	72%
Doubtful	288	11	135	10
Unhappy	1173	31	290	18
	3720	100%	1540	100%

A study of 852 couples indicated that the trouble which brought them to us was severe. More than a quarter were living separately or were divorced. Specifically, 182 couples were separated, and thirty-one couples were divorced.

In another cross section made of clients complaining of marital problems we discovered that 27 per cent reported a previous marriage and divorce. There is reason to believe this figure may be too low; some people refrain from acknowledging past failures. The clients who admitted to previous marriages and divorces showed up on our personality tests as less stable than the once married. Indeed, we could trace a definite correlation between a rise in the instability of personality and a rise in the number of divorces.

In three-quarters of all our cases of marital maladjustment it is the wife who first comes to see us, but usually we are able to persuade the husband to come in afterward. If one spouse is miserable in the marriage, the other is most unlikely to be happy. It is seldom difficult to obtain the husband's cooperation. One man, who came in some years ago upon request, is still recalled with amusement by members of our staff. He was most cordial: "Fine work you are doing here. I am very much in favor of it. But I don't see why you called me in. There wouldn't be a bit of trouble in our home if Mary would just do what I tell her to!" Perhaps 20 per cent of the time we see the wife only. The husband may be too hard pressed with his work, out of town, or uncooperative. The wife may not want him to know she is seeking help. While we prefer to see both partners, it is not necessary to successful counseling. We are quite ready to deal with the wife alone and ordinarily can help her meet the problems of the marriage by herself.

There are many instances where we deal with a half-dozen or more people. There may be the man and his wife, "the other woman" and perhaps her husband, a grown son or daughter, a mother-in-law or two. Family difficulties may involve as many as ten persons with whom the counselor must work at least briefly before a tangled situation can be straightened out. It is not rare for an erring husband to insist upon introducing "the other woman" to the counselor: "I just want you to see what a fine person she is."

Everyone concerned with marriage counseling is aware of the resistance to it on the part of many people. Intelligent men and women will destroy their marriages in the divorce court, at great expense and suffering, rather than admit they need help.

"This is my problem—if I can't solve it for myself, nobody else can solve it for me," is a common remark. People would not think of offering such an excuse if the automobile, television set, or plumbing were out of order! Marriage counselors are trained to understand and cope with the problems of marriage just as a mechanic is trained to repair a balky motor.

"We can't afford the expense," is another frequent remark. No amount of marriage counseling is as costly as the average divorce.

"The counselor will tell me that I'm crazy," other people say. They confuse marriage counseling with psychiatry—not that a psychiatrist is likely to tell a patient he is crazy.

"The counselors will try to tell me what to do," some people fear. "They will make me get a divorce," or "They won't let me get a divorce." No counselor ever intends to make any decision for a client. His function is to guide the client into thinking through his own problem more carefully, so that he can make his own decision on the basis of all the evidence, not on the basis of ignorance or a momentary whim.

Counseling is one form of education. There are many things most of us should have learned but were not taught. The counselor attempts to help individuals make up these deficiencies.

Well-informed people frequently do not understand themselves. We give modern personality and temperament tests to all our clients. They supply their own answers to the questions without advice or suggestions from anyone. Later, in studying the results of the tests, the client realizes that he is seeing himself, as in a mirror, through his own eyes. He is not taking somebody else's word—he has described his own personality. Often he is surprised, and aided, by this process of self-evaluation.

Many people do not understand the opposite sex. Frequently a wife relating a long list of grievances acquires a different view of her husband when a counselor suggests to her, "Every man normally behaves that way. Ask any woman of your acquaintance, and she will say the same of her husband. After all, your husband is merely behaving like a man. If he were not a man, you would not have married him!"

Husband and wife are always seen separately. Consequently the counselor and client can discuss the troubles in an atmosphere of calm and quiet. The counselor knows how and why other marriages have succeeded, and why some have failed. He puts this knowledge at the disposal of the client, who very often is convinced that his or her misery is unique. The counselor can be helpful, too, in serving as a neutral mediator, in interpreting one person to another; for instance he can help daughter-in-law and mother-in-law take a fresh and more impersonal look at each other.

Re-education demands time, effort, determination. It may involve changes in attitudes and habits that require long practice. The counselor can guide and encourage, but the client must do the work. Usually an hour a week for a month is enough to put a client on the right track. Then it is up to him to keep going.

The Institute has helped approximately 25,000 couples to strengthen their marriages by direct counseling in our offices, while many other thousands have been aided by our educational work all over the country. Our work has been centered not upon the problem of divorce but upon making marriages happy—which prevents divorce. We believe that almost any two normal people can make a success of marriage if they want to and know how. We believe that a majority of all divorces are unnecessary and undesirable for all concerned. We believe that a moderate amount of effort before marriage, and in most instances even after difficulties become serious, would prevent a large percentage of the divorces which now total about 400,000 a year in the United States.

Paul Popenoe, Sc. D., President
The American Institute of Family Relations
5287 Sunset Boulevard
Los Angeles 27, California

Contents

Section I: The Triangle

Thousands of marriages are destroyed every year because a husband or a wife becomes infatuated with some other person. Many divorces could be avoided if young couples and older couples, too, had more information about the nature and causes of infidelity and used a little more intelligence after they found themselves involved in a triangle.

Unfortunately, once a husband tells his wife that he no longer loves her and is desperately in love with some other woman, she is likely to take him at his word. That is the first mistake she makes and it may be irremediable. If she will recognize that such a declaration is frequently based on emotion rather than on reason, she will usually be able to win back her husband if she really wants him.

What is infatuation? If you look up the word in the dictionary, you will find that its root meaning is something like, "To make a fool of yourself." As with most words concerning the emotions ("love" is a conspicuous example) it can be stretched to mean almost anything. There is some validity in the young woman's plaintive statement: "When your parents approve of your choice, it's love; when they don't, it's infatuation." Infatuation is sometimes described as "love without respect"; frequently we hear the remark from clients: "I love him, but I really don't like him very well."

Infatuations may be classified as *ascending* or *descending*, according to whether the third person involved—the outsider—is higher or lower in social, educational, and economic status. Men are inclined to become the victims of a descending infatuation. A man's sub-conscious aim in infatuation is to make himself feel important in his own eyes. He can most easily build up his sense of importance by seeking out some inferior woman to play up to him and assure him that he is simply wonderful (whereas his wife has probably been telling him just the opposite). A woman usually achieves an ascend-ing infatuation; it is a habit of the feminine sex to search for the superior both in and out of marriage. A woman can rarely make her-self feel more important by throwing herself at some inferior man.

Infatuation is almost always evidence that the marriage itself has failed. Usually a husband is at least unconsciously trying to punish his wife by "falling in love" with some other woman. Unless the wife knows what is happening, the punishment misses its mark. This explains why the husband often manages to leave a wide trail of in-criminating evidence—a letter in his coat pocket, a vanity case, a lipstick-smeared handkerchief in his automobile. These "accidents" are not really accidental, although the erring husband may firmly believe so. If the telltale evidence is overlooked, he is quite likely to break down and confess the truth to his wife. In other instances, of course, she is alerted by a friend ("I don't like to tell you this, my dear, but I feel that you have a right to know"), or she receives an anonymous telephone call. The frequency of these anonymous calls is almost unbelievable.

Once the wife knows there is another woman in the case, she fre-quently makes every conceivable mistake.

Her wisest course is to sit down as calmly as possible and ask her-self what she really wants. If she wants a divorce she has grounds any state will accept and many of her friends will heartily approve. On the contrary, if she wants to save her marriage she should use her head and plan and think toward that objective. Consider instead the errors she so often makes:

She goes to the other woman and begs her to "please leave my husband alone. Don't break up our home and deprive our children of their father." If the other woman were sensitive, considerate, altruistic, and honorable she might reply favorably to the plea.

However, if she possessed such virtues she would not be the other woman.

In many instances the wife's unconscious motive in seeking out the other woman is to satisfy her own curiosity. She cannot help believing that the woman who has stolen her husband must be endowed with the glamour and sex appeal of a movie queen. Often she is astonished to find her rival is inferior to herself. "Why, she's nothing!" wives continually report to us. "She's not nearly as good looking as I am. She doesn't dress well. Her grammar is atrocious. She is slovenly. What on earth can my husband see in somebody like her?"

Few wives realize that their husbands in their subconscious determination to punish and wound have chosen an unworthy woman to admire, almost deliberately ensured their intrigue be discovered, and thus are saying in effect, "You can see what I think of you if I prefer this miserable creature to you." It is seldom that a woman gains in insight from a meeting with her rival. Such encounters are painful, humiliating, and unrewarding.

Although the wife may refrain from confronting the other woman, she rarely is able to resist the temptation to upbraid and denounce her guilty husband from morning until night. Her object is to make him feel ashamed of himself. But the procedure is not calculated to win back his affections or make her more attractive to him. Even if the husband has told her about his infatuation in so many words, the wife should try not to allude to it in any way. Ideally, she should behave as though the situation did not exist.

A common mistake is for the injured wife to eject her husband from the marriage bed and deny him further sexual intercourse. This automatically throws him into the arms of the other woman.

Still another mistake. The average wife assumes her husband's infatuation is based solely upon sex. This assumption may result from the wife's feelings of guilt about her own failings in the sexual area, but in any case her assumption is usually incorrect. Ordinarily an infatuation is far less dependent upon a sexual attraction than upon plain, garden-variety ego. It cannot be emphasized too strongly that the husband in pursuit of another woman is consciously or subconsciously attempting to make himself feel important while simultaneously he injures his wife.

Many wives appeal to relatives and friends for sympathy, asking them to intercede and argue with the husband. Some call on the husband's parents to expostulate with him. Others bring in the clergyman to pray with him. Most wives broadcast their troubles everywhere, apparently operating on the premise that the more they can humiliate the husband, the more attractive he will find them and the greater will be his desire to return to the hearthside. Does this make sense?

Finally the wife's mistake is to assume that the catastrophe which has befallen the marriage is entirely the fault of her husband. Seldom is this true. When a man or a woman strays—infidelity is by no means confined to the male sex—almost inevitably there is something seriously wrong in their relationship. In some vital way the husband or the wife has failed to understand and satisfy the other's basic needs.

A wife who wants to triumph over infidelity, rout her rival, and maintain the marriage should bear in mind that time is on her side. Her chances are excellent if she does not make foolish mistakes and throw the game away.

More specifically, what *should* she do? The general principles are fairly constant.

"Saw wood and say nothing," is a good beginning. Then she might review the whole marriage to find what it lacks and what she has neglected to put into it. There are certain things every man has a right to expect from marriage. Without regard to the order of importance, we might list:

Emotional security. A husband has a right to expect that his wife will not flirt with other men, that she will not be childishly and unreasonably jealous and make him miserable by her destructive jealousy. (Of course, all this works both ways. A wife has a right to expect from marriage the same things her husband does.)

Financial security. A man has a right to expect that his earnings will not be squandered, that his wife will be a competent manager and cooperate in making ends meet.

Normal sexual life. If a wife does not fulfill her husband's sexual requirements she is taking grave risks with the marriage.

Companionship. Husbands are not too exacting on this point in most instances—usually it is the housebound wife who yearns for adult company and conversation—but men, too, are entitled to have an intelligent and thoughtful companion with whom they can enjoy associating.

Children. If a husband wants to be a father, as most men do, and his wife refuses to bear children, she is not living up to what he has a right to expect.

Wives and husbands, too, whose marriages are under attack and who desire to preserve them, should give the offender every chance to break away from the infatuation without loss of face. An infatuation, it has been said, has something in common with narcotic addiction. The dope addict who is "hooked" does not take the drug so much for the pleasure it gives as to escape the pain that not taking it would induce. He fears, with good reason, the withdrawal symptoms.

The claim that "I love her and nothing can change that" is heard many times every day at the Institute. Although no wife should argue such a matter with her husband, our counselors often say to such a man, "When you met your wife and married her, you loved her. You were sure nothing could change that love. Now you tell me it has not only changed but disappeared, that you now love another woman and nothing can change this new love. Isn't it obvious logically that you may be mistaken on the point? According to your own story, you have already demonstrated the possibility."

❖   ❖   ❖

A dead love cannot only be revived, but often there is abundant proof that the first love is not really dead. More than 5000 cases dealing with infidelity crowd our files at the Institute. Each case tells an entirely different and usually highly complex story. Infidelity is seldom what it seems to the outsider.

Dick and Andrea Weymer, as we will call them, are a good example of this point. There is no question that Andrea Weymer would have been described as a selfless and ideal wife by nearly everybody except her husband.

The Weymers were approaching their twentieth anniversary when Dick announced to Andrea that he was in love with another woman. He did not know Clarice Johnson's age, her middle name, or the color of her eyes. He had seen her only four times in his life. Yet he was apparently ready to walk out on his devoted wife and family and give up a job paying $14,000 a year to join this comparative stranger. His only explanation was that he and Andrea had no common interests and could not communicate.

Since the Weymers had communicated well enough to produce four children and had in common twenty years of life together, Andrea was convinced the answer lay elsewhere. An humble, self-effacing woman, she believed she had let Dick down in some mysterious way and she called on us to find out where and how.

Her husband's revolt had come to Andrea as a breath-taking surprise. She told us everything had seemed as usual when Dick left their Los Angeles home to spend the month of March inspecting a chain of middle western factories. Dick Weymer was a consulting engineer, brilliant in his field. Andrea wistfully admitted that she was sometimes tiresome company for him; she regretted she had little time to read. But she had always left the books to Dick and kept his house in order and the children quiet so he could read in peace.

It was during Dick's middle western tour that he met Clarice Johnson. What happened on his return can best be told in thirty-eight-year-old Andrea's own words as reported in our files:

*   *

The minute Dick walked in the front door I knew something had gone wrong. Dick can't fool me about how he feels. From his droopy mouth and the way his eyes were pulled together, I could tell he had one of his nervous headaches. It makes Dick sulky to be pestered with questions, so I asked none. Nor did I bury him in family news. When I unpacked his bags, I discovered he'd brought back nothing for the children. With the two oldest, it didn't matter. But Scott and Tommy had been looking forward to what Daddy would bring them. I produced a baseball and a catcher's mitt from a supply of toys I store in a closet for such emergencies. Dick grumbled that I'd raised Scott and Tommy—one is seven, the other is five—to be materialistic and grasping.

By now I felt sure he must have run into difficulties on his trip, although the notion of another woman didn't cross my mind. I suspected business troubles again. Few of Dick's associates make sufficient allowance for his disposition, his touchiness. Since he throws all of himself into his work, it isn't human to expect him to get along without appreciation from his bosses. My compliments can't serve as a substitute; I'm too ignorant. If Dick's work is criticized, or if he imagines he is being slighted, he boils inside, really boils.

Once I remember he invented a new method of installing heavy machinery or moving it—I never got the straight of exactly what he did—which saved so much money for his employers that he was invited to be a guest of honor at the annual banquet. The company president publicly congratulated Dick, but mispronounced his last name. Next week, without a word of explanation, Dick resigned and took a position at a lower salary with another engineering firm. Later on, for some reason, he got the notion I had suggested the change, and he fumed and fussed at me for a long while. I didn't mind. Indeed, I was glad he could blame me and get the unpleasantness out of his system.

Nearly always Dick comes back from an out-of-town assignment discouraged with the work he's done, angry with somebody or other, and tied in knots with nerves and tension. I do my best to help him past the rough spot. Long ago, during my childhood, when I was being shunted from pillar to post, now with this relative, now with that one, I decided that some day I would grow up and make a *real* home for my husband and children. I always try to welcome Dick from his trips so he will want to hurry back to us next time.

The evening of his return from the Midwest I wore my newest green dress—bright green is the color he prefers on me—and a new hairdo. Dick didn't comment on the dress but he did comment on the hairdo, which he disliked. I cooked his favorite dishes for supper: fried chicken, creamed potatoes, baby Limas. Our daughter Janet baked a perfect lemon meringue pie. Dick ate crackers and milk.

For Janet's sake I urged a tiny piece of pie on him. Janet is fourteen and devoted to her daddy. Dick shook his head and snapped that both she and I should skip pastries and improve our looks. My weight is average, according to the tables printed on the penny scales, but to appease Dick's admiration for bed-slat figures I starve myself and cut out starches and sugar. Janet is thin as a bean pole and supersensitive about her appearance. I excused her from the table before she burst into tears, and joined her in the kitchen. I threw my diet overboard, ate two slices of her pie, praised it to the skies, and smoothed her vanity.

When Janet and I carried in the coffee, a storm was brewing between Dick and Ellis, our seventeen-year-old son. It seems to me those two have been at odds ever since Ellis was in rompers. Ellis was planning to go to the movies, and Dick had ordered him to stay home and study. Ellis leads his high-school class, wouldn't dream of skimping his lessons for a movie, and, like all teen-agers, resents taking orders. Ellis was standing up, stiff as a ramrod, in a humor to be ugly and defiant. I laid my hand on the boy's shoulder and got him to sit down again. He mumbled an apology, I am glad to say. I have trained my youngsters to obey and respect their daddy. In matters of discipline I stand with Dick, even when I don't agree with him.

That night when Dick and I went to bed, it turned out we were in for a siege of his insomnia. I'm scared to death of sleeping pills, but in our house they are as common as jelly beans. Dick took his usual number but couldn't close an eye. I rubbed his back and massaged the muscles of his neck. I brought him the heating pad and a pot of hot chocolate. He declined the pad, threw out the chocolate. In those black, sleepless moods, a devil seems to possess him. After working himself into a fury, Dick jerked the bedclothes from his bed and stamped off to the couch in his dressing room. I put my head under the blankets so he couldn't hear and cried myself to sleep.

Before that week was over, I was at my wits' end. Dick made the children's existence a misery and he made himself sick, horribly sick, from nerves and strain. He couldn't eat; he couldn't go to work. I tried him with milk toast, I tried him with a young boiled chicken—cooked French style with leeks and a single carrot—I tried him with my special gelatins. Finally I called the doctor. As usual, our doctor found nothing physically wrong and, as usual, recommended a change of scenery.

With our family a change of scenery means piling in the station wagon and driving to the mountains. We bought a cabin the summer Janet was born. In the old days, Dick was as big a kid about roughing it as any of my other children. It used to be the five of them could hardly wait for the camping season to begin. Ordinarily we keep the cabin closed from Christmas until June. When I suggested we open it for an early week end the youngsters were wildly enthusiastic. Dick himself seemed agreeable to the idea; anyway, he didn't say no. I hoped the mountain air would be relaxing and help him to unwind. I hoped the good times he'd had there in the past would bring him to himself. On the evening of our arrival I could see we might as well have stayed at home. Dick was indifferent to everything and plainly showed it.

Neither Dick nor I have happy recollections of childhood. I have tried to build up pleasant traditions and customs for our own children to remember in later years. We have family jokes, family rules and regulations, family singing and reading aloud; we even have a family burial ground for pets.

Every year Dick is supposed to lay and light the first fire of the family camping season. This time he forgot the fire-lighting ceremony. I managed to smuggle the logs in from the woodpile without anybody noticing. I laid the fire. I then slipped a box of matches in Dick's hand. His mind was a thousand miles away. He gave a jump, stared at me as though he was a stranger who had just dropped down from Mars. Ellis grabbed the matches and lighted the fire.

Our first meal of the season always consists of baked ham, brown bread, and beans. Scott and Tommy set the table—their task. I sharpened the knives, but Dick didn't carve the ham. He asked me to slice it in the kitchen. After the meal, he was expected to choose and lead us in a song while Janet played a guitar accompaniment. She brought her guitar to the table, but her daddy did no singing. He stared at Janet and at the guitar in the same funny way he had stared at me. She struck a chord. Whereupon Dick got up from his chair and walked out the door. Our dog hopped up and followed. Dick shoved Spot back inside the cabin and slammed the door. A moment later we heard him crashing through the underbrush.

His manner was so peculiar I was badly scared, but I knew he wouldn't want the boys to go hunting him. I went outside myself. The moon was up. In a few minutes, not far away, I came on Dick. He was sitting on a fallen tree trunk, hunched over, his chin buried in his hands. In the moonlight he looked woebegone and solitary. I went to him and put my arms around him.

It was then I learned business worries weren't what ailed my husband. The whole story of Clarice came tumbling out. Dick was dreadfully upset, almost crying. I remember wishing I could think of something to say or do that would ease him. I felt like someone in the middle of a bad dream. I simply couldn't believe Dick could fall in love with another woman on such a slight acquaintance. After a while he admitted that novelty and excitement probably had more to do with his feelings toward Clarice than tenderness and sweetness. He agreed to stop seeing or writing to her for the time being, but he then announced he intended to move out of our home to a boardinghouse near his place of business. For the next six months he says he wants to be by himself so he can mull and brood and "think things out." What he is likely to do, I realize, is think me and our children out of his life. At an age when most men draw their families closer and feel like settling down, Dick is anxious to shed his past and start all over again.

His attitude nearly breaks my heart. For he seems determined to wipe away all the worth and the memories, all the meaning, of our twenty years of marriage. Some of the things he said to me, while we sat there on the fallen log, cut deeper than the fact of his infidelity. He told me I was dull and stupid, uninteresting, that I did not inspire him. He told me that he and I had always been unsuited, that we had never loved each other and should not have married.

I guess I shouldn't speak for Dick, but the fact is he and I fell in love practically on sight. I was eighteen and a high-school senior, earning my keep by acting as a mother's helper for a cousin whose husband was a reserve lieutenant in the Navy. When my cousin's husband came back from a six-months' cruise, he told us about a handsome young sailor he considered the smartest member of his crew. On Thanksgiving Day my cousin invited Dick to turkey dinner. Regardless of Dick's present attitude, I know he carries in his heart the memory of that Thanksgiving Day, its warmth and cheer. Very soon he was begging me to be his wife. At twenty he was even more home-hungry than I was. I had a home until I was nine; then my father deserted us, and our family broke up. Dick was only two years old when his mother ran off and left him in the care of a no-account, crackpot father, an educated man but a vagabond too worthless to provide an education or a decent roof for his son. Dick joined the Navy at sixteen.

Dick and I were the parents of two children before we saved enough money for him to quit the Navy and put his full time on engineering studies. During those years I was always tired, always sleepy. I baked pies and cakes at home for a bakery chain to help out financially, and my days began at 5 A.M.

Whatever Dick wanted I have always wanted, too. I don't forget he has the family brains, while I am quite an ordinary sort of woman. Not once through the years have I objected to his restless shifting from job to job, or questioned whether his salary would go up or go down. I just manage on the amount he provides. In the whole of our marriage I have never taken a step nor made a decision without considering what his preference would be.

Maybe Dick should have married a different kind of woman, the kind who could have helped him climb higher and faster in his profession. But I doubt if Dick's conscience will give him any rest in the future if he curses our children with a broken home. He remembers too well his own painful and crazy boyhood.

❀   ❀

It was true that her husband had not forgotten his unhappy youth. At forty-one, Dick Weymer was a handsome man, but deep, nervous lines were sketched around his mouth. There was a mixture of wariness and suspicion in his manner when he talked to us about himself and his unusual childhood:

❀   ❀

I grew up as haphazardly as Huck Finn, was as ragged, and I am dead certain I washed as seldom. My father owned a fairly prosperous trucking concern in the East when my mother ran out on him and me. A short time after, in a matter of months, he owned nothing except one old beat-up truck.

The two of us set up a residence in the truck and took to the open road before any of his relatives had a chance to point out he had picked a peculiar type nursery for a youngster. My father was a great guy in some ways, in other ways an unregenerate bum. He blamed my mother for his comedown in the world, but I have always believed my dad's lamentations and tirades against the female sex were strictly camouflage. He thoroughly enjoyed our vagabond existence.

Not me. I loathed it. Kids, as you've probably observed, are essentially conventional. When I was four or five, my father knocked together a sort of wooden shack, balanced on two wagon wheels, and attached it to the rear end of the truck. He fondly called this rattletrap creation a trailer. My passionate prayer was that our "trailer" would fall to pieces, as it constantly threatened to do, and that just once we would sleep in a clean, orderly house or a decent hotel among clean, orderly, decent people. It never happened. I don't recall that my father ever paid for a night's lodging. He refused to pay for anything he could scrounge, wangle, or pry loose —and I mean, pry loose. Dad has been dead for years, but even now I have a recurrent nightmare about him and something that happened when I was six. In my dream, he and I are in the truck riding speedily away from a filling station somewhere in northern Illinois, and between us on the seat lies a monkey wrench he "forgot" to hand back to the attendant. I wake up from this nightmare, trembling, and drenched in sweat.

My father wasn't a thief in the ordinary sense of the word. But that wrench became a kind of symbol to me of his whole philosophy. My father had a deep contempt for society, for organized groups, for law and order.

Sometimes we parked our mobile shack in a hobo jungle. Other times we trespassed in a farmer's field or woods or beside his pond —my rare baths were taken in the open—until the farmer woke up to our presence and put us off his land. My father interpreted an eviction as a challenge to his ingenuity, and often we would make a stealthy night return. Frequently we were ejected three or four times from the same place and sometimes we were chased by the police. Two great dreads of my fear-ridden childhood were the police, who might drag us off to jail, and social workers, who might drag me off to an orphanage. Occasionally we were descended upon by a delegation of local ladies, charitably inclined no doubt. But they poked and pried and questioned, and wounded my pride by the condescending way they bestowed their largesse. After these visitations, I usually got sick and couldn't eat.

Perhaps once a month my father sloshed a bucket of water through our two-wheeled shack and called it a housecleaning. Ants and spiders ran about the greasy, crumb-strewn floor, acting as our janitors. I guess that background made me a fanatic about cleanliness. Sometimes now I can hear myself yelling at Andrea because of a messy ash tray or because the kids have tracked in mud, and I swear to you I have the same choked sensation I used to have with my father in that shack.

He and I seldom stayed anywhere long enough to come to the attention of the school authorities, and my primary schooling was decidedly informal. Incredible as it may seem, Dad was a college graduate and he was also clever with his hands. He taught me to make boats, trains, cranes—small-scale accurate models of the real thing—out of scraps of wood and steel picked up in junk yards. He read aloud to me from Dickens, Thackeray, Veblen, Whitman, any favorite of his available in the nearest public library. But I was eight years old before I learned to read and write; I was miserably humiliated by my ignorance and kept it secret. One day I carefully traced the word "cigarette" from a magazine advertisement, and exhibited the tracing to my father as a sample of my "handwriting." This piece of deception alerted him to the fact that literacy is not inborn, and he then taught me my letters.

Later we settled in a town long enough for me to enroll in school. There I made a friend. Bob owned a toy dump truck, and it was out of kilter. I repaired the dump truck, and Bob invited me to come to his house for lunch. His mother took one look at my clothes and tactfully, very tactfully, herded me and my small host out of the dining room into the kitchen. I choked down her food, but I can still remember my shame and anger. I never spoke to Bob again.

I learned at a tender age to keep to myself and shy away from the vast, well-scrubbed majority who would insult and patronize me. The habit sticks. Andrea says I'm too standoffish and suspicious of people. She is too naïve, too gentle-natured, to grasp the cruelty and evil in human beings or to conceive of the close infighting waged all the time in the name of competition. At the rare social gatherings we attend with business associates I hear her prattling on about my early struggles to rise from the muck. I shrivel inside and want to shout at her to be quiet. You need to be a millionaire or an acknowledged genius before you dare make capital of a background like mine.

As a child the only escape I could see—the doorway from the hobo jungle to the parlor of the gentry, so to speak—was through education. How I hurled myself at my books and studies when I had a chance! I did manage to get a high-school diploma before I went to sea. It's impossible for me to convey how much the Navy meant to me. I will never forget my joy at the antiseptic cleanliness of my first ship, or the shining beauty I found in the engine room. Perhaps I couldn't get close to people, but I could get close to a reciprocating, knee-joint engine. I knew that by education and training I could become the master of a beautiful, marvelously intricate, and efficient machine.

The big mistake I made was in marrying young. If I'd had the good sense to remain a bachelor I might have accomplished something worthwhile in my field instead of sinking into mediocrity. Andrea hasn't the faintest glimmering of the potentialities of my profession and frequently drives me almost mad by praising my not-too-extraordinary achievements. She is firmly convinced that men should be spoon-fed with compliments at every available opportunity and that all of us are grown-up boys. She often sets my teeth on edge by referring to me as a great big kid. Then, if she sees me wince, she is likely to swing to the opposite extreme and address me as Papa or Daddy. My name is Dick. I like to think I possess an independent existence, separate from my wife and children, even though I know darn well I have been as tied to home and family responsibilities as the meek Mr. Milquetoast.

Most people, I am sure, would consider Andrea a perfect wife. She stood by me while I worked my way through the university. She puts my wishes and interests first. Indeed, she puts what she assumes to be my interests too far forward. Her determination to make me comfortable at any cost to herself serves to bring out the worst in me. Sometimes when she runs and fetches my slippers I keep on my shoes out of sheer cussedness. Andrea believes implicitly that the sure route to a man's heart is through his stomach.

For me to express a food preference is a prime hazard. One compliment on a lemon pie means lemon meringue today, tomorrow, and forever.

I have the greatest respect for Andrea. Unfortunately she offers me no mental stimulation whatever. Living with her is like being aboard that ship that cruised forever between the ports of Tedium and Monotony. It has been years since Andrea has made a move or a remark I couldn't predict many minutes before she made it. Looking back, I sometimes think I may have married Andrea—she was the first nice girl to whom I ever spoke a word—because at twenty I was seeking a mother. In the real sense, I never had a mother. My mother didn't want a child. According to my dad she threw herself down a flight of stairs during her pregnancy in order to do away with me but only succeeded in spraining her ankle. After I was born she ran away, so Dad used to say, mainly because she couldn't stand to be around a young baby. A funny thing, it gave me a jolt the first time I heard that, even though I never knew her.

But the passage of time cures everything. A man outgrows his need of a mother. I've got to the stage where I want a companion.

For a while I thought I had found the companion. Clarice was exciting and stimulating to me. Although she didn't finish high school we seemed to have plenty to say to each other the few times I saw her. She liked to laugh and to dance; one night we danced until the sun came up, and she didn't fret that I might overexert myself and have a spell of sickness. Nor did she ever try to save my money; when we ate a meal together she ordered the most expensive dishes on the menu. However, I guess we weren't in love. Since we stopped writing, I've nearly forgotten what she looked like. All I can remember is that in Clarice's company I had a wonderful sense of ease and freedom. There has been too little of that in my life.

I am well aware that I am not an easy man to live with, that I am a difficult husband and a poor father. I know I get irritated too easily and lose my temper over trifles. I can't help it any more than I can help my awkwardness with our youngsters. I am proud of the children, but I seem incapable of showing it. It is improbable that any of them—and Ellis, my oldest son, in particular—feels the slightest affection or respect for me despite Andrea's loyal dramatization of Daddy as the head of the family.

Last spring I built a swimming pool in our back yard, but the kids don't seem to get much kick out of it. They don't keep the water clean and cleared of leaves, that's for sure. I set up a workroom for Ellis and equipped it with tools. When he was building his jalopy I tried to show him how to make a better job of it. He preferred to do his tinkering at a fly-by-night garage downtown. I am a graduate engineer, and my experience ranges from rheostats to rockets. Ellis took the advice of a jack-leg mechanic!

The fact is I feel almost as much a stranger with my children as I do with the people I see on a plane or pass in the street. There are times I get so hungry for warmth and comradeship, for somebody to talk to, *really* talk to, I feel a little batty.

I've worked like a slave since my earliest teens, and it seems to me I've wound up with nothing worth having. Many mornings when the gates of the plant where I work close behind me, I have the feeling I've stepped inside a prison. My throat constricts, my heart pounds, I want to run.

In the evenings when I return home I feel I am entering another prison, a prison where I am tethered by my wife's relentless, inflexible devotion.

The truth is I am almost insanely bored with my marriage and my present existence. So bored that I am sick half the time from nerves and inner pressure. I believe I should live by myself awhile for everybody's sake.

*   *

At the Institute our trained counselors immediately realized that no wife could solve Dick Weymer's thorny personality problems, that a new love was no answer for him. Clarice Johnson could not have made him happy, regardless of how fascinating she had momentarily seemed to him. The psychic wounds received during his early years accounted for his difficulties and also, oddly enough, partly explained his outstanding achievements as an engineer.

Dick's belittlement of his abilities had only a hazy connection with fact. It was true he changed jobs often, but former employers were almost unanimous in praise of his skill. At one plant he invented a process which saved the company thousands of dollars on a government project; a week after this triumph Dick walked out without saying why. At another plant, his bosses decided to make him a vice-president in charge of design; when they went to his office, they found it empty.

Dick was a perfectionist. Because he set his standards so high, he seldom felt he had lived up to them. And unless his busy employers repeatedly told him that his services were of supreme importance, he became hurt and angry. Andrea was not entirely wrong in regarding her husband as a grown-up boy. Intelligent as Dick was, much of his behavior was motivated by immature emotions and childhood frustrations. He was still subconsciously determined to wipe out not only the memory of his vagabond father but also the humiliations of the Huck Finn days. Yet as he shifted from job to job, he may well have been guided by one of his father's favorite maxims: "If you don't like it where you are, quit and move on!"

Often Dick's impulsive changes of employment did not turn out well, and very soon he would feel both foolish and guilty. Early in his marriage, subconsciously of course, he hit upon a method of getting "out from under" these uncomfortable feelings. He transferred the blame for his mistakes to Andrea. As uncomplaining as a doormat, she made the process easy. A man of Dick's type deceives himself in this way only at a price. Quite a number of his neurotic illnesses—his headaches, backaches, stomach upsets—originated in work difficulties for which he had unfairly held Andrea responsible.

The pattern for Dick's illnesses, like the pattern for his bitter loneliness and inability to communicate as an adult, had been laid down in childhood. As a little boy he simultaneously hated and yearned for the love of the mother who rejected him. He learned to use sickness as an escape. He decided that all people were cruel and ill-intentioned, and, quite deliberately, he adopted the habit of cutting himself off from contact with them. After several interviews with us at the Institute Dick acknowledged that to live alone in a boardinghouse was hardly a cure for loneliness.

He also agreed that he would not receive much in the way of affection from his sons and daughter so long as he snapped, snarled, and victimized them with his moodiness. When Dick began to mind his temper and manners around his youngsters, relations between them improved.

Andrea, not the most intuitive of women, showed the benefits of her long study of Dick when she correctly judged that the intrigue with Clarice was of less consequence than his dissatisfaction with himself.

The fact was Dick met Clarice at a time when he was seeking a dream girl. Having passed the forty mark, he had begun to wonder how many years were left in which he might find gaiety and fun. In his hard-working life, fun for fun's sake had played almost no part.

Andrea's youthful background, although quite similar to Dick's, had a very different effect upon her character. Her childhood, too, was lacking in security and love, but she did not grow up embittered and emotionally crippled. In her small-girl dreams she pictured herself as an unassertive, generous wife willing to forego any personal desires to secure a successful marriage. When she married Dick, she found the frame for that picture ready and waiting, and she happily stepped into it.

Andrea was surprised when we suggested that she had been *too* unselfish and devoted to the welfare of her husband. She had neglected to discover and develop her own individuality. She was leading too narrow a life, was too absorbed in domesticity and trifling family matters. With a little encouragement from us, she branched out and broadened her horizons. First of all, she went on a strict diet, lost 8 pounds, and improved her figure. After studying fashion trends, she treated herself to a new wardrobe. Having learned to choose smarter clothes in more becoming colors, she elicited a compliment from Dick on a dress that was not bright green.

Next she joined the League of Women Voters. Andrea did not turn into a sparkling conversationalist overnight, but she did become interested in the issues of the day. Neither she nor Dick was politically inclined and neither had ever voted. A couple of months after joining the League, Andrea surprised her family by besting Dick in a dinner-table argument. She convinced him it was his civic duty to register and go to the polls.

Shortly after this, Dick discovered that painting was fun for him, and with the discovery he burst through the walls of work and self-absorption that had so long imprisoned him. One of Andrea's League friends invited the couple to drop in on a class of amateur artists who hired a professional teacher. Andrea was mildly interested in the class. Dick was fascinated. Three hours and one painting later, the first painting of Dick's life, he invited the teacher back home with them for dinner.

The illnesses which made Dick and his family wretched and sadly interfered with his profession are almost a thing of the past. Now if he feels pressures building, he picks up his brushes and goes out painting. Sometimes Andrea accompanies him; sometimes she busies herself with her own concerns. Sometimes she praises the picture he brings home; sometimes she frankly states why she does not like it. Paradoxically, as Andrea has pulled away from Dick she feels that she has grown closer to him. Both he and she have grown within themselves. They have more to offer to each other and to their children.

*   *   *

Hoyt and Jan Summers were much younger than the Weymers when they came to the Institute for counseling; Hoyt was twenty-five, Jan twenty-three. Jan came sulkily and unwillingly. She had already made the break that Dick Weymer only contemplated; she had moved out on her husband and into a place of her own. But after a separation of several weeks, Hoyt succeeded in persuading her to seek our advice.

No two women could be more unlike than Jan Summers and Andrea Weymer. Jan was trim-waisted, deeply tanned, obviously the outdoor type. She was not a good housekeeper or cook and was proud of the fact. She had not conducted a careful study of her husband's likes and dislikes. She was unwilling to make any concessions to his preferences. Indeed she did not want to return to him. She made that clear the moment she marched into the counseling office, just as she immediately made clear her aggressive nature. She shifted the position of her chair; she adjusted the window shade to her personal satisfaction without asking permission; she rearranged the grouping of the pen and ink and other small articles on the counseling desk. When a feminine client behaves in this fashion, regardless of her youth, we can easily deduce she is strong-minded and stubborn. Jan was also very nervous. It was impossible for her to sit still as she recounted her grievances against Hoyt:

*   *

My husband patrols the block outside my apartment like a policeman. Hoyt knows he and I are all washed up, but he haunts my neighborhood. No matter what hour of the night I arrive—I am carrying several college courses in the evening—Hoyt is lurking somewhere in the vicinity. He doesn't care who may be with me when he pops up and stages a scene.

Last night a classmate of mine was coming in to discuss an assignment. When we went in the apartment house Hoyt was in full command of the public hallway. He was right outside my door sitting on his suitcase. To save me embarrassment, my friend made a rapid exit. Whereupon Hoyt, who has been insisting I move back with him, tried to move in with me. After an unpleasant argument, he managed to snatch my key and push in. I ran outside, jumped

in my car, and got away before he could follow. It was too late to
ask any of my college friends for a place to stay, so I just parked
the car and curled up in the back seat. Hoyt slept in my apartment. His bag is still there.

If Hoyt thinks he can force a reconciliation by strong-arm methods he is badly mistaken. I've had my fill of being treated like an
infant. Hoyt is only two years older than I am, and there is no excuse for his patronizing attitude.

During the two years he was in the Army, I held full-time jobs
in the various towns where he was stationed. Ever since his discharge I've held part-time jobs and gone to college, too. I don't
consider that a childish record. According to Hoyt I am unstable,
feather-headed, fickle as the east wind. In short, an all-around
mess.

Some time ago I quit listening to his uncomplimentary opinions.
Finally, I wasn't listening to anything he had to say. Frankly, I
cannot understand why Hoyt won't let me have my divorce. There
is nothing to hold us together. We don't like the same people or
the same things. I'm high-keyed and romantic. Hoyt is prosaic and
plodding. Our ideals and ideas are different. I want to enjoy the
present, to revel in it, to feel both useful and *alive*.

Most wives my age have at least two children, and one girl I
know has four. Not once has it occurred to Hoyt to suggest that
he and I might get started on a family. He is indifferent to children,
just as he is indifferent to everything else of concern to me.

Most couples our age own their homes, nice houses in nice
neighborhoods where they can entertain their friends. I was
ashamed to allow the laundry man to set foot inside the last place
Hoyt and I lived, a two-room job over a garage. It would have
cramped the style of a pair of midgets. When the bed was let
down, it occupied the whole living room. The so-called kitchenette
was closet-sized. I'm no great shakes as a cook, and I need space
to operate. If I'm shut up in a tiny kitchen I soon swamp myself in
dirty pots and pans and feel like a wild animal in a cage. Hoyt and
I usually ate our evening meals at the corner restaurant. That is,

we ate there if our schedules happened to match and we were able to have dinner together.

Hoyt is a college graduate—indeed he has his M.A.—but he took no interest in my college career. Last year I was on the student council, was a member of the building fund committee, was athletic editor of the yearbook, and was elected president of my class. Hoyt didn't bother to congratulate me on any of those honors. He considered my winning a cup in the tennis tournament the subject for a wisecrack. The trophy was sterling silver but wasn't very large, and Hoyt suggested we might use it for an eyecup.

On the night my sorority gave the annual spring dance Hoyt felt morally bound to attend a salesmen's get-together—it's a regular once-a-week business meeting—while I went stag to the most important function of the year. I had a good time at the party, anyway. Other people didn't mind dancing with me. Other people think I'm interesting and adult.

To Hoyt, dancing and tennis and golf, anything in the fun line, are trivial and unworthy of his time. But I can assure you he doesn't improve himself or add to his store of knowledge in the valuable time he saves. Hoyt reads less than I do, if you discount sales manuals and such stuff. On his rare Sundays of leisure—as a rule Hoyt divides his week ends between calling on his customers and drilling with the Army Reserve—his favorite reading matter seems to be the comics. Occasionally he tops off this intellectual feast with the crossword puzzles.

When Hoyt and I met, I was a high-school kid, and he was a serious college student in training to be a teacher. He was a track star, too. I was impressed by his combination of brains and brawn. Then, too, I was sold on Hoyt's parents; they're wonderful people and they stacked up marvelously in comparison with my parents who were "on the outs" for years before their divorce. It was strictly my father's fault. My mother did everything in her power to please him, but I can't remember a time when Father wasn't stepping out on her. My family moved around a great deal—luckily, I have always adjusted quickly to change—but wherever we moved Father soon became involved with some other woman. Everybody knew it. Everybody talked about him. Father's entanglements were terribly humiliating to me as a young girl.

My Saturday night dates were filled with suspense. I was always afraid I might encounter Father in a public place squiring somebody other than Mother. I wondered constantly what my reaction to the situation ought to be. Should I pretend not to see my father? Or was it my duty to nod and smile at his table and show how little I cared for public opinion?

As I look back, I realize I was enchanted by Hoyt's parents and his happy, pleasant home. I could hardly wait until I was wearing his fraternity pin and we were going steady. But within a week or so, Hoyt and I had a difference of some kind and I returned his pin. I can't recall how many times that fraternity pin traveled back and forth between us, or how many other boys and I went steady for a little while.

In my teens I was popular with both boys and girls, but I could never relax and feel convinced that my popularity was solid. On the evening of a first date I was already anticipating the last date. In the moment of accepting a fraternity pin I was rehearsing how I could give it back before the boy got tired of me. If somebody had to agonize over a telephone call that never came, I didn't want it to be me.

I was responsible for most of the courtship quarrels between Hoyt and myself. It was on-again, off-again with us for nearly four years. When Hoyt was drafted the same week he finished graduate school, I was terrified he would be sent overseas and consequently was wild to marry him. He didn't ask me. He did his basic training down South, then he was stationed in Oregon. On a Wednesday night he called and out of a clear sky informed me that we would be married the following Friday. There was no "Will you?" or "Shall we?"—just the bald announcement. I was so overcome by his masterfulness that I borrowed another girl's wedding dress, and we were married right on schedule. We had a church ceremony, too. All the haste and bustle seemed awfully romantic.

We had a glamorous honeymoon because Hoyt had been promoted and was being transferred immediately to the East. From then on, I followed him on every Army transfer. In those days I was proud of his ability, and I also admired his aims. Or I admired what I assumed to be his aims. Hoyt now has no sense of social responsibility whatever. When he left the Army he turned his back on a teaching career. Hoyt could have been a brilliant teacher. I am quite sure he is a mediocre salesman. I don't know how much Hoyt earns, but I do know we were practically always broke. Possibly I could have been more economical, but I am not a money-hungry character. Material possessions mean little to me. My ambition is to be of service to others. My college training—I will get my degree in June—has been in playground and recreation work. I am majoring in child psychology with special emphasis on the problem of juvenile delinquency.

Three months ago a classmate of mine—his name is Michael— asked me to help out with a recreation project for underprivileged children. Michael supervises a neighborhood club outside college hours. Michael grew up in the slums himself; he is absolutely fascinating when he talks about all the jobs he's held and how hard he has had to sweat and struggle for an education. It's a revelation to watch Michael with the clubhouse youngsters, a real privilege. Every Saturday afternoon he and I take our boys and girls—they range in age from eight to twelve—to the beach, the zoo, a museum, or something of the sort. I repeatedly invited Hoyt to join us, but he was always busy with something else.

My relationship with Hoyt has been empty and meaningless for a long time. Three weeks ago I realized that I had to put an immediate end to it. Suddenly I awoke to the fact I was desperately in love with Michael, and that Michael was in love with me. Michael is unhappily married, too. As soon as we can arrange our divorces he and I intend to be married. Nothing can stop us.

It nearly breaks Michael's heart to give up his child—he and his wife have a little boy—but he is willing to make the sacrifice for my sake. In my opinion, and I speak from experience, it's wrong for parents who don't love each other to stay together because of a child. My parents weren't divorced until I was a senior in high school. I'd have been spared years of embarrassment and the tears I shed over my mother's humiliations if she had gone to court earlier. I believe in divorce as well as in marriage. I think it's wicked for people to drag out their lives tied to past mistakes. Michael belongs to a church that forbids divorce. He is willing to give up his religion, too. That's how much he cares for me.

Michael is a strong, forceful man, who knows what he wants. He isn't fumbling and uncertain like Hoyt. He is the kind of man I should have married in the first place. Since Michael treats me like a woman I *feel* like a woman in his company. He and I agree in our ideals and ambitions and ideas. We have talked and talked about our future together, without a word of argument. Any belief of Michael's automatically becomes mine. I am proud to be his echo. When Michael told me that he disapproved of working wives —his wife, Patricia, has stubbornly hung on to a job—I discovered how little a career means to me. Hoyt would be content for me to keep on working until I'm eligible for a Social Security pension. After Michael and I marry I will probably work a few months as a temporary stopgap and to justify my education. I then will resign and make a home for Michael and bear his children and glory in being a wife and a mother. It thrills me just to think about the prospect.

I'm not ashamed of my love for Michael. I'd like to shout it from the housetops. I should feel guilty, I know. Sometimes I do feel guilty. But when I'm with Michael I feel elated, ecstatic, light as air. I feel as though I were in the center of a whirlwind and couldn't get out and didn't want to. Michael feels the same with me. He has told me so.

For a while I had hopes Michael and I could carry through our two divorces in a civilized modern fashion without hurting anybody. I have nothing against Patricia. In some ways I'm fond of Hoyt. Even though we've grown apart I hoped I could keep him for a friend. Our separation began on a friendly basis. As soon as I realized Michael and I loved each other, I told Hoyt the exact truth. I had seen too much subterfuge and deceit in my childhood to do anything else. Hoyt agreed I could take a separate apartment after I promised I wouldn't be hasty and would do some serious thinking. He even helped me settle in my apartment. He can be sweet and generous when he wants to be. I have only met Patricia once, but I don't believe she will fight a divorce.

I wish I could say as much for Hoyt. He is selfishly trying to ruin my plans and hopes for the future. Well, he won't succeed. Michael and I are entitled to happiness.

*　*

Hoyt Summers was as unprepared to find that his marriage was in trouble as Andrea Weymer had been. Jan gave him no clue to her feelings and state of mind until the night their separation occurred. It was a Saturday, very late. Hoyt was in the cramped garage apartment, sound asleep, when Jan burst in, switched on the lights and asked: "What would you say if I suggested leaving you?"

Hoyt was still half asleep. Thinking she was joking, he replied, "I'd say, go ahead. Kindly turn out the lights as you take off."

However, he soon awoke to the fact his wife was in earnest. Jan told him that his company stifled her, his conversation bored her, their marriage was a calamity. She informed him that Michael made her feel dynamic and alive and that the two of them were destined to fulfill each other and achieve great things.

Three weeks later as Hoyt described that Saturday night to us, he was still bewildered by what had happened to them:

*　*

Jan and I were happier than most couples. Or so I had supposed. I don't mean everything was perfect. Jan is rather juvenile in her thinking, and she's always gone in for too many activities, but my schedule is crowded, too. We practically never quarreled. Yet there she stood announcing her willingness to throw me over for a man who already had a wife and baby.

For a couple of minutes I was so angry I felt like closing out our whole darned show. The feeling didn't last. Jan stepped to the closet and began to pack her clothes, throwing stuff in helter-skelter. Although she had nowhere to go, she proposed to move out instantly. Jan is addicted to snap judgments and she sticks with them.

She claimed she had to get out of our apartment at once—"escape" was the word she used—and be by herself. By the time she finished her packing—we argued back and forth for hours—it was broad daylight on Sunday morning. Jan, who isn't normally a placid character, was in a terrific emotional state by then. I didn't know what crazy thing she might do unless she got some help from me. She was in no shape to drive her car. I could see she needed food. I got my car and took her out to breakfast. While she ate I hunted through the want ads for apartment listings.

We rode around and looked at several apartments, and Jan calmed down sufficiently to choose the most expensive of the lot. Jan tells everybody material possessions are unimportant to her, but she invariably picks the best, regardless of cost. When I carried in her luggage, it turned out she didn't have a dime. Payday for her is either Friday or Saturday, I forget which, but she had already blown in her whole check. Luckily I'd just collected mine and could dig up a month's rent for her. At the time I figured she would be back with me and making sense again within a few days.

On that same Sunday evening I felt less optimistic. At Jan's request she and I met Michael and his wife, Patricia, at a downtown restaurant. Patricia is a nice, hard-working girl, who is trying to juggle a home, a job, and a four-month-old baby, and I feel sorry for her. However, she was so quiet and dispirited throughout that miserable dinner I wrote her off as a possible ally. I thought she was fed up with her marriage and wouldn't lift a finger to hold it together. I didn't blame her. Up to date Michael hasn't achieved a solid job; he goes to college and does a little paid work with that neighborhood club, but Patricia partially supports him and wholly supports their child. One look, and I knew Michael was a real wolf. Bad news for me. Bad news for Jan.

Jan thoroughly enjoyed our so-called conference. I guess she felt sophisticated and adult as she explained the purpose of the jolly little get-together she had engineered. The general idea was that the four of us would discuss the situation created by her and Michael and reach some intelligent, mutually satisfactory decisions. Maybe Jan expected that Patricia and I would bow out gracefully and come through with prompt offers of two divorces. Or maybe she just wanted to keep the drama boiling. Anyway Patricia and I didn't oblige Jan, despite at least an hour of double talk on her part.

One decision, however, was reached. Jan and Michael promised they would honestly do some serious thinking and would stop seeing each other until both of them were graduated in June. That meant a two-months' respite. I then promised Jan I wouldn't burden her with my company so that she could have the freedom and privacy she considered necessary to straighten out her mixed-up thinking and feelings.

I made my promise gladly and intended to keep it. The very next day Patricia telephoned me at my office. Among other things, she told me that Michael's word was worthless. I went to Jan's new apartment. To tell the truth, I considered it my apartment, too, since she couldn't have got possession without my paying the rent.

I arrived just as Jan was serving Michael coffee and a plate of delicatessen sandwiches. Jan hurriedly explained that Michael had just popped in for a few minutes to bring back some borrowed textbooks of hers. The story was as phony as a three-dollar bill. Then and there, so far as I was concerned, my friendly separation with Jan came to an end. Michael went—I ordered him off the premises—and I don't intend to give Jan a minute of peace until she breaks with Michael, and I have definite proof of it.

Even if I didn't think she and I could get together again, I would refuse to let Michael make a hash of her life. I've conducted a pretty thorough investigation of Michael's case. Extracurricular romances are a specialty of his. Michael goes after a girl and keeps her in an uproar until his ego is satisfied. He then repents, and Patricia forgives him. Patricia has already forgiven Michael four or five times. Michael may talk about divorce, but talk is cheap. His religion will keep him out of the divorce courts. Moreover, I believe he is quite dependent on Patricia, and I know he carries snapshots of their baby in his wallet.

I've tried to give Jan the straight facts, but she won't listen. When I remind her that she moved out on me but that Michael is still living with his family, she gets furious. She seems determined to delude herself.

Jan thinks she is sophisticated and unconventional. She isn't. My parents are extremely fond of her, and they are anything but unconventional. At times Jan is headstrong and overly independent, but she is sensitive and in many ways quite innocent. Some girls might be able to handle a Michael-type romance without being too badly hurt. For Jan the price would be too steep.

It just happens that I love Jan. She's a long-time habit of mine. Her cute looks and smooth line attracted me, but what held me was the fact that underneath she was shy and insecure, and I felt she needed me. I still feel that she needs me.

Somehow Jan and I never managed to settle down and establish our marriage on a stable basis. While I was in the Army and other G.I. wives were griping at the living accommodations, I considered myself a lucky guy indeed. Jan bounced around from a bad boardinghouse to a worse one and had a wonderful time in the process. She could be packed and ready to move to a new town at an hour's notice. In twenty-four hours she had a circle of new friends and as likely as not had organized a couple of clubs.

When I was separated from the Army, I expected Jan to quit working. I hoped we would use my G.I. loan and buy a pleasant home in a good neighborhood. But Jan isn't interested in acquiring a permanent home or in homemaking. Jan's mother is an excellent housekeeper, and she can turn out a dandy meal on a two-burner grill. Jan eyes a carpet sweeper as though it were an unexploded bomb. The prospect of boiling an egg unnerves her. We've invested a fortune eating in restaurants.

Jan and I just don't know how to get the proper mileage out of money. I gave up a teaching career and went into selling, which I heartily dislike, because I wanted Jan to have the best and realized we simply couldn't make it on a teacher's salary. At the moment I must be averaging $600 a month, but I have nothing in reserve. Jan fritters away her earnings on clothes and personal stuff. Half the time I've had to pay her tuition, which is fair enough at that. It seems ironic now, but I urged Jan to enter college. In fact, I suggested her courses of study. In my college days my major interest was juvenile delinquency. To show you what a dope a man can be, I cheered Jan when she and Michael teamed up on their project for underprivileged kids.

Jan is good with children, other people's children. If we had been lucky enough to have a family of our own—I've always wanted children—I'm sure none of this would have happened.

❋   ❋

Hoyt Summers was wrong in assuming that the lack of children was solely responsible for his troubles. But he was right when he surmised that Michael's appearance on the scene was not the basic cause of his marital problems.

Jan and Hoyt simply had no real marriage. Legally husband and wife, they were living in two quite separate worlds. Jan was devoting nearly all of her thoughts and energies to her college studies and activities. Hoyt was expending his thoughts and energies upon a selling job, which he loathed. Yet Hoyt and Jan Summers possessed the common interests and the ability to communicate that Dick and Andrea Weymer had lacked. Their trouble was that they spent too little time together. Jan had far more in common with Hoyt than she had with Michael, a young man whose background and upbringing were foreign to her own.

Neither Jan nor Hoyt had put forth sufficient effort to sustain and broaden the interests that had attracted them in the first place and caused them to marry. Neither seemed to realize that marriage is a creative process, that each partner by sharing of himself contributes to the spiritual well-being of the other. Many months before there was a Michael, Jan and Hoyt became too busy as individuals to function as a team. They allowed their schedules of study and work to become so mismatched that they frequently were unable to sleep at the same hours. Their sexual relationship, a very strong bond between them, deteriorated. In their self-preoccupation they had drifted so far apart that Jan actually saw more of Hoyt *after* their separation than she had seen of him when they were living together.

Jan and Hoyt had no intimate knowledge of each other's private hopes, dreams, ambitions. Thus Hoyt was unaware that when he sacrificed a teaching career to increase his earnings "for Jan's sake," he lost standing in her eyes. And Jan was not aware that Hoyt desired a family and an established home as intensely as she did. At the time she called on us Jan knew little about her husband and considerably less about Michael and Michael's character.

Her own feelings, behavior, and motivation were also a mystery to her. Jan fancied she was mature and sophisticated, a free agent. Actually she was immature and impulsive, as inclined as a six-year-old to follow every whim. But Jan was a bright young woman. In a half-dozen counseling sessions we were able to explain her to herself.

Jan was anything but a free agent. She was firmly identified with the experiences and upheavals of her disorganized childhood. Her restlessness was an echo of the past, as was her craving for excitement and change, her quick, surface adaptability. Gregarious by disposition, Jan had learned how to earn popularity among strangers by circulating, smiling to conceal shyness, joining every club available. As an adult, she was still a joiner. She spread herself so thinly among so many organizations that she received little benefit from any one of them.

Since Jan possessed a high degree of sex appeal she thought of herself as possessing a high degree of femininity. This was not the case. In her childhood, as she battled to win companionship and recognition everywhere her parents went, Jan learned to be aggressive, which is not usually considered a feminine attribute.

In fact, Jan was afraid to be a woman. In childhood she had sympathized with her mother's humiliations. But she had only to observe her mother's position in the family to decide subconsciously that being a woman did not pay. The origin of her vehement dislike of housework and cooking was clear. Such tasks reminded Jan too painfully of her mother and of their common femininity, against which she was in futile but acute revolt.

Without being aware of it, Jan envied men. Unknowingly, she modeled herself upon a specific man—her father. In her childish memories her father had always loomed as the dominant figure. She had been wounded and alienated by his philandering, but she was fascinated by him, too. In her restless teens, as she turned from one admirer to the next, she was reflecting the shallow emotions and the instability of her father. When she turned to Michael and responded to the thrill of the forbidden, she once again repeated her father's patterns of feeling and acting.

Jan arrived at self-knowledge without undue difficulty. In six-weeks' time she perceived the folly of her subconscious wish to be male and to follow in her father's footsteps. She then was ready to admit that she had committed her vanity—and not her heart—to Michael.

After Jan acquired insight and the ability to interpret her own feelings, she became able to view Michael impersonally. She stopped hiding from facts. Michael's whole record showed that he was a far weaker man than Hoyt, a poor marital risk for any woman, a dangerous companion for any girl with a head on her shoulders. Jan's infatuation had been swiftly born and died with equal swiftness. Significantly, Michael did not protest when she bade him a permanent good-by.

Her reconciliation with Hoyt was not spoiled by recriminations and bitterness. On the contrary, Hoyt proved he could be a strong and tenderly understanding husband when he put his mind to it. Alerted to Jan's taste for variety and the dramatic, he took her on a five-day trip. To Jan's romantic mind the trip represented a second honeymoon, a symbolic and definite turning away from mistaken concepts. To Hoyt's mind the trip was worth every cent he borrowed to finance it.

During the brief holiday he and Jan talked over their ambitions and dreams, their goals, and renewed their acquaintance with each other as man and wife. When they returned, they tackled and altered their deplorable spending habits. They could not afford to operate two automobiles. Upon Jan's graduation they disposed of hers. By then they had figured out a systematic program of saving. Their savings were earmarked for the purchase of a home and the acquisition of a family.

Jan had financial courage. When she took a well-paid job in the recreation field she insisted that Hoyt resume teaching, even though it meant less money than he received as a salesman. Hoyt has now been teaching for almost two years. A year ago he and Jan bought a home of which they are vastly proud. Jan has not become a meticulous housekeeper and never will, but with the aid of a highly efficient electric kitchen, where she does not feel cramped for space, she has turned into a fine cook. So far the Summerses have no children; however, their hopes are high.

* * *

Elise and Tracy Manning, like the Summerses and the Weymers, were spending less time together than the average couple when infidelity brought them to a crisis and to the Institute. Twelve years married, the Mannings had three youngsters, two boys and a girl. Like Hoyt Summers, Tracy was a salesman, but unlike the younger man he enjoyed his work. Tracy sold enough industrial machinery to earn around $15,000 a year.

Tracy's pleasing personality explained his success as a salesman. He was a good listener and a good conversationalist, too. He was proficient at any sport you could mention: golf, tennis, billiards, horseback riding, swimming. Everybody wanted him for lunch, for cocktails, for dinner, for the talking, singing, and dancing afterward. He was the first to arrive at a party, the last to leave. When he joined a group both the men and the women brightened, sat up in their chairs, and thought: well, now the fun can begin. He was a wonderful guest, an excellent host. As Elise pointed out to us, most of Tracy's qualities were endearing—in a bachelor.

Thirty-three-year-old Elise was pretty and blond. She dressed tastefully, but not extravagantly as Jan Summers did. For eight years Elise had believed and boasted that her husband was perfection. Then in the eighth year of her marriage she learned that Tracy had been unfaithful to her. That first infidelity she forgave, but when, four years later, the infidelity was repeated, she was in no mood to be forgiving. Although Tracy insisted he broke his marriage vows only because of loneliness, she told us she found that impossible to believe:

*   *

I doubt Tracy has ever spent a lonely moment on or off the road. He isn't the type who mopes and broods in an empty room. He can't be in a town fifteen minutes before he's busy on the telephone, calling this one, complimenting that one, passing on the latest joke. In half an hour I've seen him set up a week of appointments.

The first girl he got entangled with—her name was Carol—was the cashier in a motel in Tucson, Arizona. Most wives would have sensed something was wrong long before I became suspicious. A couple of the other salesmen used to kid around, telling me that I ought to put a ball and chain on my husband. I laughed. I didn't dream I was hearing the truth. I wanted to trust Tracy, I suppose. My mother's nagging and complaining and her unjust suspicions drove my father to the divorce court when I was in grade school. As a child I decided I wouldn't be that kind of wife.

Both my mother and my older sister used to say I was too trusting and naïve. My mother-in-law—I get on better with her than

with my own mother—said flatly that no man could be trusted, her
son included, but I discounted her cynicism, thinking it could be
explained by her own experience. Tracy's father wasn't a faithful
husband. His conduct was very hard on Tracy as a small boy; he
sided with his mother and despised his father. I couldn't conceive
he would follow in his father's footsteps.

Then one night he and I dined with a wealthy customer who
owns an Arizona ranch. While the men talked business, the wife
showed me photographs of their ranch. Among them was a snap-
shot of Tracy riding out of their corral with a strange girl. When I
asked some questions, the hostess said the girl was a neighboring
rancher's daughter, but she sounded embarrassed. Later I spoke to
Tracy, and he looked me straight in the eye—he wasn't embarrassed in the least—and declared he couldn't recall anything about
the girl. It was Carol, of course. He was squiring her around among
his out-of-town friends. At times the two of them were even taking
trips together. Everybody knew about the situation except me.

A few months after that dinner, Tracy told me he had to attend
a convention in Dallas, Texas. During his absence Johnnie, our older
boy, broke his arm. It was a simple fracture, but I telegraphed the
Dallas hotel where Tracy was supposed to be. My telegram came
back, and I was notified that he wasn't registered. Two days later
he walked in, kissed me, and began talking about the blistering
heat in Dallas. I asked about the undelivered telegram. For a moment he was flustered. Then he produced a glib tale to the effect
the convention had adjourned early, and he had gone on to visit a
customer in Houston. I knew this was untrue because I'd checked
his itinerary with the local office, something I rarely do. I don't
make a habit of meddling in his business. According to the office,
no convention had been held in Dallas, and Tracy was actually
in Tucson. I dropped the subject. Maybe I didn't want to know
what he was doing in Arizona.

Shortly afterward I learned the whole story. It was late at night,
and Tracy and I were in bed asleep when the phone rang. I answered it. Carol was calling from Tucson. She was high as a kite.

Tracy got the telephone away from me and persuaded Carol to hang up. But he couldn't persuade me, hard as he tried, that she was one of his customer's girl friends. I thought she was his girl friend. He finally admitted I was right.

Tracy was deeply involved with Carol. If I hadn't been so heartbroken on my own account, I might have pitied her. As it was, I didn't blame her for the mess. I couldn't. She didn't know Tracy was a married man, the father of three children. He hadn't told her. He lacked the courage, he said.

The shock of his confession was shattering, although I concealed it. I felt obliged to offer him his freedom and I did so calmly, but the truth is I was terrified I would lose him. Tracy said he did not want a divorce. He promised there would be no more Carols in his life and that he would break with her at once. He did feel, however, that he owed her the consideration of a personal visit, and the next day the two of us drove to Tucson. I waited in a downtown hotel while he faced Carol.

She put him through a rough experience. She cried, she screamed, she threatened to buy a gun and shoot him. Indeed, she gave him such a scare that I had to drive the car back to Los Angeles. He was still shaky after we arrived. I was convinced he was truly sorry and I avoided recriminations. He asked his office to relieve him of the Tucson territory at his mother's suggestion. Both of our families knew about the trouble.

It was my mother-in-law who introduced me to Tracy. At that time she was a national officer in my college sorority—I was a lowly sophomore—and Tracy was a bachelor of twenty-six, already graduated, and well established with the firm where he still works. He considered me just a kid, and we saw each other only sporadically, but I regarded him as my most exciting date. When he went on his trips—he was sharing an apartment with his mother—I used to drop by their place and help her keep up with his mending and stuff. One time she and I redecorated and repapered his room. Tracy laughed at us, but I think he was pleased.

When he was drafted and stationed in San Francisco I bombarded him with letters, but got few replies. However, the day he received sailing orders he telephoned me and proposed. His mother and I promptly took a plane to San Francisco, where I married him in the camp chapel. A few days later his orders were canceled, and he never did get overseas. One of Tracy's favorite jokes used to be that I owed my proposal to a fluke. I used to laugh at that joke, too.

Tracy's Army assignment didn't keep him on the post at night, and I found a small apartment where we spent two wonderful years. I continued my college studies in the morning—in the afternoon I held a job—and in the evenings we bowled and skated and danced like crazy. It wasn't until Tracy received his discharge and went back with his old firm that I discovered how demanding a salesman's work can be.

Since that time I have often felt Tracy was married to his job, not to me. On the night that Johnnie was born, Tracy wasn't at the hospital; he was at a boxing match with a covey of customers. When Ruthie had her tonsils out, he was on a fishing trip with his boss. A lot of his so-called business activities don't seem to me to have much to do with selling. Until the children came along, Tracy kept me busy wining and dining out-of-town clients, who usually appeared without their wives. Tracy often arranged dates for these married men. And after a long evening I would jump out of bed next morning to go gift-shopping for the absent wives. I didn't mind buying a pretty blouse for a woman I hadn't met, but I hated helping a philandering husband to salve his conscience.

Tracy lavishes much more attention on his customers than he does on the children or me. The customers come first. He dislikes liquor, but he drinks to put drinking men at ease. He dislikes rich food, but the proof of his high regard is a high-priced restaurant. I'm quite sure that Tracy's company expense account doesn't cover his entertainment spending, but I don't really know. Tracy likes to live splendidly, and he wants everyone's good opinion. He can't bear to appear unpleasant, and it is almost impossible for him to say no. Because it was a project of his civic club, Tracy spent every

Saturday last summer teaching underprivileged kids to swim. He has yet to find the time to take our Johnnie and Stevie on a weekend camping trip.

Tracy is liberal and freehanded, but somehow the family money is usually managed so the children and I get the worst of it. Our present house is far too small. It wasn't a bargain in the first place; I'm convinced Tracy bought it because a real estate friend was in trouble and needed to make a sale.

In all fairness, I don't believe Tracy realizes he spends more on his clothes than he does on me and the children. I'm sure he would deny it. Buying good suits, he says, is an economy, but he pays more for a suit than his boss does. Tracy just doesn't know what he spends; we have no family budget.

Last April he bought several hundred dollars' worth of luggage and a set of new golf clubs and drove away on a three-weeks' trip. This left only eleven dollars in our bank account. In the second week, I went to work in a department store to tide us over, and my mother came to stay with the youngsters. It wasn't the first time I had taken a temporary job. But Tracy never knew; I didn't tell him.

Not long after his return from that trip, I began to suspect there was another woman in the picture. I don't know why; I just sensed it. I met Phyllis one evening without tumbling to the fact that she was interested in my husband. She was escorted by an out-of-town customer; the four of us went dancing and then dropped by our house for scrambled eggs. Phyllis is a bleached-blond divorcée with a nine-year-old daughter; she had recently been hired as a receptionist at Tracy's home office and was very wide-eyed about the fascinations of the business. Just remembering those eggs I scrambled and served to her practically makes me choke.

Phyllis was, of course, the other woman in the picture. That news was delivered to me by the postman. One morning I opened a bill from our dentist and was sure an error had been made. I called the dentist's secretary. The error had been mine when I opened the bill. Tracy was paying for a teeth-straightening job for Phyllis' little girl. I don't believe a bill for a mink coat would have made me half as angry.

I called Phyllis on the telephone, and she was delighted that at last I knew the score. She informed me that Tracy was also paying the rent on her apartment and that she expected to marry him as soon as I obtained a divorce.

When Tracy came home that night I had hysterics for the first time in my life. Our living room looked like a department store. I had pulled his expensive clothes out of the closet and jammed some of them into his expensive suitcases. As he came in the door I threw the unpacked jackets, his silk slacks, and his custom-made shoes on the front porch and tried to push him after them. Tracy tried to take me in his arms and comfort me. I hit him, I screamed, I wept. But why go on?

That dreadful scene occurred two weeks ago. Tracy is still in the house. He insists he is all washed up with Phyllis, that she means nothing to him and never did, that he loves me and our youngsters, that he deserves another chance. Again and again he has promised there will never be another woman. Unfortunately I have heard those promises before.

At this point I don't know which way to turn. I feel completely baffled. I don't understand Tracy or why he treats me as he does. I don't understand the way he acts at all. In spite of my suffering and disillusionment, I am still fond of him in some ways. I would hate to bring up our children without a father, although I have no fears about my ability to provide for them as well as he has done. If I take a few refresher courses, I can get a teacher's certificate. The children and I can learn to live without Tracy, I suppose. I don't quite see how I can learn to live in peace with a man who is unfaithful, untruthful, and untrustworthy.

❉   ❉

Tracy Manning, who was thirty-eight years old, looked younger. His muscles had not yet begun to run to fat. When he walked into the waiting room of the Institute his round, sunburned face was drawn in a scowl, but seemed cherubic. Reluctantly, he had this to say in his defense when he talked to us:

* *

Like a good many other men, I lead two lives. I have a home life with Elise and my kids. I have a business life that is separate and apart from my home. In my business life I meet women, lots of them, but I don't take up with stray girls at a convention the way some of the fellows do; I would rather sit and chew the fat and trade jokes. I'm no Don Juan, whatever Elise may think. I'm in love with her.

Carol once meant something to me, I'll admit, although I only saw her a couple of times a year and thought of her as a friend rather than a sweetheart. She has a good, sound business head. I used to discuss my deals and cry over my worries with her in a way I couldn't do with Elise. One time early in my marriage I hinted to Elise that some little thing about my job wasn't absolute perfection, and for the next six months I was fighting off her attempts to get me into an entirely different line of business. That experience taught me to keep my mouth shut.

Carol fooled me about what she wanted from our association. I had no idea she was looking for permanence. She liked tennis and horses, she liked to swim, she played golf like a man. We had many good times together. Elise hasn't been on horseback since Johnnie was born. She gave away her golf clubs when Stevie came along. Since our daughter joined the family, Elise has rarely put on a bathing suit. She lacks the time, she says. I can't imagine Carol ever being too busy for sports.

Well, there's no point dwelling on the past. I gladly split up with Carol for my wife's sake, although in the final showdown I got the impression Carol had more genuine affection for me than Elise. She showed more flesh-and-blood feeling. Elise offered me a divorce as calmly as though she were offering me a second cup of coffee. Her coolness wasn't flattering. After all, she was my wife and had caught me in the wrong. She had earned the right to raise the roof, but she didn't even raise her voice.

Elise isn't an easy person to understand. When she was a girl, she seemed to be crazy about me. When the children began to come, I soon felt I had been crowded out. Today I don't know how Elise really feels about me, what she really thinks. Apparently she doesn't think much of me at the moment. My hope is her thinking will change.

For the most part, I would call Elise a self-contained and a self-maintaining woman. I can't believe that either she or the youngsters miss me during my absences. All three of my kids are bored with me and show it. I suppose it's natural enough. They look to their mother for their pleasures. I'm just that man who comes and goes. When I arrive home from a trip it's nothing special to my family. No fireworks are shot off. Frequently, after two weeks on the road, I walk into an empty house. There isn't even a note for me to read. It's a lonesome sensation. I get the feeling I might as well have stayed away, that my family can do without me. Other men in my line of work have the same experience. I'm not kicking, I'm merely trying to understand Elise's side of the present foul-up.

I cannot comprehend why she forgave me four years ago without batting an eye and yet can be so hard on me now. My interest in Phyllis is completely dead and was always trivial. I saw Phyllis outside the office a dozen times at the most, and I don't propose to see her again.

When Elise first discovered the situation, I'm willing to admit that I deserved exactly what I got. In fact, I didn't mind the punishment I had to take. Elise's hysterics seemed to prove she cared enough about me to blow her top. It was the first time I ever realized she was capable of violent jealousy. I know I shouldn't have stepped out on her, and maybe I shouldn't have lied to her. I only told the lies when I was cornered, and then I told as few as possible.

If Phyllis hadn't had a nine-year-old daughter, the honest truth is our acquaintance would have stopped in the office. I didn't ever promise to marry that young woman. I promised her nothing. Nor was I paying the rent on her apartment. I lent her one-month's rent, and although I didn't expect the loan to be repaid there is quite a difference. Phyllis was having a tough time supporting her daughter; they were newcomers to the West Coast and had no friends, and I was sorry for them both. One afternoon the little girl came by the office after school, and I bought an ice-cream cone for her. The child was more grateful for the ice cream than my sons were when I gave them the money for a plane ride.

I drove Phyllis and her daughter home that afternoon. On the way she complimented me on my sales record. I was surprised and pleased she had noticed. When I learned she was broke, a chronic condition with her, it seemed natural to stop and lay in a stock of groceries for her. It then seemed natural for me to stay long enough to sample her cooking.

I quickly became aware I had made a mistake, that Phyllis was a talented gimme-girl and a troublemaker to boot, but I didn't know what to do about it. In the hope she would latch on to somebody else, I introduced her around, and my strong hunch is she has already consoled herself. Phyllis is the type who is bound to light on her feet. It's preposterous for Elise to let that girl worry her and upset our marriage.

I'm not a bad guy. In the main, I'm a pretty good guy. I wish Elise would think about my virtues for awhile. I don't smoke. I'm strictly a two-drink man and I would gladly stay on the wagon except that in my business I can't afford to be a kill-joy. I support my family comfortably. Elise has never had to work. She is now talking of returning to college and getting a teacher's certificate, which is ridiculous. I'd prefer she didn't work. Anything in reason she and the youngsters think they need I am able to provide. It's true that we could use a larger house and some day we'll probably be moving into one. If Elise doesn't get what she wants, it's her own fault. If the money doesn't go for one thing it goes for another, I often tell her. Sometimes I wonder whether she isn't extra thrifty in order to point up my extravagance.

There is a streak of the martyr in Elise. She still remembers I was at a boxing match the night of Johnnie's birth, but seemingly she doesn't remember that she went into labor two weeks early, and I got to the hospital as soon as I could. As a rule, I'll admit, I let Elise take full charge when the kids are sick, and I duck out on the hospital waiting. My philosophy is to avoid depressing places and depressing thoughts, and look on the bright side of things. Elise is the opposite of me in many ways. When I'm on the road I know she feeds herself and the kids hamburger when I would rather they all ate steak. It would make my own steaks taste better.

I didn't expect marriage to be 100 per cent perfect. To be honest, in my youth I didn't intend to marry. I was comfortable sharing an apartment with my mother and I enjoyed running around with all the girls. To me, marriage seemed too grim, too confining. Devoted as I am to my mother, I can recall occasions when she made it hot for my father because he didn't earn enough to suit her. Of course he had no right to run around with other women the way he did, but I didn't think it was his fault he lacked the money-making knack. When my parents were divorced and my father didn't fight for my custody or even ask for visitation privileges, I tried to kid myself it was because he couldn't afford my keep. But in my heart I knew the real reason he didn't want me around. My father, who was a great athlete in his day, considered me a weakling and a sissy.

By the time I reached college age I was able to show him different. I had an athletic scholarship for two years out of the four. I wasn't heavy enough for football, but I was on the tennis and swimming teams.

In spite of Elise's tact, I know she doesn't think of me as being special in any way. I wish she could be proud of me. I've climbed high in a hotly competitive business. The product I have to sell, the identical product and just as good, is offered at a lower cost by several of our competitors. My customers cheerfully buy from me. Why? They buy because I sell them service. In other words, I sell them on myself.

Since I can sell myself in a rugged commercial field, I'm fairly sure I can sell myself back to my wife. Elise is too level-headed not to come to her senses soon. She doesn't want a divorce any more than I do. And I don't need a psychologist to tell me so.

* *

Tracy Manning was the kind of client we can seldom help. He was unwilling to grant there was anything particularly wrong in himself, in his marriage, or in his wife. In our opinion he was fearful of tinkering with the jovial public personality that made him a social and business success. He wanted to think and live on the surface, despite the fact that the two affairs upon which he had embarked—both of the affairs were prolonged and there was some evidence of still other infidelities—clearly indicated that all was not well with him and with his marriage.

Tracy and Elise took the personality tests we offer all our clients, and he was disconcerted and displeased with the findings. His own answers to the tests, as explained to him, strongly suggested that his jolly, back-slapping ways were mostly a pose, that inwardly he felt insecure and afraid. After scoffing at our interpretation of the tests and thereby subconsciously arming himself to evade the pain of self-knowledge, Tracy wanted no future counseling.

However, Elise decided to continue on her own and make an effort to understand the reasons for the failure of the marriage. She realized that a divorce would be hard on her three children, just as her parents' divorce had been hard on her. What Elise did not realize, until after her counseling, was that in her own way she had been as unsatisfactory a wife to Tracy as her mother had been to her father. In some ways Elise as a wife resembled Andrea Weymer. Elise did not nag, complain, lose her temper, spend too much of Tracy's money. Her house was not untidy, her food was not poorly cooked, but her virtues were negative, academic. They were not the virtues calculated to meet the needs of a man like Tracy.

Tracy required an unusual amount of affection and reassurance. His ego was weak, and he was chronically uneasy about the impression he was making, as are many people who vie for the popularity prize at every party. A mamma's boy, a disappointment to his father, Tracy in his bachelor days had sought proof of his virility and masculinity in each fresh romantic conquest. Similarly, in college, he had felt impelled to excel in sports.

Elise started out in the marriage under good auspices. She was her mother-in-law's choice as well as her husband's, and she was eager to please. If she had recognized and fulfilled Tracy's emotional needs, she could have made herself indispensable to him. Unfortunately, in an attempt to avoid the mistakes of her nagging, bad-tempered mother she built up a rigid conception of marriage that had very little application to her and Tracy. Her conception of herself as a wife was sugary and artificial.

When she had a legitimate complaint, she hid her annoyance under a sweet smile, hoping Tracy would respond with gratitude and ardor, since she, too, had a strong need of approval. He sensed her phoniness. Instead of voicing her valid objections to some of the more excessive demands of his job and trying to work out a compromise, she kept still. He interpreted her silence as a lack of pride in him.

Tracy needed honest feeling from Elise. When she discovered his first affair, her calm behavior screened inner tumult, but left him with the puzzled belief she was unmoved and indifferent. If she had taken a positive stand and expressed her outrage, it is possible there might have been no second affair, although Phyllis' appeal for him seemed quite understandable. Both she and Carol were interested in his work, or pretended to be. He welcomed the sympathetic ear he did not find at home.

Moreover, Elise made a fairly common but serious error when the children were born. She allowed Tracy to regard his own youngsters as rivals. She made him feel like a fifth wheel in a concern that could operate nicely without him. She was almost asking him to look for consolation in the eyes and arms of other women.

Tracy was highly sexed. Underneath a cool exterior, Elise herself was warm and affectionate. Not once in the twelve years of marriage had she rejected Tracy's love-making, but she had never made any loving advances to him. A conventional woman, she believed it was her duty to wait for his overtures. Elise was both amazed and chagrined when she learned from the answers Tracy gave in one of our temperament tests that he considered her very cold. In taking the same test she had scored herself very high in the areas of sympathy, tenderness, and affection.

By studying these tests and delving into the past, Elise gained insight into herself and into Tracy, too. After much hard thought she finally understood what he really wanted and needed from her and where she had failed him. Then, since she desired to save her marriage, she was able to effect radical changes and improvements in her whole relationship with Tracy. When she changed, he changed, too, even though he persistently denied that changes were necessary or had occurred.

Common sense, combined with a little guidance from us, directed the changes Elise made. In the first place she introduced her husband to the fun of knowing and playing with his own children. It was not hard. He was genuinely fond of children and of sports. She found time for swimming, hiking, and tennis, and insisted that he make time to enjoy these recreations with his family.

In the second place, she stopped ignoring his business and began to talk about his commercial triumphs and problems. She discarded her snippy disapproval of his customers and once again helped with their entertainment. Above all, whenever she felt warmly toward him she showed it.

Tracy needed responsibility. She gave him financial responsibility and thus helped bolster his masculine pride. Instead of secretly taking a temporary job in a financial emergency, she asked him to weigh their income against their expenses and arrive at a workable budget. She then began to spend more on herself and the children and gave him the satisfaction of feeling like an extra-good provider. As a long-term goal, Tracy listed a four-bedroom house on their budget.

They now own the new place. According to Elise—we never see or hear from Tracy—he is a very proud home owner. Their new home is graced with a swimming pool, and Tracy is always eager to get back home and take a plunge with the youngsters. Elise sees to it that he never walks into an empty house after an absence, but recently he was assigned more work in the local office and is out of town much less. He may have asked for this new assignment, but we do not know. At any rate, Elise is sure there is no danger of his ever becoming interested in another woman. She and the children occupy too much of his time.

❅   ❅   ❅

Shocked and wounded as Elise was by her husband's infidelity, it is doubtful that she ever really wanted to leave him. On the other hand, Marian Renfro desperately wanted a divorce from her husband, Hal, when she appealed to us for help. A tiny, fading redhead in her thirties, she was terrified of Hal and of his ungovernable temper.

The two had met back in the days of World War II as defense workers in an ammunition factory in St. Louis when Hal was twenty, Marian eighteen. The first time he saw her she was wearing gray wool slacks and a fresh white shirt. Her voice was low; her smile was reserved but sweet to him. A yellow ribbon was tied in her hair. It was love at first sight for Hal. To his bewitched eyes, he told us years later, she looked like an auburn-haired doll strayed from the toy box, or like Little Red Riding Hood lost among black and greasy forests of ammunition and machinery. But she had held a man's job, been businesslike and efficient.

After a long, stormy courtship, Hal induced Marian to marry him. Thirteen months following the wedding he was sent overseas as a fighter pilot. His romantic and possessive nature may be guessed from the fact that he took along and wore two wrist watches. He kept one watch set to Marian's time in St. Louis. On particularly hazardous missions, scraping the hedge tops in France and looking down the throats of ack-ack guns, he would think, "Hal, this is it. Good-by Marian, good-by my kitten, my baby doll." Then he would glance at her watch and try to picture exactly where she was in their apartment at that hour, exactly what she was doing in St. Louis.

It may have been as well that he did not know. When he came home after eighteen months overseas, he found Marian was six weeks pregnant. Nearly fifteen years later when Hal talked to us at the Institute he vividly remembered the agony of that homecoming. Wiry and unusually tall, in his middle thirties but still looking like a fighter pilot, his tanned face was drawn in lines of pain as he described his arrival home from the war:

*   *

We landed in New York at Mitchel Field. I fast-talked myself aboard a west-bound C-54, and before takeoff sent a telegram to Marian. It was early morning when we touched down in St. Louis, around 5 A.M. Marian wasn't at the airport where I hoped to find her, but I thought she would be waiting in our apartment—an even better deal.

She wasn't there. Yet my telegram lay on the coffee table, and it was open. All the apartment lights were burning. I was sick with longing for Marian, bursting to have her in my arms again, and my message told her so. I didn't ask myself why she had run out on me. Maybe, wanting Marian with such an ache and hunger, I was afraid to speculate on the whys and wherefores.

For several minutes I stood fighting stomach butterflies. Suddenly I was mad. I could feel anger rising in me, tightening in my chest, throbbing behind my eyes. I shook it off, tried to use my head. Marian has a brother and two sisters. I gambled she would be with Thelma, her older sister. My barracks bag was stuffed with truck I'd fetched back to her—perfume, costume jewelry, a music box, and such. I dumped the bag, grabbed up some of Marian's gifts, and took off after her.

It was six o'clock when I rang the bell at Thelma's place. Inside I could hear whispering and moving, although the lights were off. I banged with my fist. A light went on. Finally my sister-in-law answered. Thelma was in her nightgown and yawning. She pretended my wife wasn't there. But I could see inside. On the sofa, big as life, lay Marian's fur coat—the dyed squirrel I couldn't afford but had bought her the week I got my overseas orders. At that sight, my temper blew like a boiler full of steam.

I shoved Thelma from my path. Then, as hard and accurate and fast as I could, like I was back in France making rapid passes at a railroad bridge, I pitched Marian's gifts on the floor and all around the room. I did a lot of damage, quick. One of the packages, I remember, held a pretty china teapot. That package hit a primary target and got a secondary, too. It knocked over a fancy piano lamp with a crash and ended by sailing—wham!—through a windowpane. Thelma was screaming. Her husband, a fat oaf, ran from the bedroom and jumped at me. I knocked him down. In the uproar their youngsters were crying and carrying on. Throughout, I kept yelling for Marian.

She had locked herself in the bathroom. At last she unlocked the door and came on out. Her face was waxy pale, and her voice was trembly as she said she'd come along with me if I would stop busting things. In the taxi, we sat far apart. I'd flown some mighty hot terrain and lived, I'd got a D.F.C. and three oak leaf clusters, but she didn't mention she was glad I was alive. We didn't speak except for me saying I was sorry I made such a commotion and Marian saying to save my apologies for her sister.

When we reached our apartment I got no belated welcome home. Just to show what a fool I can be, I still halfway hoped I might. I'm the kind that needs a wife's love more than most husbands, as Marian is well aware when she denies me. I held her close and kissed her lips, and that was all. She turned her face aside, and I could no longer prevent myself from noticing how she wouldn't look me in the eye. I asked her what was wrong. Nothing, she replied. Nothing except she was tired. I now asked what I didn't want to know—was there another man? No, said she. I didn't believe her, although I tried to believe.

That night I slept alone in our double bed, and Marian slept curled up in a chair. That is, I guess she slept. Her eyes were tightly shut whenever I went and looked at her. I stayed wide awake while my wife's past history—the past I did not hold against her and never will—moved in a turmoil through my thoughts.

On our first date Marian told me a lot about herself, and on each subsequent date she told more. It was information I had no desire to hear, but I couldn't hush her. Many times since, she has insisted her object was to warn and drive me off. If that is true, she did not succeed. When Marian declared to me that she was rough and tough, when she called herself a tramp and worse, I knew different.

Marian wasn't sexually innocent when we met, which did not change my feelings toward her one iota. I wasn't a saint myself. If anything, my determination to have her for my wife, which ran like a fever in my blood, was increased. For I knew my girl had been misled by youth and ignorance and lack of family care. That she needed to be protected and looked after. Her dad died before she could remember much about him, but her mother should have tended her and did not. At fourteen years of age Marian was molested by a man in his thirties. She was a baby sitter in his house; she remained in his employ a period of months. For that fact and for her later experiences I blamed the men involved and I always hated her mother.

After Marian finally accepted my diamond—I had to force the ring on her finger—I made it my business to guard and watch her. Although by then the draft board was breathing down my neck, I agreed to a three-months' engagement at her demand. When we got married at the St. Louis City Hall, I wouldn't allow her mother to have any part whatsoever beyond attending.

Marian quit work, and our life together was perfect. Perfect for me that is, though maybe not for her. When I was drafted, I sublet the apartment, and she followed me to flight training at Randolph Field in Texas. She took a job to fill the hours we couldn't be together. So far as I was concerned, our life continued to be rosy. She never raised her eyes to another man. Of that I am sure. She doesn't know it to this day, but the rooming-house janitor kept tabs on her for me. Any suspicion of Marian I had ever felt was lulled by the time my overseas orders came through. I did try to persuade her to join my parents who were living in Los Angeles, and she halfway promised she would. Instead she went back to the apartment in St. Louis.

As I lay alone that first night home in the double bed where my marriage began, I knew I should have *made* Marian go west and live with my folks while I was gone. She was not to be trusted, but I had stuck my neck out and taken a chance and I had lost. I knew without quesion there had been another man in her life while I was overseas, but I thought I could think him out of existence by keeping my jealousy under control and my temper in check and saying nothing.

It wasn't a case of my forgiving Marian, but rather a case of favoring myself. I preferred to have nothing to forget. Although I had kept faith with her during our separation, I figured it might have been because I was so busy flying and so scared all the time. Or it might have been because no other woman has ever really appealed to me since I met Marian. Consequently I could hardly request a personal halo be issued. What had happened to me had happened to other guys, plenty of them, and they'd lived through it. I could do the same, I figured. These were among the considerations that occupied my mind that long, sleepless night. I still didn't know, of course, just how bad my luck was.

Around noon next day while I was in the bathroom shaving, Marian moved out of the chair and crawled in the bed. I grinned, went to the kitchen, and made a pot of coffee and fixed a tray for her the way she'd done for me one time on our honeymoon. She drank the coffee and ate the eggs and said thank you. But when I tried to get in bed with her it was no deal. She froze. At once my fine resolutions to control my temper went glimmering. I smashed the dishes and the tray. I kicked the sideboards off the bed so that the springs and the mattress dropped to the floor with her. I hollered at her until the janitor rushed up from the basement, threatening to call the police.

For the next week or so our life was pure misery. I abused Marian, I pleaded with her, I slapped her around but not hard, I knelt on my knees to her, I showed my worst side, I showed my best side, and I got nowhere. I got no love, no truth, no explanation. In our apartment, and believe me I looked and watched and listened, there was no sign of the other man. I went through her desk and every scrap of her correspondence; if she picked up the phone I was there; whenever she walked two steps I walked beside her. Nothing.

Then on a Saturday afternoon I was scrubbing the kitchen floor— I must have been making up to Marian for something mean I'd done to her earlier—when the doorbell rang. I jumped up but Marian beat me to the door. It was a woman, wan and thin and cheaply dressed. Selling something, I thought, losing interest. Marian stepped out in the hall with the woman, and I went back to scrubbing. Some minutes must have passed by before I wondered, hey, what goes on? Then I saw Marian had closed the door behind her. I charged across the living room to investigate just as she came back in. There was no expression on her face. The bell rang again. Marian shrugged her shoulders in a sort of helpless way she has. She then said a crazy woman was outside, that I had best ignore her. I opened the door. Marian made no move to stop me.

The woman was leaning sad and despondent against the wall. I went over to her and introduced myself. In five minutes I had the whole story. The woman begged me to force my wife to leave her husband alone. She said she and her husband had three small children they could barely afford to support and now Marian was carrying his fourth child.

With that, the woman went away. When I entered the apartment, I had no wish to bust things. Marian was sitting on the sofa, with her eyes watchful, looking toward the opening door. I had no impulse to holler at her. I walked to the sofa and started to say something, but found I had no voice of any kind. I sat down on the floor. I laid my head in Marian's lap and cried as though I was four years old. I had always calculated Marian might bring me pain and trouble, but I hadn't calculated she would bring me another man's child. I didn't see how I could tolerate somebody else's young one. Not when she and I had spent so many of our honeymoon hours deciding to postpone our own family until my war service was done with. The postponing was my idea mainly. If my wife was fated to be a widow, I didn't want her to be burdened with the support of a child.

Marian's hand, small and soft, lay quietly in my hair. She shed no tear. In all our years together I'd never seen her cry but once—a time her mother was carried to the hospital. At last I pulled myself together. I asked did she love the other man? Did she wish two divorces and marriage to him? Slowly, she shook her head. I asked her if she wanted to bear his child. She said no. I asked if she wanted to stay on and live with me as my wife, if she loved me at all. She wasn't sure, Marian replied; she didn't know. To tell the truth, I myself wasn't sure I wanted her to continue as my wife.

Generally I am not a drinking man. There wasn't a drop of liquor in the apartment. Telling Marian I would have to think about our situation and then she and I would talk further, I went off to the nearest bar. When at length I went roaring home, I was in a mood to wreck the joint. Plus God knows what else.

Marian was gone. I was glad, I guess. Relieved, anyway. School could keep or not, but me, I just didn't care. In the morning I cared plenty. You took her for better or for worse, I thought; the worst came, and you ran out on her. What was going to happen to my girl, pregnant and helpless, that I had turned my back on and left to shift for herself? I began a two-weeks'-long hunt. Marian's family is so large I hadn't even met them all, much less visited in their homes and noted down addresses. My mother-in-law knew her whereabouts and wouldn't tell me. Eventually I found Marian twenty miles outside town on a farm belonging to her brother. She was in bed, weak and recovering from sickness. One of our problems was solved, anyway. There would be no child.

A week later Marian and I left St. Louis, traveled out to California and free lodging with my folks. We were penniless. I had sold our apartment furniture for nickels and dimes. I cut all our ties with the past. I wouldn't permit her to say good-by to a single member of her kin, including her mother especially. I wanted us to have a brand-new start, a fresh beginning.

We have lived in Los Angeles ever since. The sole bright spot in our marriage is the fact we now have a child, Mary Ann, six years old. Steadily everything else has worsened. Marian fought with my mother or vice versa until we had to move. With a G.I. loan I bought us a nice house in a nice neighborhood. Marian won't clean, nor will she cook. Any cooking or cleaning in our house falls on me, in addition to supporting the family. With another G.I. loan I established a business at which I should be doing well. I'm doing rotten. I can't discuss my business affairs or money worries with my wife. If orders are coming in satisfactorily, Marian can easily curb extravagant purchases. But let my inventory climb too high, let my creditors start pecking at me, and she craves everything we can't afford. Other men, smarter men, she says to me, could provide her with the luxuries.

Very often, the stuff Marian insists on buying has been suggested by her mother, who has now moved out to California. So have her two sisters and her brother. It's a free state. I couldn't put a fence around it.

When I refuse Marian cash for something she wants, she takes a job and buys the object—the last thing was a totally unnecessary mirror—with her own money. That gets me upset and mad, as she knows. She parks Mary Ann with her mother—we hardly ever see my folks—and off she goes to work. It's the only time these days she ever looks sweet and clean and pretty. Around the house she wears her hair in strings, no lipstick, and a shiny nose.

Marian insisted that we start our family, have Mary Ann. I thought we should wait until I was in the clear financially. While Mary Ann was a baby, Marian acted like a mother. She now treats Mary Ann as I wouldn't treat a mongrel dog. She doesn't spank or hit her. She just demands perfection. Last week Mary Ann didn't put away her toys promptly. So Marian gathered up her dolls, every single one, and gave them to the rubbish man for his children. Our little girl was brokenhearted.

When Marian is working—at the moment she has a job in an insurance office—my life is misery. Instead of scheduling my calls on customers like other married businessmen, I keep hot-footing it to the insurance building. At lunch time, at coffee-break time, in the afternoon when I drive Marian home. A couple of weeks ago at a coffee break I caught sight of her perched on a stool in the diner, rolling her eyes at a man on either side. I drove off on my calls sick and shaken. That afternoon Marian said both men were her lovers, that their company was preferable to mine.

That is not true. She said it to torment me. She also torments me by telling me of the men in her past—some of these men, too, I am positive are inventions—but she talks at length of how they loved her more and better than I ever have. She tortures me with threats of divorce. Five separate times I have been served with divorce papers. On such occasions I've spent days arguing sense into her and then have paid off her lawyer. I have divorce papers in my pocket right now, which is one reason why I came asking for advice.

The other reason is our doctor suggested it. For two months and five days Marian and I have had no sex life whatever. This is the problem in our marriage which has really got me licked. She is suffering from a vaginal discharge the doctor can't cure and says is psychosomatic. It is her way, he says, of escape. I don't intend her to escape. I want you to tell me what to do. I will make concessions, changes. I will master my temper. I will turn myself inside out for her sake, tell her. You can also tell her for me that ailing or healthy, joyful with sex or starving without sex, I will never let her go.

*   *

As small a woman as her husband had described, Marian Renfro was too deficient in vitality and force to claim beauty. She sidled into the counseling office as though prepared for instant flight. Her lifeless hair floated in a page-boy bob; her lipstick was applied with scrupulous care. Her nails were bitten, untended. Her voice was cool, and she seemed completely unmoved when she spoke of her husband's protestations and avowals which we reported to her:

* *

Hal doesn't love me, whatever he says. Nobody on this earth has loved me in my whole life. Every man who ever spoke to me of love, including Hal, merely meant he admired and wanted my body. The rest of me—my thoughts and dreams, my feelings—didn't matter.

Hal knows noise gets me so nervous I could die. With his nasty, evil temper he keeps our home in a worse uproar than there used to be in the ammunition factory.

I earn my own money, no thanks to him. Several months ago I bought a round, gold-edged mirror my mother saw advertised in a bargain sale. Fearful of Hal's objections, I left the mirror hidden underneath the sofa, intending to put it above the living room mantel some time he wouldn't notice. Our little girl—Mary Ann is a sweet child but nosy—crawled behind the sofa and at once ran to her father. Whereupon Hal commenced an argument which ended by his throwing my new mirror straight through the big mirror of our dresser.

Now we have no mirror in the house except the little one above the medicine cabinet. Furthermore, while fragments of the mirror were lying strewn in millions of pieces, Hal decided we ought to make love. It was his idea of the way to mend our quarrel. It wasn't mine. I told him to sweep up the glass. He got the broom and did the sweeping. Then when I still refused him, he went ahead and took me, anyway.

My husband is like all men. Sex is all he ever thinks about. He is demented on the topic. Naturally I expected sex with marriage. I don't mind sex in moderation. The sweet, loving part of sex—the part Hal wants to rush through or skip—I yearn for and enjoy. My feelings don't interest my husband. Often he doesn't even ask permission. He steals up while I'm unaware, ironing maybe or preparing supper. He grabs me from behind, carries me to the bedroom, slams the door with an elbow and throws me on the bed. He then complains I am cold to him. Cold? Cold doesn't half describe it. Often Hal makes me feel as though I wasn't even alive but was one of those department-store dummies. I'm glad I am too unwell for any more of Hal's kind of love. I hope I stay that way.

Since I can remember, I have wanted and searched for love. Real love, true love. My sisters and brother found love. All of them are handsome and of normal size. I am the sole exception. I am only 4 feet, 11 inches tall. People, men especially, those with ideas in mind, have called me pretty. My hair and my features are pretty to me, I guess; my size is hideous. If I'd been an inch or so shorter I could have got a job as a circus midget. My father used to say he should put me in a side show with the fat lady and the other freaks. Then all of them at home would laugh. As a child I was called the runt of the litter. Everybody teased and made fun of me. Everybody was stronger. My sisters and brother could lift me like a feather. We had a window seat in our house, a kind of hollow storage box, with a hinged lid. They would put me in the box, lower the lid, and sit on it just to hear me struggle to get out, scream in fear, and cry. When finally I learned to stop struggling and crying, they played the game no more.

At about twelve or thirteen I acquired the hope I might grow to be 5 feet tall. I thought 5-foot people were different from me. Sometimes I still think so. Anyway, I drew a secret 5-foot mark in crayon on the basement wall. Each day after school I would hurry to my basement corner and stand on tiptoe and stretch and stretch and try to force myself to grow up to be as high as my secret mark. Then one afternoon my mother caught me at the stretching, and she laughed. She passed the story to my father—he died later that same year but was sick so long I can scarcely remember him—and he laughed, too.

I wasn't overly fond of my father. My mother worked to the dropping point because of his sickness and so little money coming in and all us kids. I was not a good child. I used to wish my father would either get well or die. Often I didn't think too kindly of my mother either. She didn't seem to care very much for me or any of her children when we were small. She must have hugged and kissed me as a baby, but I don't know. Once when I was four or five I ran to her with a bleeding finger I had cut against a knife blade on purpose. I begged her to kiss my finger well, as I had seen a playmate's mother do. My mother, who was tending my father, frowned and pushed me off. Then and there I vowed I would never again seek a kiss from her. I have kept my vow.

In our house no child's birthday was celebrated. In vain I pestered my mother for a party. The year I was eight, my brother's wife gave the party for me and baked a cake with candles. I then told my poor mother I loved Arline better than her. I've tried to make up to my mother for the hard thoughts I used to hold against her in childhood. That's the reason Hal's treatment of her and insulting, unfair remarks get me frantic. He puts the blame for my misdeeds before and after our marriage on my mother and in every other quarter except where it belongs. The blame is mine.

When I first got myself into trouble on the baby-sitting job I was at fault. Nobody else. I was fourteen, I could have rejected the advances of the man. He had two children and a wife, and I knew it. Somehow I couldn't help the way I behaved with him. It was as though he and I made a pact. I was willing to accept the sexual relationship he wanted in exchange for the kisses and sweetness and tenderness I wanted. Seeking and thirsting, I believed the man loved me.

He didn't love me, of course. He fooled me. When my sister Thelma learned what was going on and confronted him, he denied he had so much as touched my hand in greeting. It is needless to mention other men in my past who have fooled me. But here is how Hal convinced me I was loved for myself, cherished.

I was doubtful he would want to marry me when he heard my story. But he did. The night he gave me my engagement ring he was supposed to work the late shift. He put me aboard the trolley and asked if I was going straight home. Surprised, I said yes. Well,

after a long ride I walked up on our porch. In the darkness the
swing was creaking, and in the swing sat Hal. He had taken the
night off and hired a taxi and raced out there to see if my word was
good. Where is the love in that? Hal doesn't know I know that during our honeymoon he hired a janitor to spy on me. When he was
ordered overseas I hoped he wouldn't be shot down or wounded,
but I did hope that he wouldn't come back to me. That long ago I'd
had just about all I could stand of him.

Hal doesn't trust me in a solitary thing. He boasts he is generous
financially, but he won't hand me the cash to replace the mirrors
he broke. I know he is earning more than he lets on. The other day
I stumbled on a roll of bills he had hidden in his tool box for fear I
might go through his trousers and count his money. He complains
I don't keep house and cook. It's true. I'm too nervous and discouraged to drum up the interest or energy.

Mary Ann discourages me, too. She looks exactly like Hal except
for being small like me. She and her father are close in temperament and disposition. Hal was terribly spoiled as a boy. His grandmother told me he sat in her lap and his mother's lap until he was
in the third or fourth grade. I don't want Mary Ann spoiled. She
loves me little if at all, which doesn't affect my duty as a mother.
Since Mary Ann is bound to be a midget-sized woman like me, she
needs better training than I received as a child. She needs to be a
lady. On top of everything else, Hal interferes with my attempts to
discipline our daughter.

Divorce may be bad for most children, but Mary Ann will benefit
by being separated from her father. Tell Hal that. You can also
tell him he makes me feel like the mustard seed in the Bible. A
mustard seed crushed beneath a heavy millstone. I long to be free.
Please, please tell Hal not to fight my divorce suit.

❖   ❖

Marian and Hal Renfro were destroying themselves and the future of their young daughter by living almost entirely on an emotional level. Hal was a college graduate, and Marian had completed

her sophomore year with better than average grades. Yet neither employed intellect in managing their marriage and their lives. Of the two, Marian, who resented her small stature so fiercely, seemed to be in more serious need of gaining personal insight. We did most of our counseling with her.

Neglected by a well-meaning but overworked mother, Marian grew up with no sense of personal identity. Her craving for attention and love earned for her not comfort and warmth but the laughter and teasing of relatives she regarded as stronger, bigger, wiser, and of more account than herself. Early she developed an abnormal sensitivity. Almost greedily she collected and stored in her childhood memory only the impressions that would solidify her feeling of being adrift in a huge world. As a teen-ager she feverishly hunted for the love she was convinced she had never received, throwing herself at the head of an employer old enough to be her father. She presented herself to him as a worthless girl, as later she was to present herself to Hal.

We suggested to Marian that unless she could love and respect herself, she could not love another. Without the ability to give love, whether or not she divorced Hal, it was likely her existence would continue to be chaotic and unhappy.

After several interviews Marian acknowledged she had never loved a human being—not her husband, not her child, not her mother. Her adult clinging to her mother represented a sort of expiation for the hatred she had borne her mother, her father, her sisters and brother, during the crushing loneliness of her childhood years. A heavy load of guilt—it is not "right" to hate your mother and wish death to your paralytic father; it is not "right" to be promiscuous and break your marriage vows—added to her emotional confusions.

With our encouragement and aid, Marian went to work to get rid of her wasting self-contempt, to build up her ego. We explained to her a psychological law which might be called "the necessity of body acceptance." Short people, tall people, fat people, lean people, crippled people, even unusually attractive people sometimes become obsessed with the notion that the bodies in which they must live are disgusting. Marian's figure, though slight, was graceful and pretty. We insisted that she sit up straight in a chair instead of shrinking and cowering; we advised her to compare herself with other women she passed on the street. At length and very gradually she learned to be at peace with her small stature. After she talked to us again and again of painful past experiences which were embedded like thorns in her memory, a psychological process known as desensitization occurred. The old memories returned less often and hurt less.

In her treatment of her daughter, Marian was mimicking her mother's indifference—why should Mary Ann have a happier life than the little girl Marian once had been?—as well as skirmishing in her continuous warfare with Hal. She got at her husband by attacking the child. In her treatment of Hal, Marian was attempting to cut him down to her size.

In a way, Hal invited some of the abuses Marian heaped upon him. Hal, like Tracy Manning, was strongly sexed. Yet Hal regarded himself as an average, affectionate husband handicapped, but only slightly, by an uncertain temper. We never fully understood Marian's powerful sexual appeal for him, but there is no doubt it existed. His conception of loving Marian, however, was nothing more than self-gratification.

Several good books on the nature and meaning of sex were recommended which brought enlightenment to him. He was advised that unselfishness, consideration, and trust were important factors in love between a man and a woman. He took the advice. Tenderness from Hal aided in effecting Marian's recovery from her psychosomatic malady, and eventually their marital relationship was resumed on a basis satisfactory to both. Most of Hal's explosions of temper, inexcusable in an adult, had resulted from Marian's rebuffs of his sexual overtures. When their sex problem was resolved, the rough edges of his temper smoothed.

By that time he and Marian were admitting equal blame for the abominable state into which their marriage had fallen. Once he grasped that marriage meant sharing in all departments of life, Hal confided his business worries to Marian. He was pleasantly surprised by her reaction; she wanted to help and did, with thriftiness. She continued to work for a while in order that his business might be established on a firm foundation. She budgeted willingly and paid a fair share of the household expenses instead of throwing away her money as well as his.

Their in-laws, particularly Marian's mother, still cause occasional family arguments. But after Marian understood the reasons for her dependence, she was able to loosen some of the ties that bound her to her mother. Hal has helped her. When a criticism of his mother-in-law forms on his lips, he deliberately turns the sharp remark into a compliment. This technique has led Marian to find admirable qualities in Hal's parents.

Mary Ann now has a chance to see both her grandmothers. Marian no longer dreads spoiling her daughter, since she has learned to love and understand her. Not long ago Mary Ann came home from school in tears because she had the smallest feet of any child in the room.

Marian sent her little girl back to school filled with joy and pride. Cinderella, Mary Ann informed her schoolmates, had such tiny feet she won the prince.

* * *

Outside of fairy stories self-knowledge and understanding, sacrifice, and hard work are more efficacious means than shoe size for a Cinderella to win—or even rewin—the prince.

Doris Bradley had tried everything, short of a fairy godmother, to rewin her husband, Paul. She finally decided she would rather lose Paul completely than share him any longer with Florence Moore, who had once been her best friend.

Paul and Florence had been carrying on an affair for almost three years when Doris came to us in desperation. Ironically enough, it was Doris who introduced her husband to the other woman in his life. She and Florence first became acquainted in a park where they took their children. The Moores's boy and girl were practically the same ages as the Bradleys' son and daughter. Inclined to be reserved and shy, Doris found Florence so friendly and full of fun that she could not feel shy with her. In a matter of days the two young women were doing their marketing together. Because Doris had a job and her friend did not work, Florence took over the bargain-buying for both families when there was a sale during the week.

Paul Bradley, an outgoing, gregarious man who worked for an automobile agency, had long felt that he and Doris stuck too close to their own fireside. Although he often urged that they circulate more and enlarge their circle, he showed very little interest in his wife's glowing tales of her park-bench friend. Sensitive as well as shy, Doris suspected that her husband believed any acquaintance she made on her own would be tiresome and dull.

On the Saturday afternoon when she finally invited Florence and her family to drop in on them, Paul almost did not stay at home. Saturdays and Sundays were his best days to demonstrate cars. It was only after considerable persuasion that Doris prevailed on him to put off a couple of prospective automobile buyers in order to meet the Moores. She was delighted when Paul found Florence sparkling and amusing.

The two families clicked from the first. Soon they were spending nearly every week end together, generally at the Bradleys'. In the beginning Doris did not notice how Paul managed to juggle his appointments in order to be at home whenever Florence was expected. Doris not only trusted her husband, but she was also kept busy cooking a big dinner for the crowd. While Florence often invited the Bradleys to her house, they usually went there after everybody had been fed by Doris. Florence was not keen on cooking. She was the cold-cuts-potato-salad type, whereas Paul was the roast-beef-apple-pie type, preferring good hot food and sitting down at a table to eat it.

It was Florence's husband, Ralph, who first became suspicious.

He dropped hints to Doris, but she tried to dismiss them. She was unsuccessful. She began to wonder whether Paul actually was demonstrating automobiles on all the nights he stayed out so late.

Paul's hours were long and irregular and fitted poorly with her long hours. Doris rose at six o'clock in the morning and drove the children to a cousin's house, a distance of twenty miles, before reporting to her secretarial job. She worked hard all day and was tired by the long drives to deliver and pick up the youngsters, so tired she was practically dead on her feet by the time she prepared an early supper. After Paul ate and hurried off on his evening round of appointments, she and the children promptly went to bed. Until Ralph Moore's hints made her uneasy, she had always been sound asleep when Paul came in. But then she started waking up, no matter how quiet his entrance was. She would look at the clock and see it was midnight or later.

She asked Paul why he could not get in by half-past ten, as he had previously done. He explained he had several prospects working the swing shift in aircraft plants. Once he did not arrive home until 6 A.M., just as Doris was getting up. He told her he had gone bowling with a bunch of the fellows, and then stopped in a bar with the head of the sales crew and lost track of the time.

At this point Doris suggested that they stop seeing so much of Florence and Ralph and see some of their other friends for a change. Paul refused. Regularly each Saturday and Sunday Doris continued to entertain Florence and her family and continued to pretend the Bradleys and the Moores were still friends.

Then came the evening when the pretense could no longer be maintained. Doris walked in the kitchen unexpectedly and found Paul and Florence in each other's arms. He stepped away from her and smiled at Doris and said Florence was his second-best girl. He waited for Doris to smile back. She merely turned and stumbled out of the kitchen.

Somehow she managed to get the dinner on the table and feed the four youngsters. Mercifully, Ralph was out of town on that occasion. It was not until Florence had left with her children and

Doris had put hers to bed that she and Paul had a chance to talk. He confessed the whole miserable truth, admitted that he and Florence had been meeting in motels for many months, and then announced that he wanted and needed both his wife and his mistress. It seemed to Doris that Florence meant more to him than his home, but he declared he wanted to maintain their marriage and begged for her forgiveness.

They talked all night. In the morning, Florence drove over. She and Paul promised to stop seeing each other. From then on, there were no more of the communal week ends, but Paul and Florence immediately broke their solemn promises. They continued to see each other on week ends without the nuisance of families. They saw each other at every available opportunity.

For well over a year, Doris lived with constant reminders of her husband's infidelity. The woman cashier at the automobile agency supplied her with unwanted bulletins on the number of times Florence phoned Paul at work. The agency manager relayed the news to her that Paul's work was slipping and wondered if she could help straighten him out.

After months of suffering and strain she went through an evening when she could bear no more. She told Paul he would have to choose between Florence and her, and next day she came and talked to us. At that time she was on the verge of a nervous crack-up. Our counseling report on the interview notes that she wore an expensive, lavishly embroidered cashmere sweater in combination with a rumpled tweed skirt and that her shaky hands aimlessly buttoned and unbuttoned the sweater as she related the events that led up to her ultimatum:

*   *

Yesterday was my tenth wedding anniversary. I had vague hopes Paul and I were going to spend a pleasant, normal evening like other married couples. He brought me this sweater I'm wearing and a bouquet of pink roses. Then, in one of the sweet ways he has, he gave a small gift to both of our youngsters and told them to thank me since it was because of me they were here on earth to get presents.

My cousin came to dinner, and afterward she offered to stay with the children while Paul and I went dancing. I was terribly tired—we're in the midst of the annual inventory at my office—but Paul loves to dance, so I pumped up some enthusiasm and said yes. There is only one place near us with an orchestra. A block before we reached it, Paul slowed down the car and asked if I wouldn't prefer the movies. The tone of his voice, very offhand and casual, was all I needed. When Paul is thinking about Florence I can read his mind. I've had plenty of practice. The moment he spoke I knew he had taken Florence dancing there recently—she is a far better dancer than I am—and he was trying to be nice on our anniversary and prevent himself from comparing the way she and I dance.

We went to the movie. It was a good comedy, but I just couldn't get interested or concentrate. Right in the funniest part of the picture, Paul suddenly got up from his seat, explaining he had forgotten to pass on an important message to someone at the agency. The offhand tone was in his voice again. He went out to the phone booth in the lobby and—I knew it as well as if I had followed—talked to Florence for eighteen minutes.

On the way home, I asked him how Florence was. He gave me a hangdog look and said Florence was fine. Then he put his hand on my shoulder and said he was sorry—strange as this may sound, I think he *was* sorry—but that he just couldn't help making that phone call. It seemed he hadn't heard Florence's voice for two days. I pushed off his hand.

When we got home, my cousin took one glance at us and knew something was up. She reported the children had been angels and grabbed her hat and flew. I saw Paul brace himself as though I might start a fight, which was quite unnecessary. I hadn't the energy to quarrel with him. I hadn't the wish. I wasn't even angry. What would be the use? I felt empty, like a thrown-away paper sack.

But when Paul started to undress for bed, something inside me must have snapped. As he dropped his necktie on our bureau, I heard myself tell him to make up his mind between Florence and me that very minute. I'd had all I could take, I said. Why didn't he go to Florence and leave me in peace? Immediately Paul launched into his old story of wanting and needing us both. His words, as usual, made no sense to me. He begged me to reconsider. Just let him think it over until morning. I shook my head.

He looked at the door, looked at me. He went in the children's room and turned on the light and looked at them. He came back in the bedroom and put on his necktie again. He knotted it, carefully. Then he got out his bags and started to pack his clothes. His favorite shirt was in the dryer, and I offered to iron it for him. His eyes got kind of bright, and he said not to bother.

I didn't cry. I felt exhausted, numb, as though I'd run a million miles and then come in at the tail end of the race. It didn't seem to matter that my husband was leaving me and our children for another woman, that my marriage was breaking up before my eyes. I sat down in the boudoir chair Paul gave me last Christmas—he gave Florence a chair just like it—and I fell asleep while he was still packing.

When I woke in the morning his bags were unpacked, and his clothes were hanging in the closet again. He had wrapped a blanket around me, but he was gone from the house. I can't tell you how many times Paul has packed his bags, announcing he intends to leave. Every two or three weeks he decides he can't live another minute without Florence, but then he changes his mind and unpacks.

It still seems incredible to me that a man like Paul, generous and kind and considerate in so many ways, could treat a wife as I have been treated. When we got married, Paul was like a god to me. I was a dumb little country girl holding my first job in a big city and was scared to death of men and of sex. Paul was so gentle we soon solved the sex part of our marriage. Or so I once believed. I once believed he loved me.

Now I realize nothing about me ever did suit him. From our

honeymoon days, he has tried to make me over in every respect. And I have tried with all my might to change into the kind of wife he wants. I took dancing lessons at Paul's request. I took evening college courses in English. Paul enrolled me in a charm school. I attended faithfully. He told me what to talk about in company, and I stuck to the topics he selected. He favored fancier cooking than my mother taught me, so I took cooking lessons, too. Paul has always selected all my clothes and told me the proper accessories to wear. He thinks I lack clothes sense, and it's true. The fact is I am lacking in everything. For the first few months of our marriage I was flattered by Paul's suggestions, but I long ago figured out he was ashamed of me.

For years and years I struggled to improve my marriage and myself. It was like running backward all the way. Finally, I just couldn't run any longer. I was worn down to a nub even before Florence appeared. I cannot compete with her.

Paul doesn't advise Florence what to wear or how to act. It isn't necessary. He loves her the way she is. I'm a failure as a wife. As a person I don't hold a candle to Florence. She is beautiful, she's charming; if she wants my husband she can have him.

Paul is only staying with me for the sake of our children. For their sake, I, too, tried to hold our home together. I'm now at the end of my strength and my interest. If Paul chooses to get a divorce and marry Florence, I will be perfectly satisfied. I will have my children and for the first time in years I will have a chance to relax and get some rest.

*   *

Paul Bradley was thirty-six, seven years older than Doris. He obviously was not happy about his situation when he talked to us. His hollow eyes and distracted air testified to the tension, indecision, and self-contempt he told us he was experiencing:

*   *

For months I've swung back and forth like a pendulum; my nickname ought to be Tick-Tock. Many a night I've sat in our living room until sunup, smoking cigarette after cigarette, with my mind twisting this way and that. One minute my spirits are at zero, the next minute I feel equal to carrying my burdens and acting as a decent husband and father should, the next minute I have to battle the impulse to sneak out of my home and never come back.

I know I ought to be satisfied with my marriage. Just as I know all the right is on Doris' side, and she deserves better than me. Regardless of how I've behaved toward Doris, I am very fond of her. I'm not of a critical, complaining disposition. It makes me feel like a heel to sound off against Doris, who has never brought anything but good to me and our children. She is a fine housekeeper and a wonderful mother. She is unselfish and considerate. There is nothing she won't do for me or the kids—she will crawl out of bed at any hour of the night to draw a bath for me, and she never forgets to lay out sandwiches for when I get home.

But Doris is a downbeat character. Nothing that is fun is fun for Doris. Or if so, I've never discovered what she considers fun. Seemingly she doesn't get a lift out of ANYTHING. After ten years of marriage, I don't know whether Doris is enjoying a movie or is there as a favor to me and would prefer to be at home. Generally I suspect she'd rather be home catching up on her shut-eye. Doris requires ten- or eleven-hours' sleep at a minimum. She would turn down an invitation to a ball at the White House if it interfered with her rest. Any kind of social function starts her yawning. I used to ask a crowd over for the evening sometimes, but she took no interest in talking to anybody. She invariably excused herself and fell into bed the minute she finished serving a splendid dinner. She is an unusually talented cook, but guests expect more than good food. So does a husband. I've tried to teach Doris how to have fun and companionship and get along with people—in the past I arranged all sorts of lessons for her—but she never caught on.

If Doris has a favorite TV program she has yet to mention it. On the rare occasions when we watch TV together, her head begins nodding immediately. I don't recall the last time I heard her laugh out loud. She doesn't even smile very often. Once I took her to a championship football game where the winning touchdown was made in the final two minutes. She missed the excitement hunting for her gloves. Another time I took her to the Sadler Wells Ballet, and she spent most of the second act resting on a couch in the ladies' room.

It seems to me Doris and I are temperamentally unsuited. We were acquainted only six weeks before we married. I was twenty-six. I wanted to settle down and raise a family. I'd had my fill of girls who chased me because they admired the color of my pay check.

Doris was cute as a button, and in those days she kept her stocking seams straight. She was shy and modest, a refreshing change from the fluffs I'd known. She is a top-flight secretary now and has always been darned efficient. She was stable and reliable, and I knew I could depend on her in the future if the financial going got rough. Doris handles money better than any person—man or woman—I ever knew.

This isn't to say she tries to stint my spending, for she doesn't. The main reason she works today is because I'm extravagant. I was raised poor. To me marriage meant living in a nice house, bigger and with better furnishings and equipment than could be swung on one salary, a good place to entertain friends. We don't entertain, but we've sure got the background, thanks to Doris. I wish you could hear my parents sing her praises. Awhile back my dad ran into tough luck, and, without mentioning it to me, Doris sent him money from her heart.

Doris is generous with cash, but in several important ways she is stingy with herself. I'm warm and affectionate by nature. She isn't. To me our honeymoon was a humiliating fiasco, although I kept my mouth shut and I didn't blame Doris. Her mother brought Doris up to be a good woman but stuffed her head with a lot of foolishness about the brutality of men. I tried to be patient and for a while I thought we had the sex problem worked out. I was mistaken. After the birth of our second child Doris seemed so distressed by my advances that I have troubled her as seldom as possible.

I don't deny Florence has a strong physical appeal for me, although there is more to the attraction than that. Perhaps I could have resigned myself to the fact there was little sex in my marriage. But I cannot get along without companionship. I grew up in a noisy, crowded house—I'm the youngest of six—jammed with friends of both sexes and all sizes and ages. Doris grew up with one little sister who was crippled, and their mother kept their house as neat and quiet as a hospital.

Our present home is just as quiet. Whatever time I get in, it's like stepping into a morgue. I tiptoe into the kids' room and make sure they are covered—I can always count on finding my son's blankets heaped on the floor—and then I tiptoe into the master bedroom. I'm keyed up and anxious to talk about my day. Doris doesn't open an eye. Of course I could wake her and ask her to do something specific for me, but she'd fumble around half asleep and there would be no satisfaction in that. I look down at my sleeping wife and feel as lonesome as any bachelor all by himself in a hall bedroom.

In my loneliness, I guess I was waiting for Florence some while before I met her. Florence is willing to go anywhere or do anything at any hour of the day or night. She is like a Fourth of July sky rocket. She is as wide awake as a ten-year-old on the Saturday the circus comes to town. Her husband is also perpetually weary. I'm sure that is what first caused Florence and me to take a second look at each other—the look between a man and a woman that counts. Back when our two families were spending week ends together, the children would eat and then run out to play. At that point Ralph would collapse on the sofa while Doris dozed in a chair. Florence and I would put on some records and dance. I had planned for Doris and me to celebrate our tenth anniversary in a fancy night club. We wound up at a neighborhood movie. Florence looks like a million dollars in her clothes. Doris automatically ruins the style of anything she puts on. She didn't notice the sweater I gave her was cashmere. She didn't bother to change to an appropriate skirt, and there was a run in her stocking. I would like to be proud of the appearance of my wife.

Maybe it's wrong, but I can't help enjoying Florence's gaiety and high spirits. I will never forget some of the laughs we've had. At times we've grabbed each other by the hand and laughed ourselves sick at a funny happening on the street or a funny remark made by one of my customers. Florence isn't capable and efficient like Doris. If I fell under a truck and got my legs cut off, Doris would turn to and support the kids and me. In such an emergency Florence couldn't even take care of herself. She doesn't know how to work, her housekeeping isn't extra, and nobody would describe her as a wonderful mother. Our boy and girl are the best behaved and best dressed in the block. Her kids are wild Indians, and often they are downright shabby.

I know Florence lacks Doris' fine qualities, but I can't get Florence out of my head or my heart. Anything and everything brings her to my mind. The smell of her perfume on another woman. Passing a street cart of flowers and recalling the thrill Florence got the day I bought her a handful of daisies. She now calls daisies "our flower." Doris accepted my anniversary roses with no change of expression, without remembering I gave her pink roses at our engagement party. Several nights ago around 3 A.M., too restless for bed, I was listening to the radio in our living room. A disk jockey put on "Star Dust." I thought about the way Florence sounds singing that song. In the dark of the living room, I could hear her voice, see her image, and feel the tears roll down my face.

I can remember the promises I've made Doris—and then broken —as well as she can. I have tried to forget Florence and make something of my marriage. The prospect of losing my two kids torments me daily. I am so badgered by my conscience that I am practically insane. My sales record—I used to enjoy selling—has plummeted. If I don't soon unscramble my mixed emotions, reach a solid decision and stick to it, I'm bound to be dropped by my agency.

I will never meet a better woman than Doris. I will never meet a better companion than Florence. I've lost my capacity to think. What do you think I should do?

* *

Naturally we did not *tell* Paul what course of conduct to pursue. Our job is to help our clients find their own way. We suspected—on the basis of one significant piece of evidence—that Paul had already made the important decision. Although he was not yet consciously aware of the fact, it seemed almost certain that Paul intended to stick with his wife and children. The evidence? We humans are likely to do what we want to do, whenever possible. If Paul had *really* desired to leave his family, get a divorce, and marry Florence, he would have packed and moved out of his home long before he and Doris came to the Institute for advice. Nothing was holding him.

Paul and Doris discovered—as did the other couples with similar problems we have discussed—that the first step in saving their marriage was for each to follow the age-old precept, "Know thyself." In the process of learning about themselves, they made some surprising discoveries.

Paul, easygoing with friends, always ready to laugh and joke with a customer, tolerant with strangers, was startled when personality tests and our counseling proved to him that he was exceedingly critical of those close to him—in this case, Doris. When he married her, he had not conducted himself like a bridegroom. He had behaved like the impatient teacher of a dull-witted student. What bride would enjoy being bundled off to a charm school?

Loving her husband and vastly impressed by his "big city" knowledge and manners, Doris had willingly thrown all her strength and energy into satisfying his demands. She had failed to please him. Continued failures shattered her confidence, destroyed her self-esteem. Since she woke with a sense of failure each morning, quite naturally her energy leaked away. Instead of becoming more socially adept under Paul's anxious, insistent prodding, she became less adept. The neatly turned-out girl he married changed into a listless wife who neither knew nor cared how she looked. Once

Doris was convinced she could not win in the game of pleasing Paul, she stopped trying. The smallest social challenge sent her to bed exhausted.

At our advice Doris went to her doctor for a complete examination. No physical cause was found for her chronic fatigue, nor did her hard work at home and on her job explain the need for ten- or eleven-hours' sleep a night. Doris' weariness was neurotic. She was escaping into sleep from the problems and dissatisfactions of her life and marriage.

The medical examination did disclose a physical reason why she shrank from Paul's love. During the birth of her second child her cervix had been damaged. A sexual relationship was painful to her. She had been too dejected in spirit to confide this fact either to Paul or to her doctor. Minor surgery repaired the damage. The couple then resumed their sexual relationship on a mutually pleasant basis.

Paul fancied he was staying with the marriage solely for the sake of his children. The truth was that Doris herself possessed qualities of character and temperament which held him. As soon as we helped him to realize this, Paul *wanted* to make something of his marriage, stop punishing his wife—he was punishing Doris for his unjust disappointment with her—and cure himself of his obsession for the glamorous Florence. At our suggestion he balanced the qualities he admired in Doris—her generosity, stability, efficiency—against the least admirable qualities in Florence. Again and again he deliberately concentrated his thoughts upon Florence's irresponsibility, her indifference to her husband's comfort and peace of mind, her open neglect of her two youngsters. Slowly but surely the scales were tipped in Doris' favor. Gradually the images of Florence and the fantasies which had enthralled him faded from his mind.

When Paul recognized that his criticalness had reduced Doris' confidence to the vanishing point, he made amends. A few kind words paid rich dividends. At a single compliment Doris fairly bloomed. The alteration in her appearance was astonishing to us.

With every interview we could see a difference. Her sagging figure straightened, her drooping mouth lifted, even her hair seemed to acquire a new shine. Her long-dormant sense of style revived.

Enormously grateful to Paul for the encouragement that cost him little, Doris changed in other ways. Whenever Paul wanted to go out for an evening, they went out. On Saturday nights they usually invited a crowd to their house. Doris stayed up until the door closed behind the last, lagging guest.

Her drowsiness diminished when she learned of its neurotic origin. But because her schedule obliges her to rise early while Paul can lie abed until nine, she needs more nighttime rest than he. By rearranging her schedule she gets it. After Paul leaves the house in the evening, she puts the children to bed, curls up on the sofa, and sleeps until the alarm rings at 9:45, fifteen minutes before Paul's return. That gives her time to freshen her lipstick, comb her hair, and look her best for a home-coming husband.

Over a late-evening snack, she and Paul talk over the events of his business day and hers. When they get to bed it is often 1 A.M., but they retire together. Doris happpily overlooks the inconvenience to herself. She has the satisfaction of knowing she is a successful wife at last.

*   *

We have just discussed couples whose marriages appeared to be failing because of extracurricular love affairs. In every case other factors figured in the trouble. Next, we will take up a group of our clients who complained that their marital difficulties were caused by in-laws.

Section II: Getting Along with In-Laws

Probably no people have more difficulty getting along with their in-laws than Americans. Primitive peoples faced the problem more frankly. Some tribes had a strict rule that a man and his wife's mother should never be in the same house together. Sometimes the husband and his mother-in-law were not even allowed to speak to each other. At the opposite extreme, in the older Japan and other Oriental countries, the husband's mother was the ruler of the home. If she did not like the girl her son married, she could, in effect, divorce that girl. She could order her to leave, and choose another wife for her son. Between these extremes, there must be a very broad middle ground on which a better family life could be built in this country.

We have not yet found that ground. In every section of the United States the in-law problem is critical. The Jesuit sociologist John L. Thomas of St. Louis University made a study of 7000 divorces in the archdiocese of Chicago. He concluded that, during the first year after the wedding, more marriages were broken up by in-law troubles than by anything else.

The younger and the older generation alike are in need of enlightenment, education, tolerance. The wife who expects her husband to repudiate his mother, to ignore her completely, is as unrealistic as the mother who assumes she will have the same control over the young couple as she once had over her own "child." As soon as the wedding is announced both sides might well begin rehearsing the new roles they will play.

The prospective mother-in-law should give the newcomer a feeling of acceptance in the family—genuine acceptance. Sometimes she overdoes her cordiality, introducing the girl to her friends with fulsome and obviously insincere praise. Other times she insists on taking the side of the bride-to-be against her own offspring in all differences of taste. It is not easy for the older woman to establish the new relationship on an ideal basis. In general, if the mother can build up an air of companionship, respect, and affection, and demonstrate her willingness to let the younger people live their own lives, she will be making the right start. It is not necessary to go so far as did the mother-in-law who explained that she had finally learned how to get along with the young people: "I keep my pocketbook open and my mouth shut."

Traditionally it is the wife's mother who is the troublemaker, but several recent American studies have indicted the husband's mother as a greater source of difficulty nowadays. The young bride has had a lifetime of experience in getting along with her own mother. She may have learned docilely to accept being bossed, or she may have developed a sort of "mother deafness" in which she goes her own way and pays no attention to what mamma says. It is virtually impossible for her to transfer either of these attitudes to her husband's mother, whom she is inclined to regard as a complete outsider, a prospective meddler, and a dangerous rival. This chip-on-the-shoulder behavior of the younger woman is reflected and perhaps intensified by the stale mother-in-law jokes which are almost as old as the race.

If husband and wife can talk over in-law problems calmly and objectively, they can usually solve them without too much rancor. But this is difficult. Whenever an in-law problem arises, indignation, resentment, and hostility are likely to burst forth. At this stage, a disinterested and experienced marriage counselor can often be invaluable. Frequently the distressed couple merely needs to be reassured that a proposed course of action is wise and justified and will be acceptable to all friends and relatives. A sound rule to hold in mind is that any serious in-law problem should be resolved by the blood kin. In other words, the husband must speak to his own mother and put her in her place if necessary. His wife cannot do it; nor is it intelligent for him to take up the cudgels with *her* mother.

A clever wife can often get action by approaching the subject of her mother-in-law indirectly. Picking out a quiet time, she can say to her husband, "I have been wondering if you feel I am dominated too much, in some ways, by my mother? Tell me frankly, and you and I together can work out a solution." Maybe he will reply with astonishment, "I never dreamed of such a thing!" Maybe his reply will contain some sharp criticisms. In either event he will probably follow his comments with, "Do you think I am paying too much attention to my own mother?" Then the two can talk the whole matter out, focusing on definite points of annoyance one at a time and agreeing on a policy concerning each.

Although nowadays young couples are less frequently obliged to share a roof with their elders than in the past, physical separation does not necessarily ensure their privacy. At the Institute we listen daily to the laments of young people who are expected to devote every week end to parents. There are certain rules that our counselors wish that all in-laws would memorize:

Make your visits "short and sweet," not too frequent, and never unannounced. Do not be too ready to accept an invitation in general terms, "Come to see us often." Go when you are invited and specify in advance a definite period of time for your stay.

When you visit a daughter-in-law, behave as though you were in the home of a friend or acquaintance. Any young woman would resent having someone peering into her closets, pulling open the bureau drawers, taking the lids off the pots on the stove to see what's cooking, dropping suggestions about the planning or furnishing of the house, and so on. A mother, like any other considerate guest, can make herself useful by helping with the housework, and perhaps hope to set a good example by doing things rather than by dispensing a flood of unwanted advice. But even in her best-intentioned efforts to be helpful, she will sometimes irritate her son's wife. She may suggest, "Do let me have some of John's socks. I will be glad to darn them. I have been doing it all my life." Generous as the offer sounds, the younger woman may twist it to mean, "I'll bet you don't keep his socks darned. You've probably got an overflowing mending basket, and it's up to me to help you out."

Holidays often produce the first crisis in a new family. Parents take it for granted that the young people will come to them for Thanksgiving Day or Christmas. Perhaps the newlyweds have other plans, or perhaps both sets of in-laws are in competition. The young people should be allowed to make their own arrangements. If they say, "We'd love to spend Christmas in your home," they can be safely welcomed. But if they are silent, they should be privileged to have their own Christmas and feel they are a family in their own right.

Now we might direct a few remarks to daughters-in-law, unpracticed in dealing with the older generation. Remember that your mother-in-law has known your husband a great deal longer than you have. She has invested a quarter of a century in him. Maybe she built her life largely on ambitions and dreams for him. She cannot turn her deep-seated feelings on and off like an electric light. Show her a little patience and understanding.

The problems that arise when the two couples are compelled to live in the same house are obvious. In a survey the Institute once made of several hundred couples who had shared a home with parents, less than half expressed themselves as satisfied with the arrangement. Not surprisingly, the families living on a farm were happier than those dwelling in a city apartment. More space was available, and there were more tasks to occupy the older people.

When two generations must live together, they should start with a clear understanding of whose home this is. Is the young couple living with parents, or are parents living with them? That basic difference will control many decisions and should be taken into account in all planning.

There should be a clear division of labor between the two women. One may enjoy cooking, the other may enjoy cleaning. This might suggest a method of dividing the labor. Or the women may take turns, one doing the cooking this week, the other next week. Harmony depends on clear understanding and definite respect for the division.

A fairly common situation now is for a widow to move in with a married daughter. Two-thirds of all wives outlive their husbands and, therefore, should plan for life alone. It is far more desirable for older women to maintain their own homes, but sometimes this is impossible. Sometimes, too, their daughters or sons unwisely insist that Mother give up and come to live with them.

When an older woman moves into a youthful household she should recognize from the first that it is imperative for the young couple to make the major decisions, especially in training and disciplining their children. She should attempt to lead as full and rich a life on her own account as possible. Adult education classes, volunteer activities in community and church groups, building up a new circle of friends of her own age may be the answer for her. She should always endeavor to keep herself well groomed and attractive. In earlier life, women take more pride in their appearance than do men, but in later years, interestingly enough, women show a greater tendency to let themselves slip and become more unkempt than men.

Young people have a right to remain in control of their own social life. Sometimes the older woman might take dinner in her room when the young people entertain their friends; other times it might be pleasanter if she went out. Some young couples do their entertaining on the night church suppers are held so that Mother can dine there.

There should be no sense of martyrdom on either side, although there sometimes is. If young people build up Mother's self-respect and feeling that there is a place for her, not merely with them, but in the world outside, and if the older woman will concede that the "children" are grown up and parents themselves, usually the home becomes big enough in size and in spirit to shelter two adult generations.

In these days only a minority of parents must live with grown children. But all parents have an influence upon the marriages of their children. The examples they have set in their own marriage leave a powerful and frequently a lasting impression.

All the statistics, spot checks, and samplings of the thousands of marital cases handled by our counselors over the past quarter century show that divorces run in families. The five couples involved in triangles discussed earlier were chosen at random from our files. Yet more than half were the products of broken homes.

*   *   *

Jill and Bob Lester, who were besieged with in-law troubles when we first saw them, both came from broken homes. Pretty, twenty-five-year-old Jill had already begun divorce proceedings against Bob when she called at the Institute. She was not happy about her action. At the time of our opening interview Jill was suffering from excruciating headaches, could not keep food on her stomach, and was steadily losing weight. She was concerned about the effect of the impending divorce on her baby and on Bobby, Jr. She did not think her mother's divorce had done her or her two sisters any harm, but she admitted that none of them could even remember having a father. It developed that Bobby, Jr., who was five years old, did remember his father and often cried for him. Jill was afraid Bobby would blame her later on, and she wondered if he would keep on missing Bob. But then she quoted from her mother who believed and often said that constant quarreling was worse than a good clean break. It seemed her mother had already hired a divorce lawyer, the same lawyer procured several years earlier for Jill's sister, Betsy.

Miserable as Jill was, she told us she was extremely grateful to her family:

* *

My mother and both my sisters have been wonderful to me. Every single one of them is on my side. They've done everything for me. Alice—she's my oldest sister—got me a filing job in her own firm. Alice is the brainy one in our family. All the men in the company have tried to hold her back, but she's earning more than Bob. I'm not specially interested in my job, but Alice and Mamma both say I'll be interested in time.

Mamma is taking care of my baby and Betsy's baby, too. Her baby is the same age as mine, three. All of us—except Bobby, Jr., who's staying in a boarding home—live in this apartment development Mamma superintends. With Mamma working and all, the care of the two babies is hard on her nerves and her health, but she hardly ever complains.

Mamma has always said she would do anything in the world for Betsy or Alice or me to make up for our having a no-good father. My mother isn't really strong. When things get on her nerves she has sick spells. That's why Bobby, Jr., has to live in this boarding home. He's active and noisy, and three children would be just too much for Mamma.

None of my family ever did like Bob. They keep reminding me Bob and I fought like cats and dogs almost from our first day. I can't begin to remember the number of times we've been separated. Once I had to leave him twice in the same month. Still and all, Bob and I were married six years, and we have two children. That's hard to forget, whatever Mamma says. I just can't help missing Bob sometimes. I find myself remembering the nice things he has done for me—like the way he acted when our community property was settled.

In court when we divided our things, Bob insisted I take both the icebox and the stove. He was entitled to the stove. And then Bob made his own lawyer furious by standing up and telling the judge $75 a month wasn't enough alimony for a woman with two small children to support. Bob earns $250 a month, which isn't very much, but he insisted—he practically shouted—we should be allowed half of it.

Of course there's a method in my husband's madness. He's trying to get me back, like after all our other separations. Mamma says to pay no attention to Bob's sweetness now, that he's just being tricky and underhand, the way men are. Actually, Bob hasn't changed one particle. His voice and his manners have always driven me crazy. I used to nearly die of humiliation when Bob and I would go out some place and he'd yell at the waiter we were starving and needed instant service. Then if I tried to hush him, he'd get mad and start yelling at me. Right after we eloped, Bob gave a birthday dinner for Mamma and made so much noise in the restaurant she went home without touching a bite and made the others go home with her. She hasn't stopped talking about that evening yet.

Mamma calls Bob "the Banty Rooster," strutting and crowing to make himself seem important when he isn't. Bob is 2 inches shorter than me, and the two of us look simply ridiculous together. Mamma and both my sisters told me so, long before we were married, but I wouldn't listen. Afterward I regretted it. People used to stare at Bob and me—even when he wasn't shouting and showing off—until I could sink through the floor. How can a wife be proud of a husband shorter than she is? Bob makes me feel like a telephone pole!

It's far too late in the day for Bob to change his spots and start being nice. Both my sisters say it's unfair and downright mean of my husband to be sending me flowers now. I can see straight through Bob. He's determined to win out over Mamma, no matter if the arguing and fighting and wrangling pull me to pieces.

When Bob and I were living together, it was a different story. There weren't any flowers then. Bob yelled at me and picked on me and criticized until I hardly knew which way was up. My hair didn't suit him, my clothes didn't suit him. He complained of my cooking, he showed me how to use the vacuum, and he even told me the way I should change the baby's diapers. He was harder to please than Mamma in one of her moods, and when I don't please people it makes me almost sick.

I've always been that way. When I was a little girl and would come in a room, I would go around and kiss everybody there— the women, the men, the children. Because Mamma had to work, my sisters and I were always being moved some place new, and I guess I must have thought if everybody liked me I could stay where I was. Moving so much and changing so much kept me kind of scared as a child.

I've done everything to make my marriage a success, and it hasn't worked. Last year Bob complained so much about my family inter- fering that the children and I moved to Tacoma with him. *His* fam- ily lives in Tacoma. Two months of that was as much as any human could stand. Bob's older brother moved in with us. Edwin is stuck up, and Bob fawns on him sickeningly. Edwin thinks I'm a nitwit, and Bob laughed every time Edwin made fun of me. Then one night Edwin insisted I darn his socks—why should a wife do a brother-in-law's mending?—and Bob backed Edwin up. We had a terrible fight, all three of us. Then Edwin called up my mother-in- law and asked what she thought, and she said I should darn the socks. What business was it of hers?

After that quarrel, I packed up and brought the children back home. Mamma and both my sisters agreed with me about the socks. So did my three aunts; they live near us.

Betsy is the beauty of our family. Her ex-husband never did ap- preciate her. Betsy works in a place with lots of attractive salesmen, and they fall all over themselves dating her. She goes dancing nearly every night. I thought I ought to postpone dating until my decree was final, but Betsy insisted waiting was silly, and Mamma finally agreed I needed recreation, so I wouldn't be forever moping around and crying over a past that can't be mended.

It isn't as though there was anything *wrong* in my dates. A few kisses is all I ever allow. I don't care too much about sex. In my opinion sex is—is messy. Mamma thinks the same. And you should hear Alice and my three aunties on the subject! None of them was ever married.

I'm sure you understand the kind of advice I need. I want to work out some way I can earn enough money to make a peaceful, *single* life for me and my two children. And that means Bob isn't in it. After all my family has done for me, I can't possibly change my mind again about the divorce. Mamma would never forgive me. Besides, I can't take Bob's yelling and arguing and criticizing a single minute longer.

*   *

Contrary to what Jill Lester thought about the kindness of her family, 5-foot 5-inch Bob held them responsible for most of the trouble between Jill and himself. A stocky young man, his angry, unhappy voice shook the windowpanes in the counseling office as he said:

*   *

I was tall enough for my wife until her mother got at her. Jill doesn't want to divorce me and take away my children, whatever she says. It's her mother and her meddling sisters and her nosy aunts who want to push me out of the family. Nobody—*nobody*— is going to push me around. I know what's best for my own wife, I guess. I know how to handle Jill and make her happy. All I need is to get her and my children back where they belong.

Jill's family have teamed up on me and poisoned her mind. They're the ones who've convinced my wife it's practically indecent to have a husband and sleep with him and listen to his opinions. Why shouldn't Jill listen to me instead of her bossy mother? If I try to show her how to use the vacuum, she quotes her mother at me.

It's the same with everything else. I want Jill to wear her hair long, and last spring her mother persuaded her to get a skinned-cat cut. Blue is my favorite color for Jill, and one time her mother deliberately talked her into spending *my* money on a pink dress. When I told her exactly how she looked, she up and left me. She and the children stayed away six weeks that time, while she and her mother and her sisters and her aunts hashed over what a heel I was. Whenever I tell Jill to do something, she and the kids are gone again. What kind of marriage is that?

Jill's mother wouldn't like *any* son-in-law. She got rid of Betsy's husband in their first year, and doesn't seem to notice Betsy is unhappy and is turning into a cheap little gold digger who will wind up some day in an awful mess. There was nothing wrong with Betsy's husband. It's because of my mother-in-law that Alice—that hot-shot career girl—is turning into a crabby, frustrated old maid who's always jumping on men because she doesn't know how to catch one. Alice is twenty-nine, and she's already darn near as bad as those dried-up old aunts of theirs. I'll bet my bottom dollar my mother-in-law's everlasting bossiness had a lot to do with her own divorce. I sure would like to meet Jill's father some day. I pity that man.

A short guy has enough headaches without being driven nuts by in-laws. I haven't ever had it soft in my own family. After my parents were divorced, Father sent money for my older brother to go to college, but he didn't even answer the letters when my turn came. Edwin is a big six-footer and played football, and I guess my father was proud of him. Edwin was forever beating me up when we were kids. I used to crawl in through the basement window when I got home from school for fear he would be waiting in the front hall. Last year Edwin made trouble between Jill and me, and I guess I should have thrown him out on his ear, but I couldn't figure how. I'm still halfway afraid of Edwin.

In business I'm always at a disadvantage, with big guys grinning to themselves and thinking I'm barely out of short pants and don't know beans. I've lost several jobs for getting into fist fights over that very thing. Maybe that's why a lot of guys my age are better off financially. If I can't be the *head* of my own family, with my own wife and kids looking up to me, I've got no confidence to hold any kind of job or even feel like a man. Jill claims my voice is too loud and my manners are bad. Why can't she realize if I don't speak up and make my presence felt, I'll be shoved off in the corner every time? Believe me, business is no cinch. And you have to yell around her family and mine if you expect to be heard!

I want you to help me straighten out this mess with Jill. This time I'm afraid she really will go ahead and stick with the divorce. Tell me how to get my wife and children back. I'll do anything you suggest—whether it's reasonable or not. All Jill and I need is to get our relatives off our necks and to be by ourselves.

*   *

Neither of the young Lesters had a happy childhood home to remember or happy childhood experiences. As a result they were not emotionally prepared to defend their own home and love against outside attack. Both their families had interfered outrageously in their marriage, with Jill's mother as the chief offender. She had actually told Jill how often and when to grant Bob his marital rights and checked up by telephone. Few young couples could have got along smoothly under such conditions.

Nevertheless, Bob's and Jill's own personality difficulties complicated their problems. Like so many of the couples we see, these young people had no course by which to guide themselves. They knew nothing of life and marriage, nothing about each other or their own natures. Bob was disconcerted when we proved to him by his own words and actions that he was as dominating as his mother-in-law. In addition to his bossiness he was intensely critical of the shortcomings of others—a typical symptom of insecurity and weakness. When Jill reacted to his cutting criticism by withdrawing her love and attention, he became even more insecure, and hence more critical. Neither he nor Jill realized their quarrels were inevitable unless they changed their attitudes.

It was not Bob's right as a husband to tell Jill how to choose her clothes and wear her hair, to show her how to cook and clean, to criticize and superintend her every act, any more than it was her mother's right. Bob was endeavoring to prop his own faltering ego at his wife's expense. He had a bad case of small-man trouble, fostered by a neglectful father and an elder brother whom he simultaneously feared, envied, and admired. When we first talked to Bob he believed the way to prove his strength and manhood was to behave like a household tyrant and a social boor.

After some weeks of counseling Bob came to understand the origin of, and reason for, his belligerent attitude. He perceived that his aggressiveness had not only endangered his marriage but handicapped him in earning a living. Jill was not the kind of girl who could tolerate rudeness and bullying, and few employers will put up with it. When Bob saw these truths, he determined to alter his personality and his attitudes. In an amazingly short space of time, he did so. Previously he just had not applied that kind of thought to himself.

Nor had Jill done any positive thinking about herself or her marriage. For instance, she was unaware of how her personality had suffered from her parents' divorce and her unstable background as a child. This girl had subconsciously set herself the task of winning the complete approval of everybody at all times—an impossible assignment. She was much too sensitive to criticism directed at her or at anybody even remotely identified with her. Consequently she was excessively embarrassed by other people's adverse opinions of *her* husband.

In the first years of her marriage, she ran between her husband and her mother trying to evade the criticisms of both and to please and win the approval of both. When that effort inevitably failed, habit turned her toward the person who had dominated her thinking the longest—her mother—when she should have been turning toward her husband and searching her own mind. In her concern with satisfying everybody else's wishes and gaining universal approval, Jill lost all track of her own wishes and her own right—indeed, her duty—to live and make decisions and choices as an adult. Not only did she hurt Bob; she outraged the spirit of marriage when she went to her family to report marital differences she should have thought through herself.

It was obvious Jill did not really desire a divorce. When she asked for it, she was literally yielding her own will to the wishes of the majority—her family. We did not argue with Jill. We did talk to her in a casual way about the possible disadvantages of her future without Bob. After only two consultations, in which Jill probably did the first concrete thinking of her life, she admitted that as a divorced woman with two children she would face tougher problems than those she was trying to escape. By then she also realized that by divorcing Bob she would subject her children to an upbringing as unsatisfactory as her own had been.

Another important point: for the first time Jill saw she had been regarding Bob not as a person, but as a husband who made her unhappy. She had been giving less attention and thought to him than she had given to any of her relatives or even acquaintances.

Jill was soon ready to try marriage again with a different attitude. But she lacked the courage to break the news to her mother. And she still could not endure the fact that Bob was 2 inches shorter than she was.

The second difficulty was solved in a very simple way. Bob bought a pair of the so-called "elevator" shoes and, so far as ordinary observers were concerned, became as tall as Jill.

The other difficulty was equally easy to solve. Jill said nothing to her family of her intention. She had acquired the spunk to decide that her plans were none of their business. One dark night she packed her bags, gathered up her youngsters, and eloped with Bob the second time.

That was a year ago and the reconciliation has lasted. Just last week Jill telephoned that she and Bob had not had a real quarrel since the reunion, and that their financial situation had greatly improved. Bob's additional height, plus Jill's pride in him, supplied the young man with sufficient confidence to seek and obtain a much better job. Jill and he were especially gratified that her mother called in person and congratulated her son-in-law on the new job.

* * *

Jill and Bob Lester found that their raging battles over their in-laws almost miraculously subsided after they recognized and set right the flaws in their own personalities. Susan Fleming had no desire to search out and correct her faults. All she wanted from us at the Institute was three quick lessons on how-to-get-rid-of-your-father-in-law. She was positive that her husband's father was set upon wrecking her marriage. She was determined to put a stop to his daily phone calls to her husband, his presents to her small daughter, his advice on how to manage the Flemings' financial affairs. It did not occur to twenty-eight-year-old Susan that she and Andy, her thirty-year-old husband, might have had something to do with the erosion of their marriage.

The Flemings had been married for six years and their daughter, Pamela, was two, when Susan appeared at the Institute. She and Andy were eager to move out of a small apartment into a home of their own and then have a second baby. But, Susan informed us:

* *

Barney, my father-in-law, does his darnedest to make all the decisions for Andy and me. He thinks we should postpone an addition to our family and hasn't hesitated to announce it. In my opinion, the size and timing of our family should be the exclusive concern of my husband and myself.

Three years ago when I was pregnant with Pamela, Barney wanted to select my hospital and pay my bills. I ignored his recommendation, but he isn't the type who takes hints that his interference is unwelcome.

I'm sure you've heard of Doctor Read, the English physician who has popularized "natural childbirth." Well, I purposely picked out a local obstetrician who used the Read method. When my parents mentioned the fact to my father-in-law, Barney went into a spin. He got hold of several old-fashioned doctor friends who told Andy natural childbirth was mostly hypnotism. Andy began to insist that I change to a different obstetrician. I finally convinced him that natural childbirth had nothing to do with hypnotism and that

I would be allowed whatever anesthetics were necessary. Andy then quieted down.

I had my way. I won't pretend my experience was an unqualified success. There were complications; my labor was prolonged, and Pamela's delivery was unusually difficult. However, I've never regretted my decision, and with my next baby I intend to try natural childbirth again. Barney will have nothing to say about it, and we will pay our own bills.

From the very beginning, Andy and I have had to fight against the overweening generosity of his parents. We were still on our honeymoon when Barney tried to give us an electric refrigerator and an electric stove. I preferred to equip my own kitchen—I like gas for cooking—and I got Andy to tell his father that in plain words. Barney wasn't a bit discouraged.

We see Andy's parents much more than we see my parents. Whenever Barney has the urge, he and my mother-in-law pop in on us. Nearly every Sunday we eat lunch or supper with them. Andy is working for his Ph.D.—he teaches English in a junior high school—and his week ends should be devoted to research and reading. My in-laws own a mountain cabin as well as an enormous house in town. At least once a month when the weather is warm we pack up the baby and spend both Saturday and Sunday at the cabin, and Andy doesn't get in a lick of study.

I detest our trips to the mountains. Little Pamela gets thrown off schedule. And even after the visit we aren't free from Barney's . . . hovering. My father-in-law is a worrier. If Andy and the baby and I drive in by ourselves, Andy is obliged to telephone back to the cabin the minute we arrive at our apartment. Otherwise his father will be on the wire clamoring to hear if something is wrong.

Barney has a worse case of telephonitis than any woman of my acquaintance. Four o'clock, the hour Andy gets home from his classes, is my favorite time of day. Barney knows our schedule by heart. Invariably, just as Andy is kissing me or kissing Pamela—before I have a chance to tell the new cute thing she's done—the phone rings, and it is his father. "Is my son there?" Barney asks breezily, without even saying hello to me. As I hand over the phone I sometimes feel like pitching it out the window. While my domestic news gets cold, he rambles on and on—dropping his inevitable pearls of advice in Andy's ear.

Everybody in the family—including, I regret to say, my own parents—kowtows to Barney. Not me. I don't regard financial success as particularly important, and neither does Andy. Instead of going into partnership with his father, Andy elected to teach. I was thrilled by this independent decision. While he worked for a master's degree and took courses in education, I held a job to help support us. I also did the housework and cooking, which wasn't exactly an easy task.

Lots of wives wouldn't put up with my husband's faddish ideas on nutrition. To please Andy, I cook and serve our main meal—meat and potatoes, a heavy dessert and salad—at seven in the morning. At six in the evening we eat a supper as light as the baby's. Andy thinks this is healthier. Frankly, there are times I feel stuffed in the morning and hungry as a wolf at night. But I haven't really minded the radical adjustment.

I'm so proud of Andy I gladly make concessions for his sake. Someday, if Andy applies himself and continues to study hard for his Ph.D., he will wind up as the president of a small college. That is my dream for him.

I've never been afraid of hard work and, if I say so myself, I'm good at budgeting. By looking a long way ahead and figuring closely, Andy and I have been able to get a good deal out of our money. Three years ago we bought a city lot and planned to sell Andy's stocks and bonds so that we could build a house. Of course Barney put in his oar. With the assistance of his accounting department, he produced facts and figures showing it was cheaper for us to hang on to Andy's stocks and bonds and continue to pay rent. We sold the stocks and bonds, despite my father-in-law's wails of anguish.

Last spring we finally located a satisfactory architect and used the cash from the investments to start our house. Since then, Barney has done a flip-flop. The house has become his pet project. He and a contractor friend visit the building site practically every morning. Barney then picks up my mother-in-law, and the two of them drop by the apartment, whereupon I receive a full report on the blunders our carpenters are making. Day before yesterday my ironing was interrupted for an hour while Barney expounded on the poor quality of our termite protection or something similar. Yesterday the doorbell rang just after I had put Pamela in her crib and was washing my hair. I peeked through the curtains, saw Barney's sporty foreign car at the curb, and went on with my shampoo. But I felt awfully guilty.

Next month Andy and I should take possession of our house. I don't think of our first real home with much pride or joy. Instead I'm likely to think of it as a battlefield, a source of endless friction between my father-in-law and me. Barney is well aware that Andy and I admire modern architecture and furnishings. But he insists upon considering our fondness for modern interiors a childish phase. The fact is, we dislike clutter so much that we don't even have any pictures on our walls. For decorative accents in the apartment, I've hung mobiles Andy and I designed and made ourselves. Whenever my father-in-law enters the foyer, he stops short and stares at the mobile in the doorway. It's a length of copper wire twisted into the shape of a fish, a Chinese symbol for good fortune. Usually he smiles. Quite often he then clears his throat and gives us a lecture on taste and the beauty of antique furnishings. Barney collects antiques, and I guess he does own some fine pieces, but I'm awfully tired of that lecture.

Two weeks ago, just before Andy's birthday, his father read a glowing description of a 1901 Steinway baby grand in an auction catalogue. Andy plays the piano. I play the violin. We had set our hearts on a blond-wood spinet, and Andy had told his father about it, but Barney went to the auction and bought the Steinway for us.

There isn't room in the apartment to crowd in a baby grand piano. My in-laws are now keeping it in their recreation room. But on moving day I'm sure Barney expects our van to pick up Andy's birthday present.

Last week I suggested to Andy it might be a good idea to transfer our checking and savings accounts and do all our banking in the neighborhood where we're moving. Andy agreed—until he talked with his father. He then decided to shift our joint checking account to the branch bank, but to leave his personal savings account on deposit at the old bank. We don't consult *my* father on such matters. Indeed, we don't consult my parents at all. Both my mother and my father respect our rights as a separate family with a child of our own.

For a while I will confess I had my hands full coping with both sets of Pamela's grandparents. My folks were just as bad as Andy's about showering the baby with toys and clothes, though, of course, she received nicer presents from his side of the family. After many discussions, I impressed it on my father and mother that they were to confine their gifts to birthdays and holidays.

Barney hasn't paid the slightest attention to my wishes. He never visits us without bringing Pamela something, and it isn't fair to my parents. Sometimes the gifts are small and inexpensive, but Pamela is already getting spoiled. When Andy's parents come to visit, her eyes grow big as saucers, and you ought to watch the way she throws herself on Barney's lap. I don't like to seem like a hard-hearted mother who withholds pleasures from her child, but Barney forces me into that position.

I admit that my father-in-law's incessant meddling may be meant kindly. No doubt there are wives who could take Barney in their stride. Perhaps I could be a little more patient if Andy himself wasn't so easygoing and philosophical, so sold on peace at any price. Peace for himself, that is. "Fight with Barney all you like," is the tack Andy takes, "so long as I am not involved." Andy is convinced that I become too upset over trifles. Possibly that is true, but I can't help it. The bitterness I feel toward his father is damaging my whole relationship with Andy. It is damaging me too. I've arrived at the point where I hate Andy's father, really hate him.

My father-in-law treats my husband as though he were an unmarried college boy. When Andy accepts the treatment, I just can't bear it. Around the baby and me, Andy behaves like an adult. But when his father appears on the scene he acts like a small, bashful boy. I want a husband who is mature. Every woman does.

* *

Her husband did not look immature. Wearing glasses and well-cut tweeds, Andy Fleming looked like a scholar. Taking his pipe out of his mouth and laying it on the counseling desk, he said gently but wearily:

* *

Ever since Susan and I started building our house, her favorite indoor sport has been picking fights with my dad. She and Barney are furiously competitive people. I try to be a peacemaker and bridge their rapidly multiplying differences, but you know what happens to bridges. They get walked on.

Susan now acts as though there were only two viewpoints: my father's and hers. Apparently it doesn't occur to her that I might have a viewpoint too. And in reciting her grievances, she overlooks one important fact: she wins most of the arguments. Whenever she feels strongly on an issue I throw in with her—and my father, who can be a model of tact when he wants to be, subsides.

Susan has told you something of our finances. Let me tell you a little more. For a long time I had a small packet of stocks and bonds which my father, a shrewd businessman, looked after. At Susan's urging I sold the securities and prepared to build a house. That was three years ago. Susan could not find an architect who suited her, and it was only recently that construction got under way.

Where has the "house fund" been since I sold the securities? In postal savings at 2 per cent interest! When Barney took care of those stocks and bonds I was making 10 per cent on my money. In other words, the blow we struck for financial independence cost us three years of dividends. Not that I mind—but facts are facts.

Just the other day Susan suggested that I transfer our checking and savings accounts to a bank in the neighborhood of our new house. The savings account is small, but it was opened by my parents when I was born. I consulted my dad, and I know Susan resented it. Barney, very practically, advised me to leave the savings account where it was. He pointed out that the bank officers have known me since childhood and this acquaintanceship might be valuable, if I ever needed to float a loan.

Far be it from me to say Barney is perfect. Who is? But when I was courting Susan she used to be fond of both my father and my mother. Barney is a self-made man, and from the very first he rooted for Susan's spirit and drive. He is still tickled by her scrappiness. I am willing to grant he comes by the apartment too often, that he picks up the telephone too quickly, and I guess he does have too many suggestions about our new house. But that's only natural when you consider he's an expert in the field. Until he retired—and he still has fingers in several business enterprises—Barney was at the top of the heap in the construction business. He promoted several of the biggest real estate developments in the Los Angeles area. Susan doesn't appreciate his riding herd on our builder, although he's been a lot of help. A couple of days ago he caught the crew skimping on the aluminum banding which is supposed to protect us against termites. The builder promptly made amends, but that could have been serious.

Regardless of what my father does, he rubs Susan the wrong way. She still gets annoyed when she recalls how Barney wanted to give us an electric stove and electric refrigerator shortly after our marriage. But she doesn't recall that the offer was made at a period of wartime shortages when any kind of kitchen equipment was hard to find. And she has also forgotten that when I asked Barney to get us gas equipment for the kitchen and let us pay for it, he did just that.

Susan sometimes blames my father for things that aren't his fault. She considered it extremely impertinent of him to suggest we postpone having a second child. Well, there was more to it than impertinence. Barney's concern, my concern, her own parents' concern, was Susan's health. Susan has never forgiven Barney for getting into the act when Pamela was on the way. He spoke up because Susan's parents appealed to him to do so; they were scared stiff, and with reason. Susan had chosen an inexperienced obstetrician, just out of medical school. His theories may have been sound, but his obstetrical techniques were not. After Susan had been in labor for thirty hours, we had to call in a specialist who delivered Pamela by instrument. And Susan narrowly escaped death.

In some ways it may be true, as Susan claims, that my father treats me like a kid, but I wish she could appreciate that my father has always encouraged me to follow my own bent. Barney early reconciled himself to the fact that I wasn't a go-getter. When I chose teaching, I'm reasonably sure he was disappointed, but he never said a word.

While I was growing up, my mother and father and I were a pretty tight little corporation. As a matter of fact, I never really had a girl until I met Susan in college. After I got my B.A. we were married. I've never been sorry, but our first year together was rough. Susan insisted that I turn back the allowance I'd been receiving from my family. She had a supervisory job at a radio station, and she managed to hire me as her assistant. I was working, I was beating my brains out for an M.A., and we were both so starved for sleep that we walked around like zombies most of the time.

It seems to me that Susan and I should get more enjoyment out of our lives. I spend nearly all my free time on study and research. Even if the weather is sweltering, Susan won't drive to my parents' mountain cabin more than once a month.

Ultimately—let's face it—I will inherit a sizable chunk of money that my dad has earned. I can't see what Susan and I prove by cheating him and my mother out of spending a little dough on us right now. They won't be around forever. Yet Susan kicks up a fuss

if Barney and my mother bring a couple of inexpensive toys to little
Pamela. After all, she's the only grandchild on either side and isn't
one bit spoiled. But Susan has her own parents so intimidated they
are afraid to give our baby presents except on holidays.

I've never before spoken critically of Susan's parents—and
I must say I've been pushed hard by her mother. I know my ideas
on diet may sound extreme, although I can run 5 miles without
raising my blood pressure, and I haven't had a cold in years. I've
always given Susan plenty of credit for being sweet enough to
adopt my ideas—to please me, she also stopped smoking—but I
sure do weary of the way my mother-in-law chatters on about my
eating habits and drags up the subject in company. People "oh"
and "ah" and make me feel like an animal in the zoo. Susan hangs
on the telephone trading recipes with her mother, and the two of
them talk back and forth about what on earth to feed me. While
Susan often comments on the length of my father's telephone conversations, she spends more time on the wire with her mother.

I know my father's twice-told tales bore my wife, but her
mother's thrice-told tales are just as boring to me. Furthermore, I
hold it against my mother-in-law that Susan started off with such a
poor grounding on sex. I spent a good part of our first year sleeping
on the living room sofa. Susan was terrified by the physical side of
love. Whenever I approached her, she was likely to become upset
or to be so terribly tense that often the result was a nervous illness
of some kind. For at least six months, outbreaks of hives kept her
miserable. That made me miserable, too, and I certainly wasn't
flattered.

Susan's nervous illnesses have disappeared, but she gets little
pleasure, if any, from our sexual relationship. However, she and I
didn't come here for advice on sex. What I want to know is what to
do about my father. I'm sure Susan would like to cut Barney out of
our lives. But she has an awfully strong sense of justice. If we go to
my parents' mountain cabin for a day, we have to take her parents
driving for an afternoon. If we eat a meal with my family, we have
to eat a meal with hers. Since she feels such an obligation to her

parents, I believe she can be led to understand the sense of obligation I feel toward mine.

*   *

Both Susan and Andy Fleming started out in marriage with one
strike against them. Each was an only child. Only children, reared
without the necessity of sharing with brothers and sisters, often
grow up more self-centered and more selfish than the average
youngsters. Susan had a second strike against her. Her parents were
old enough to be her grandparents. Her mother's ideas on sex were
hand-me-downs from the Victorian era, and she passed on these
ideas to her daughter. Where men were concerned, Susan's mother
expected the worst.

Susan's father, a cellist with the local symphony orchestra, had
lagged behind financially. Her mother, an ambitious woman, was
unsurprised but disappointed and very vocal about the disappointment. As a small girl Susan was encouraged to think that she, the
only chick, was entitled to the best of everything. As she grew up,
she discovered with dismay that her parents could not afford to give
her the best. The discovery cut deep. Paradoxically, in Susan's
artistic household considerably more emphasis was put on material
things than in the household where Andy's father was a flourishing
businessman.

During her courtship Susan was charmed by Andy's father,
whom she rightly considered an ally. However, it was a foregone
conclusion that the marked similarities in their personalities—they
shared drive, competitiveness, and a taste for planning ahead—
would lead to clashes.

Very soon after her marriage Susan almost unconsciously began
to compare the financial success of her father-in-law to the "failure"
of her own father. She loved her father but was secretly ashamed
of him. Because she was ashamed of her parents and her background, she blamed herself for being a snob. Her guilty feelings
caused her to proclaim her family loyalty. Her family loyalty, exaggerated out of all proportion, then made her demand that every-

thing must be "fair," regardless of how awkwardly the "fairness" might work out for others. To salve her guilty conscience, the standards of her family must prevail. Thus, a postal savings account seemed sensible to her and a brokerage account almost wicked.

It was natural for Susan to want Andy to be independent of his parents, but she carried her conception of independence to such an extreme that her insecurity and jealousy showed through. No injustice was done to Susan's father when Andy's father, long acquainted with financial operations, was consulted about their investments.

Susan was on sounder ground when she complained that Andy changed character in his father's company. Admiring his father's brilliance and versatility, temperamentally disposed to be modest and unassuming, Andy did not particularly mind taking a secondary position to the older man. Susan, a loving, highly possessive wife, *did* mind, and very much. She instinctively recognized that as Andy applauded and hung onto Barney's words, he himself seemed diminished in stature. Her competitive instincts were aroused and drove her two ways: (1) Andy, her husband, must come first; (2) she must come first with Andy.

Susan was startled to learn from consultations with us that she put too high a value on money. At the beginning of her marriage she attached so much value to earning a livelihood and accumulating a savings account that she neglected to consider Andy's and her own happiness. During the first important year of marriage, quite unnecessarily she pushed Andy and herself to the point of physical exhaustion and collapse. Sheer fatigue probably had almost as much to do with starting their sexual relationship on an unsatisfactory basis as did the prudishness she borrowed from her mother.

We helped the couple resolve their sexual problem. Susan's joy in the fact so increased her confidence that she became more clear-eyed on her in-law problems.

It did come as a distinct jolt to her to find out that Andy had silently put up with numerous annoyances from *her* parents. It had not entered her head that Andy had made more concessions in

their marriage than she had. When Susan adjusted the meal schedule to Andy's unconventional preferences, she gave herself full
marks for being cooperative and flexible, and bowed out of making
any further adjustments. This amusing human trick, quite common
in marriage, might be called "rationalization by *non sequitur.*" In
effect, Susan had been saying to Andy, "We eat as you choose.
Therefore we must budget as I choose, discipline our child my way,
and let me decide on our recreations."

It was Susan, not Andy, who yearned for the prestige of a Ph.D.,
something to boast about. So that he could gain time for the studies
he did not enjoy, Susan had maneuvered for him to resign from
coaching the junior-high basketball team, teaching tennis to the
young students, and so on. These activities he did enjoy.

Susan blamed her father-in-law for crushing Andy's individuality.
Until it was pointed out, she was not aware that she had hampered
Andy from strengthening his ego and blighted any growth of de-
cisiveness on his part. When she realized the true state of affairs, she
choked off her steady flow of wifely suggestions. She released him
from her ambition for an advanced scholastic degree. When Andy
resumed coaching the basketball team and helping his students on
week ends, he and she had less time to spend driving to the mountains and less time, too, to spend with her parents.

Gratified by Susan's efforts to improve their situation, Andy had a
long serious talk with his father. The older man was amazed to
hear that he was a problem to his daughter-in-law. A little miffed
at first, he soon recovered his good nature and agreed to reduce the
quantity of his advice and put the brakes on his generosity. This
informal contract between Andy and his father did not turn out to
be exactly watertight. However, the pressure was eased when Susan
and Andy took possession of their house and required no further
building advice. Incidentally, their moving van did not stop by to
pick up the Steinway baby grand. On her birthday, Susan received
from her father-in-law a blond-wood spinet that adorns the living
room in their modern, ranch-style house.

Andy's father made one definite promise, and he kept it. He

abandoned the daily phone calls to his son. Susan then gave up the daily phone calls she had been making to her mother. Nowadays she calls both families two or three times a week—a stubborn young woman, she still maintains some of her notions on "fairness"—and perhaps once a week they visit both families.

After Susan conceded that the baby was not really "getting spoiled" and that in fact she had jealously wanted to hug all Pamela's affection to herself, she realized that the problem of doting grandparents was not of vital importance. At any rate, she acknowledged she could not solve it. She then withdrew her objections to the numerous small gifts Pamela was receiving from her paternal grandparents and gave the maternal grandparents more leeway. Although for a while Pamela was buried in toys and gimcracks, the heavens did not fall.

Susan is now expecting that second baby, for which she was so eager. No doubt this child, too, will be on the receiving end of needless gifts from four loving grandparents, but Susan will try to take it in stride.

*   *   *

The problems of Susan and Andy Fleming were far less complex than those of Margaret and Ron Anderson, who also suffered from sexual maladjustment and interfering in-laws. Both Margaret and Ron regarded themselves as misfits. They had married because they felt fairly comfortable with each other and awkward with everybody else.

In college Ron, 6 feet 1 inch and athletic looking, had been able to talk Mozart and Picasso, but he did not know the difference between a double play and a drop kick. Margaret's two older sisters, who were little and cute, had been the belles in her family. Margaret was supposed to be a son. At news of the birth of a third daughter, Margaret's mother had been so disappointed she had hysterics in the delivery room.

By the time Margaret followed her sisters to college and into their sorority, she was nearly 6 feet tall. She was good at sports: skiing, tennis, swimming, and golf, but at dances she was, as she ruefully described herself to us, "that giantess skulking in the corner trying to look like a midget."

Margaret and Ron met at the annual homecoming dance, the one night most of the students stayed up all night. Margaret's date, a castoff of her sister Edith's, had gone to sleep. Ron's girl had stood him up.

Three months after the dance, Ron was drafted. By then he and Margaret were pretty well acquainted. His mother approved of her and of her family's social standing. In those days Margaret liked Ron's mother and his whole family. Their home seemed gay and informal compared to her home, where each night the family was served one cocktail before a dinner eaten by candlelight and ending with finger bowls, at which point all the females retired to their rooms while the man of the house went to his club to play bridge.

Ron and Margaret corresponded for the two years he was in the Army and became engaged by mail. Three days before their marriage, Ron panicked and suggested they break up. Margaret was panicky, too. She consulted her college counselor, who thought they should wait awhile. But by then five hundred invitations had been mailed. Also, both Margaret's sisters were married, and Margaret, at the age of twenty, was afraid if Ron did not marry her she might be an old maid. The wedding went through, as scheduled.

After ten years of marriage and three children, Ron unexpectedly asked for a divorce. Five days later, Margaret's pretty face still mirrored shocked bewilderment as she told her story to us:

*   *

At first I thought I was coping with just another of Ron's depressions. During all our years together, Ron and I have never had a serious quarrel. My sisters and I weren't allowed to whine and bicker, and I got the habit of liking peace as a child. I've managed to sidestep arguments despite the fact Ron is high-keyed, intensely critical of little things, and very moody. On an average of every six months he sinks into an ocean of gloom.

Whenever these dreary periods descend I keep the youngsters quiet and out of sight—Deborah is nine, our twin sons are six—supply Ron with everything he requests, however wild and unreasonable, pour forth my utmost in the way of sunlight and cheer. Ron always seemed to respond and in the course of time climb back to normal.

I had no idea he considered his existence a misery and our marriage hopeless. All he wants, so he says, is to leave our home and be entirely free and independent, whatever that may mean. I still feel stunned by his attitude.

I won't pretend Ron and I have been as happy as some couples—we just aren't the blissful type—but we are better off than many couples who stay together. We have our children. We have a pleasant home and an interesting, if small, circle of friends. Ron has been dissatisfied with his work for a long while—he is in charge of design at a large firm that manufactures ceramics—but he knows I would have stood behind him in any change he cared to make. I have a small income from my grandfather's estate, and I have repeatedly offered to lend Ron the principal if he ever wanted to establish a business for himself.

I have tried to be a good wife and mother and an efficient housekeeper, something I was obliged to learn from scratch since I grew up in a houseful of servants. I have done my best to be an agreeable companion to Ron, somebody loyal and generous and understanding. I have become a fair cook. I wield a paint brush and hammer under Ron's direction; every time he gets restless he redecorates our house again, which keeps it in a constant state of upheaval. I don't object to that, or to the fact that our décor reflects his ideas, not mine.

When Ron is sick, I nurse him faithfully. His depressions often wind up with an asthmatic attack, a siege of sinus, or a digestive upset. He has an ulcer like his father before him. Last month his boss threatened to reduce the annual bonus, and Ron was sick in bed for a week with worry and a flare-up of his ulcer.

In the early days of our marriage I took on the burden of handling our finances. Ron declares he can't abide the mundane chore of paying bills. I deposit his weekly check of $125 along with my dividend checks in a joint bank account. Often Ron forgets to advise me of his withdrawals and to fill out stubs. Twice last year I heard from the bank that our account was overdrawn. I didn't make a fuss about the financial crises. I sold enough bonds to get straight with the bank and allowed Ron to continue in the serene belief our checking account must be stocked by elves.

I have consistently defended Ron to my parents, my mother in particular—she hoped I would marry an ambitious, he-man type instead of an introverted artist—but my parents scarcely represent a threat to Ron. They live in Seattle, a thousand miles away. On the rare occasions they do visit, Ron carries on outrageously, taking an opposite view on every issue merely to be annoying. Once my father mentioned his tailor, and Ron pulled a poor mouth and pretended he acquired all his clothes in the bargain basement—a ridiculous pose since at the time he, too, was wearing a tailor-made suit.

Ron's parents live within a few miles of us. To please him, we see them at least once a week. Ron feels perfectly free to pick all kinds of flaws in my parents, despite their unfailing courtesy and generosity to him. I have never breathed a word against his people although Gertrude, his mother, can be considerably more difficult than my mother. She is more demanding and harder to satisfy. Last Christmas Ron spent hours shopping for an expensive Chinese brocade jacket he hoped Gertrude would fancy and then, in five minutes, he bought me an album of Count Basie records that he wanted himself. He bought nothing for our children. Selecting their presents, as usual, was my job.

Whenever Ron is in his mother's company he puts forth a special effort to be animated and amusing. I don't mind that. But I often receive the impression he and Gertrude are deliberately conspiring to make me feel stupid and uncomfortable. Two Sundays ago

Ron praised a frilly, bright-red dress Gertrude was wearing until she blushed with pleasure—my mother-in-law has excellent taste, which I suppose Ron inherited from her—and both of them managed to make me feel like a big horse, wrapped in gunny sacking. Next, they plunged into a musical conversation, a subject where they shine and I don't—my college major was math—and in the midst of the colloquy Ron suddenly asked me who composed the "Pavane to a Dead Princess." Naturally I didn't know the answer, and naturally Gertrude did. Once again, and purposely I believe, Ron flattered his mother at my expense.

On the way home that day, in the hearing of the children, he wanted to know if I'd had a good time. I told him I'd had a dandy time and that his mother was charming. In some ways, strange as it may seem, I think Gertrude *is* charming. She is clever and original. She is also a real expert at the art of making trouble and needling without getting caught at it.

When Ron began to pick on Deborah in the car for the way she smeared her face eating candy, I suspected I was hearing an echo of Deborah's grandmother. And when Ron jumped on the twins, whom he usually leaves more or less in peace, I knew darn well he was spreading a little of Gertrude's insidious brand of poison. During our visit she had made quite a thing of describing the beautiful manners and astounding poise of her next-door neighbor's small boys. Complimenting somebody else's kids is Gertrude's zigzag method of getting across a disagreeable message about the inferior way I'm rearing ours. Ron doesn't see it, of course. I've always kept my mouth shut on the subject of Gertrude. Ron is devoted to his mother, and he detests his father, whom I rather like, though I've taken pains not to defend him. Something else Ron doesn't know is that my feelings have been hurt for years by his envy of his elder brother, Jerry. Jerry is unmarried and leads an unencumbered existence in a bachelor apartment in New York. No wife, no kids to cramp his style.

In a sense, it was through Jerry that I discovered Ron's opinion of me as a wife. Last Thursday, when Ron didn't show up for dinner, I jumped to the conclusion there had been trouble at the plant again. I telephoned his office, but the switchboard was closed. For a week or so I'd been conscious of the growing tension that generally precedes one of Ron's depressions. By eight o'clock I was definitely worried and thought I'd better go and hunt for him. Usually he heads for the beach.

I rounded up a sitter and slipped away from the kids by the back door, which took quite a little doing. They're nervous youngsters. They'd sensed the tense atmosphere, and all three were prepared to be real evil. Ron insists I spoil our children, but can't see his changeableness frightens them. One minute he grabs and squeezes the twins till they can hardly breathe, the next he retreats, scowling, into the silences. He plainly shows he isn't extra fond of Deborah, and she feels it, too. According to her teacher, Deborah should be near the head of her class but instead she's near the foot. I guess neither Ron nor I is a good parent.

Well, I drove twenty-five miles to the Pacific Ocean. Ron had parked his car and was walking along the beach. The tide was coming in and soaking his shoes, and spray was splashing his favorite sport jacket without his noticing. When I asked if something had gone wrong at the plant, Ron went into the old song-and-dance about how he loathed his boss, how the boss's wife stifled his creativeness, and how his work was dull and meaningless. As far as I could tell, we were going through the same old routine.

Eventually Ron agreed to get in his car and follow me home. It was when we walked into the living room that the blow fell. Ron pulled from his pocket a letter he had written his brother Jerry. In an offhand manner he remarked that maybe I should read the letter before it went in the mail.

That letter was my announcement that Ron had decided our marriage was on the rocks, that he intended to arrange for a divorce. After the divorce, so he wrote, he would fly to New York, find a new, more satisfactory job, share Jerry's apartment, and resume leading a bachelor life. In the twelve pages it took Ron to detail his plans for the future and describe his bleak past—he wrote in glittering generalities, there were no specific complaints—he scarcely mentioned me, his daughter, his sons. He sounded as though we didn't exist.

Ron has now decided maybe he won't mail the letter, that joining Jerry might be a mistake. Ever since Thursday night he and I have been talking in circles. As of this moment Ron wants to table the divorce question temporarily, keep his present job awhile, but turn his studio in our back yard into a separate apartment to be occupied solely by him. I've vetoed that cockeyed plan, but I've applied to take a course in selling real estate in case we do split up, so I can supplement my personal income and support the children. I'm too proud to accept further financial assistance from my parents. I believe I would be in favor of a divorce and a total separation, if I weren't ashamed to have my mother find out. I'd hate to have her learn she was right in disapproving of Ron.

I have never let her know that she and Gertrude enjoyed Ron's and my wedding far more than we did. To us, the elaborate ceremony and our carefully planned honeymoon were dismal indeed. Ron has a strong sex drive, no tenderness whatever. Furthermore, in a funny kind of way, he is a prude. We spent our first night in the bridal suite of the hotel where my parents and my two sisters began their married life. I came out of the dressing room in a filmy nightgown—I wasn't frightened or embarrassed—and Ron hurriedly handed me a bathrobe to put on, saying that somebody might look in and see me through a window. We were on the fifteenth floor, and all the shades were drawn.

The remainder of our honeymoon, spent at a lodge in the mountains, was worse. Ron and I would begin the night together in the double bed, but then he would have an attack of asthma and would have to leave me and go sleep on the floor in front of the fireplace. With an asthmatic seizure, Ron has to breathe warm air. I understood that, but as a bride I felt humiliated, discarded. To me our sexual relationship has always been unsatisfactory. I've never achieved a climax, which is something Ron doesn't know since I've pretended with him, considering it my duty as a wife.

On every single occasion Ron has kissed me I have known his mind was on sex, but I've never refused his kisses. Nor did I ever reject the love-making that followed. I can't see why Ron thinks our marriage is a failure.

*   *

Margaret Anderson was not so successful as she believed in hiding her true feelings from her husband. A handsome man, with a crew haircut and dark-blue eyes, he had this to say:

*   *

At times during our ten years together Margaret has professed to love me, but her love is all show, no feeling. If I ever marry again, which seems doubtful, I want a living wife, somebody warm. Margaret seems to be bloodless, unfeminine, not like a girl at all. Our sexual relationship has been perfunctory with us both. She has just pretended to enjoy herself when we made love, though she doesn't know I know it. She has dutifully accepted my advances, but inwardly she has been untouched, as cool as one of those Fourth-of-July sparklers.

Awhile back there was a popular song called "The Great Pretender" that puts me in mind of Margaret. Our marriage was a big pretense from the beginning. Margaret and I never did love each other. Maybe we aren't capable of romantic love. What we had in our courtship days was liking, respect, and a desire to present a mutual self-protection front to the world.

I worked in the university library at the time, and Margaret hung around in the stacks with me. We talked books and seemed to be companionable. During my Army service Margaret and my mother were my only correspondents. My father couldn't be bothered to write. When I was decorated, my mother saw to it my exploit was covered in the local press. She sent me the clipping and a long letter I treasure to this day. In a brief postscript my father cracked a corny joke to the effect I should be careful if I couldn't be good. I tore his postscript from the bottom of my mother's proud, affectionate, and, in some ways, awfully funny letter. She warned me to avoid cold night marches for my asthma's sake and to drink plenty of fresh milk for my stomach's sake, as though an humble G.I. had the say.

During my overseas service Margaret and I drifted a long way apart. At the time of our marriage, we really didn't know each other very well. Margaret can't say I rushed her to the church. I had a strong last-minute hunch I was the bachelor type like my elder brother, dubious husband material.

After my first six months with Margaret, I had practically decided I wasn't temperamentally suited for marriage, anyhow marriage to her. But by then she was pregnant with Deborah, and that seemed to be that. Margaret's sisters beat her to the altar, but she was determined to present her parents with the first grandchild in the family, and she succeeded in her objective. Occasionally I think that might be why she married me.

Margaret tries to kid me into thinking she believes I'm quite a talented fellow. More than once she's offered to set me up in business, but I don't want her patronage.

Despite Margaret's dry, insincere little compliments on my work, she has no faith in my creative ability or taste. I go for subdued, earthy colors in house decoration and clear, bright colors in clothes, my mother's colors. Margaret unfalteringly chooses the reverse. I've never seen her wear a dress that wasn't a wishy-washy blue, gray, or brown. Yet a few months ago she wanted to put a vivid provincial-style wallpaper in our contemporary modern bedroom. We had just painted the interiors throughout our house in a shade of off-white that took me two week ends to mix. When I expressed my opinion of the junky provincial number, Margaret immediately told me she was only joking and was crazy about our off-white walls.

Margaret and I are both detached and remote from people. I have never in my life had a friend, a genuine friend. When I was a kid, my mother tried hard to get me in with other boys. My father, a Yale graduate, didn't earn enough for us to live in a decent neighborhood, and the kids nearby were toughies. At a time my mother could hardly pay the grocery bills, she wangled me a membership in an exclusive country club, and every afternoon I would walk two miles to get there. No bus fare. I didn't have much fun. I had the feeling the other kids, those with successful fathers and pocket money, suspected me of wanting to cadge ice-cream cones and soft drinks from them. On my birthdays Gertrude would arrange for the sons of her college classmates to be transported from way across town to my party. Half the time my father would show up and spoil the occasion by making snide remarks about my guests and about me.

Margaret's childhood was soft, but apparently she, too, was short on companionship. She had a nurse until she was thirteen years old, and she went to a girls' day school until she was ready for college. She now has a few so-called friends who condescend to come to our house because of her family's social connections. I don't enjoy Margaret's friends—and their parties bore me. Our entertaining is an even worse bore. We don't have buffet suppers at our house. The table is laid with a lace cloth and our wedding china, gold-banded Lenox, too delicate to be exposed to our dishwasher. I would prefer informal pottery and the guests waiting on themselves, instead of Margaret turning herself inside out to provide a sit-down dinner the way her mother does.

Something always goes wrong when we entertain. At our last party the sitter arrived late, and Margaret, busy in the kitchen with the cook she'd hired for the evening, shooed the kids into the living room where I was dispensing cocktails. You couldn't hear yourself think for the uproar they made. When I tried to remove Deborah from the scene, she screamed so loudly it's a wonder the police didn't show up. I don't know how to handle Deborah, who is now at the pudgy, unattractive stage and is stubborn as a mule. A few minutes after I'd got Margaret to put Deborah in her bedroom, the sitter appeared and took charge of the twins. Gregory was jumping up and down on one end of our white sofa, ignoring the guests seated at the other end. Robin was rubbing the woodwork with his dirty hands. Margaret maintained later the guests didn't mind the turmoil, but the evening was a horror to me.

When I finally got to sleep—I'm an insomniac—I had one of my recurrent nightmares. In this nightmare I see myself hidden in the branches of a leafy tree, looking down on a crowd of people below and feeling snug and secure when suddenly I realize that above is a huge, cold, expressionless eye watching me. When I woke in the morning, I was too sunk and sick to go to work.

Perhaps I could endure the emptiness and lack of love in my home if I received any satisfaction from my work. Instead, I'm steam-rollered by my boss and his wife. My employer admits that my designs are 50 per cent responsible for his business success, but he hasn't transferred any company stock to me, something he has been promising for years. Nor will he speak up and protect me from the noisy verbal assaults of his wife. Last spring I was asked to make rough sketches for a new line of dinnerware. By sitting up night and day for two weeks I was able to turn out finished drawings and both the boss and his wife were delighted with them. Next day, Mrs. Boss denied she had approved the drawings, and I had to get my crew to work out another series. After six weeks of seesawing back and forth, endless misunderstandings, recriminations, and three other series of drawings, the boss and his wife settled for the designs they had seen in the first place. By then it was a miracle I didn't have two ulcers. Nobody should be expected to be creative in the kind of atmosphere where I work.

I realize I've been oversensitive since boyhood. To me mole hills *are* mountains. A week ago, driving Margaret to the shopping center, I stopped at an intersection for a red light. When we got the amber signal a car in the rear zoomed around me like a bullet, and I got so flustered I killed my engine. Then the light turned green. Immediately we were in the midst of blowing horns, and traffic piled up. A policeman came over and bawled me out. When we finally drove on, Margaret said nothing. However, she gave me a look of calm contempt that reduced me to the status of a worm and shriveled my very soul.

That night I told Margaret I was wretched in our marriage and had been for years. We are so far out of touch that she didn't even hear me. She yawned and went to bed. I wrote that letter to my brother not at all sure I would send it, but determined to compel Margaret to read it and fix her attention upon my unhappiness with my work, with her, and with our marriage.

My three youngsters all dislike me, with Deborah leading the list. You can hardly blame her. I've developed into a father almost as bad as mine, impatient, sarcastic, critical. Deborah is asthmatic like me, and I know my attempts at disciplining her sometimes start her wheezing, but surely a sulky kid of nine requires discipline.

When I ask the twins if they love me, they shuffle their feet and look uncomfortable, or else they run off. On their last birthday Margaret suggested I give them a present. I spent an afternoon selecting a fine Erector set. It was a waste of time and money. Margaret's gift to the twins was a surprise and a roaring success—a six-month-old puppy. My gift impressed nobody.

Margaret is well able to be both a mother and father to our youngsters. She is completely self-sufficient. If she won't accept financial assistance from her parents, she can go to work and sell real estate as soon as she gets her license. I think I should quit my job, clear out, and go somewhere else. If I'm to be a misfit all my life, there's no reason I should hang around and make my family unhappy, too.

*   *

There is a saying that people are often impelled to marry their problems. Both Margaret and Ron Anderson felt inadequate and inferior. Both wanted friends, but repelled friendship by snobbishness and coldness. Both were too much in need of self-understanding to understand and help each other. Through counseling, the two not only salvaged their marriage, they became the woman and the man each instinctively desired to be. In their case, the route to self-understanding was long and rugged.

It was plain the cause of their unhappiness lay in the past.

Somewhere in their childhood their personalities had been distorted. In the cold, formal atmosphere where she grew up, Margaret, sympathetic by nature, was taught to curb her warm impulses. Also, she early acquired the knowledge that her parents had wanted her to be a boy. She did her best to oblige by denying her femininity. Simultaneously admiring and fearing her father, she chose this aloof man as a model. She sought to win parental approval with proficiency at sports where men excel. Her unusual height added to her social uneasiness and her confusion as to just what her position was in the world. Indeed, her personality had been damaged as much by her being too tall as Bob Lester's had been by his being too short. Envy of her sisters, who were pint-sized and surrounded by swarms of boys, probably was also a factor in leading Margaret to jeer at fluffy, feminine attire and to choose tailored suits, slacks, and the like.

By the time Margaret entered college, she was very mannish. Another truism is that mannish women usually attract soft men. At the university Margaret attracted Ron, moody, indecisive, and possessing artistic interests generally considered feminine.

Ron's mother, Gertrude, wore the pants in his family. Perhaps unconsciously Gertrude had badly wanted to be a man. She took revenge for her disappointment in her own sex by attacking the manhood of her husband and sons. In psychoanalysts' trade talk, Gertrude would be classified as a "castrating female." She damaged all three men in her family. Both Ron and his father suffered from asthma and ulcers, ailments associated with tension and nerves. The elder son, Jerry, was probably the unhappiest and most maladjusted of the three. He had twice attempted suicide. For Ron, with his depressions and his problems, to team up with an even more depressive Jerry would have been unrealistic indeed. However, we did not tell him so. Through counseling, he was guided to make his own decisions.

It would have been futile for us to attempt to provide Margaret with a list of rules on how to conduct herself as a good wife and mother. For ten years she had slavishly followed a lengthy list of self-imposed rules. On the surface Margaret's batting average as a wife appeared to be high—no scenes, no quarrels, no tedious responsibilities to burden Ron, pep talks when he was low spirited. What was lacking in the performance were sincerity, insight, feeling.

The truth, which Ron keenly sensed, was that Margaret had not the slightest appreciation of the daily humiliations he suffered as he was bullied at work by his employer's dominating wife and babied but inwardly scorned at home. When Margaret realized and acknowledged the insincerity of the sympathy she had long professed to feel for Ron, she perceived something quite obvious—her marked resemblance to her mother-in-law. Instead of strengthening her weak husband, she had further weakened him. Completely self-sufficient, Margaret had been depending on Ron for literally nothing, and he knew it. Ron needed to be needed, he needed prestige, he needed to assume responsibility and to be a man.

Margaret did not want to be a Gertrude. She proved it. She transferred to Ron the task of handling their finances and paying their bills. At first he was unenthusiastic; it was easier to hand over his weekly pay and let Margaret worry about the bank balance. In the first month of his management the tardy payment of a premium jeopardized an insurance policy, and he urgently requested that Margaret take over again. She declined.

Ron now takes pride in supporting his family—Margaret's $100-a-month income is reserved for luxuries—and he boasts of his skill in juggling the family funds. The responsibility has been as important to him as it was to Tracy Manning when Elise turned over the family finances to him.

It was harder for Ron than for Margaret to understand his real personality, the reasons for his difficulties. Curiously enough, the recurrent dream where he saw himself up a tree, hidden and looking down on other people, was helpful. During the course of his counseling this dream was interpreted to mean that Ron envisioned himself as superior to and above other people, withdrawn from life, while another part of him (the eye) understood the impossibility of escape. Gradually Ron realized he actually wanted to be an active participant in life, that his childhood experiences and his mother's influence had persuaded him to stand on the side lines, sarcastic, critical, hostile, and—fearful. By the end of our interviews Ron had grown more understanding of his father, whose loud, rough kidding he decided was a screen for timidity.

When Ron perceived how Gertrude had enfeebled him, he did not lose his affection for her, but he did become aware of her capacity to do harm. He then saw how unwilling his mother was for his small sons to act like noisy, normal boys. More watchful of his mother, these days Ron turns aside Gertrude's hints on how the children should be reared. He now has ideas of his own.

After Margaret began to depend on Ron for help with the youngsters, he rapidly improved as a parent and soon took the initiative in arranging games for the boys, helping Deborah with her homework. The dramatic improvement in Deborah's scholarship showed how badly she had needed a father; she is now in the top group at school. Deborah still has occasional attacks of asthma as, for that matter, has Ron. But their attacks seem to be less severe, and Ron's depressions have almost disappeared. All three children are less nervous. Ron now knows better than to ask young boys whether they love him. Gregory and Robin demonstrate their love by the way they run to the door when he comes home. And Margaret now knows better than to ask Ron to buy a birthday present for their twins and then outshine his choice of gift with a beguiling puppy.

When Margaret learned to guard against the masculinity within herself that lessened Ron's masculinity and her respect for him, the couple's sexual relationship became a pleasure to them both. With the change in Margaret's pattern of feelings, her behavior changed in ways too numerous to mention. For one thing, she dropped formality in entertaining and now is satisfied with buffet suppers like others in their neighborhood. At these affairs Margaret and Ron have built up genuine friendships among people with similar interests to theirs. Margaret still wears slacks and tailored suits, costumes that become her, but she also wears the kind of dresses Ron admires in the colors he fancies.

Ron has abandoned his incessant decorating and redecorating of their home, inspired by his restlessness and discontent. But not long ago he papered the master bedroom with a provincial print that Margaret liked.

The turning point in the marriage came on an afternoon when Ron arrived home boiling with complaints about his employer's wife. The old Margaret would have rushed in with tons of sympathy and millions of suggestions. The new Margaret serenely informed Ron that the problem was his, and it was up to him to solve it. All evening Ron brooded. Next morning, however, he told off the boss's wife in no uncertain terms, and his show of strength was rewarded. Alarmed that a valuable employee might quit, the boss fulfilled his long-standing promise and cut Ron in for a share of company stock.

At present Ron is better satisfied with his work, although he and Margaret are talking of the time he will set up in business for himself. The two now talk to each other. It is no longer necessary for Ron to write a letter to his bachelor brother to capture his wife's attention.

* * *

If Ron Anderson had known Chad Russell, he would have discovered they had much in common: Chad, too, was moody and felt inadequate at home and at work; his wife, too, was beleaguered by mother-in-law troubles.

Ava Russell considered Chad's mother the worst hypochondriac she had ever met, and Ava could lay claim to wide experience in the field since she was a registered nurse before her marriage. She particularly resented Chad's credulity and tender heart where his mother's innumerable illnesses were concerned.

A slightly built woman, with snapping, blue eyes and a square, firm jaw, Ava had other complaints to air the day she visited the

Institute. She felt that Chad took no interest in her activities or her feelings, that he kept his own feelings and activities a secret from her. She objected to his overwhelming interest in hi-fi. She interpreted his turning on a record whenever she was within earshot as a ruse to keep from hearing her talk.

Some weeks before we first saw Ava, life with Chad had become unbearable to her, and she had moved herself and her two small sons into her mother's apartment. Her plan was to stay there until she could rent a place, locate an efficient full-time maid, make connections with a hospital, and get back into nursing again. She looked defiant and almost triumphant as she announced to us:

* *

Chad is now at liberty to play the hi-fi every evening as loud and as long as he likes. I won't be around any more trying to talk over Haydn and Bach. Chad can mope and gloom to his heart's content. From now on he is also free to visit his mother and listen politely while she harps on her imaginary ailments and her unsatisfactory, unsympathetic daughter-in-law.

Until I married, I thought I could get along with anybody. When I got acquainted with Lady, Chad's mother, I found out different. I'm a down-to-earth, literal sort of person; when I speak I deal in facts. Plain facts are too prosy for my mother-in-law. Lady prefers fiction and drama.

She lives only two blocks from our house. Her multiple illnesses were timed to strike her just as I was dishing up dinner. She would send a hurry-up call for Chad, and he would arrive at her bedside in advance of the doctor. While our dinner cooled, she was tightly holding his hand and describing her backache, her migraine, her heart attack, her gallbladder pains, or whatever the current malady happened to be. As soon as Lady collected sufficient sympathy, she would rally and pass on to Chad the latest wild tale she'd concocted about me. How I insulted her by hanging up the phone in her ear; how I criticized her cooking or new hat; how I imposed on her and my sister-in-law. Lady's most cherished delusion—she constantly circulates this fable among our friends—is that I make a practice of dumping my youngsters on her and on Chad's sister. The truth is my two children haven't stayed with my sister-in-law half as often as her three children have stayed with me. And Stephen and Malcolm haven't seen their grandmother for weeks; she's been too ailing. Chad knows the straight of the baby-sitting dispute. I've told him often enough.

The last quarrel between Chad and me was started, as usual, by his mother's overactive tongue. In the past I've tried—with indifferent success, I'll admit—to be patient with Lady's tireless inventions concerning my personal misdeeds. She loves to compare my failings with the virtues of a neighborhood girl she once hoped Chad would marry. On a Saturday afternoon Lady saw this girl— her name is Helen—in the drugstore and spent an hour running down *my* mother. The gist of Lady's long-winded tale, according to Helen whom I've made a friend, was that my mother's housekeeping was so bad the other tenants in her apartment house had complained, and the management asked her to move. My mother works —she and my father are divorced—and she doesn't pretend to be a demon housekeeper. However, there wasn't a shred of truth in the story.

After this basket of news was dropped in my lap, I phoned Chad at his office. Chad is fond of my mother, or he has always appeared to be. Judging from his reaction—Chad didn't say a great deal, but then he never does—I was convinced that for once he was on my side. He promised to have a talk with Lady and order her to stop using Helen as a mouthpiece to broadcast slanders on my mother. Anyhow, that was my impression of our conversation.

Chad was late getting home that evening. I'd bathed and put the boys to bed and was in the bathroom emptying the tub when he came in. I called and asked him how the meeting with Lady had gone. Chad didn't reply. Instead, he turned on the hi-fi full blast. I had to raise my voice and shout through the uproar. What had Lady done? Had she promised to quit insulting my mother? What had she said?

At that point, without warning, Chad dashed into the bathroom. Ordinarily, he is calm as a clam. When he is annoyed, his habit is to turn gloomy and quiet. It's unlike him to give way to temper; I'd never known him to move so fast. He rushed at me like a cyclone. Before I took in what was happening, while I was staring goggle-eyed, he picked me up and threw me into the bathtub. Water splashed everywhere. I wasn't hurt except for cracking my elbow, but for a moment I was badly scared. I thought Chad had suddenly gone insane. But then almost at once he pulled me out of the tub, and I saw his face. It was bewildered and ashamed. There were tears in his eyes. In a twinkling I understood the reason for his performance. My mother-in-law was the answer.

I had caught Lady in a malicious lie, but she was still in control of my husband. Somehow, she had got around Chad again and put herself in the right with him, and me in the wrong. It was clear she had spelled out the get-tough policy to Chad, and he had obediently followed her suggestions. Perhaps I could forgive Chad for acting like a brute—indeed I frequently think a show of honest emotion on his part might clear the air—providing I knew he had acted on his own volition. How can I possibly forgive him for permitting his mother, who hates me with a passion, to become a third and a dominant partner in our marriage? After all, I have some pride.

When I married Chad, I didn't dream he was tangled in apron strings. On the night his ex-girl friend Helen introduced us—we met on New Year's Eve and married on Valentine's Day—I had just broken my engagement to one of those big, grown-up boys with oceans of charm and no strength of character. I was good and fed up with the type of male who expects some woman to lead him by the hand through the storms of life. I wanted to marry a real man, a strong man. Chad was so sweet and so generous—if anything he is *too* generous—I couldn't help falling in love with him. In those days, the days before he became so ingrown and self-centered, he was extraordinarily thoughtful and kind. He lived many miles from the hospital where I was then on duty, but during our short courtship we saw each other every night except one. On the evenings I had charge of the floor I could spend only a few minutes with him, but Chad wasn't discouraged by that fact. The only night he missed the long drive was the night before our wedding, and that time he sent flowers. I easily persuaded myself he was strong and dependable and adult.

I soon learned he wasn't adult at all. On our honeymoon Chad had a tonsillectomy he'd been needing a long while. The hotel doctor happened to be a friend of mine and gave us a courtesy rate. Chad wasn't hospitalized, and inside twenty-four hours he felt fine. Nevertheless, he yearned for his mother. It was all I could do to prevent him from inviting my mother-in-law to join us in the bridal suite.

When we got back from our trip, Lady had already selected and virtually spoken for the "bargain" house we now own. Financially speaking, I suppose our house is a fair investment, but it's located in a moribund community. Everybody else's children are in high school, and most of the other wives are twenty years my senior.

After we settled in the house—I was too dumb to object to the purchase—I discovered how maddeningly childish Chad can be. For one thing, he expected me to shoulder the responsibility for getting him up and off to work in the mornings. Chad is a talented sleeper who can't be aroused by the noisiest alarm clock. I doubt an earthquake would budge him. I didn't mind waking him—once. He demanded to be called six or eight times, at five-minute intervals. If I got impatient and jerked off his blankets or if he took exception to the tone of my voice, he would roll over and stick to the bed for another hour or so. Sometimes he didn't even go back to sleep, he just lay there and sulked. Naturally, he was frequently late to work. Never did he blame himself for being late. He blamed me.

Since Chad's income isn't remarkable—he is an expert on air conditioning, but is earning considerably less than he should be earning—we should stick to a careful budget. We are up to our eyebrows in debt and installment payments. Holidays and anniversaries register big with Chad. He showers the boys and me with gifts he can't afford. He is equally munificent with his mother on her birthdays. Periodically he goes on spending sprees and buys unnecessary luxuries for himself—a motion picture camera, a new tool, a record album. The movie camera enthralled him—for six weeks. He then presented it to the twelve-year-old son of our postman.

Chad seems to have a compulsion to give away things he enjoys owning. He also seems compelled to lend his tools, although I know he hates doing it. A year ago he lent his power saw to a neighbor who has never been known to return anything. Ever since, Chad has been wishing he could think of a way to get back the saw. The way to get back the saw, as I told him almost daily, is to go and ask for it.

The door-to-door salesman Chad can resist has yet to ring our bell. My cupboards are bulging with gimmicks and gadgets I don't know the purpose of. Last month Chad signed up for a new type of electric mixer, although we already owned two satisfactory mixers. I didn't complain, I just put the box containing our third mixer on the top shelf. But Chad got so upset, apparently at his own foolishness, that he went barreling out of the house. I had a notion he was headed toward his mother, so I followed.

To my surprise, Chad walked into the park. He sat down on a bench and covered his face with his hands. For a moment I was tempted to walk to the bench and put my arms around him, but then I changed my mind. In my opinion, a man should behave like a man. I turned around and went home.

Chad's mother is responsible for many of our difficulties, but not all. Maybe the real trouble is I can't figure Chad out and don't understand the way he behaves. I can't seem to reach him, however hard I try. Talking to Chad is like hollering down a well. All you receive in return is the echo of your own voice. Even Lady complains he is remote and erratic and almost impossible to get at. For no reason I can fathom, he ducks my most trivial questions. If I ask whether he intends to work late or leave his office early, I receive a blank stare. If I ask whether we can accept an invitation to a party, he just grunts. Often he scarcely appears to be aware that I exist.

On the infrequent occasions Chad made love to me in recent months—and this does hurt—I had almost no sense of intimacy or closeness. No sense that he and I were loving companions, sharing a thrilling experience. It was as though I were in the embrace of a stranger. All of the rightness and meaning have gone out of our sexual relationship.

I've never had the feeling, even during my pregnancies, that Chad was protective as a husband should be, that he cherished me. He seemed as delighted by the birth of our first child as I was. Yet he didn't stand by me when his mother made trouble at the hospital. I forget the details of that argument but, as I recall, Lady was determined to name Stephen for the husband she henpecked into his grave. I preferred to name my own baby. To this day, I don't know which name Chad preferred. Ever close-mouthed, ever the neutral, he declined to commit himself.

I hate to bring up my boys without a father, but I have no hope of saving my marriage. The only reason I'm here at the Institute is because my mother, who believes divorce is the last resort, begged me to come. I'm sure your interviews with Chad will be a waste of time. Chad is both unwilling and unable to speak frankly about himself.

*   *

Ava Russell's thirty-year-old husband was a big man with nervous hands. His eagerness to tell us his side of the story did not bear out his wife's complaints about his taciturnity. His words poured forth so fast he stammered as he said:

*   *

I've been pushed around all my life, usually by some woman. I've always wanted peace—and I only found it once. That was just after I got out of the Army. In the Army I was really pushed around—by professionals. Rules, regulations, regimentation. Do this, do that, and do it on the double! When the Army finally sprung me into private life, I decided I was going to *have* a private life. I wasn't going home to my mother and her rules and regulations. I built myself a small house in a growing community on the desert. I did air-conditioning installations for local builders, and I didn't have too many jobs, but I earned almost as much as I earn now in the city. I got up when I pleased, I went to bed when I pleased. If I wanted to, I stayed up all night listening to my record collection, watched the stars fade and the sun come up. That was the life!

Then I met Ava. I will never forget our first evening. I went into the city to attend a New Year's Eve party, and there we were introduced. Ava was wearing a black dress with a lacy-doily dingus at the top and a long, full skirt. Socially I'm a bust and I'm also a poor dancer, but in a few minutes she had me out on the floor and we were laughing together. I knew at once she was the girl for me.

During our courtship she was sweet and companionable and so helpful to me. Every night in the week she would phone, and I would drive all the way in from the desert to see her. She was kept busy at the hospital, but to me Ava's minutes were worth any other girl's hours. In those days my comfort and my wishes rated high with her, even in small things. If the evening was cool, Ava fetched me a cup of hot coffee from the nurses' kitchen; if the evening was warm, there was a pitcher of lemonade waiting. I was sure that she would be the kind of wife who would cheer for and support my ideas. Ava told me she shared my love for the desert and, daydreaming, I pictured the two of us living in my little house—listening to music and looking at the stars.

Before we had been married a week I discovered Ava was as bossy as my mother and my sister. She had been determined all along that I would take a job in the city, and I did. I came back to my mother, my sister, my family, a steady job, and the old neighborhood. Ava now thinks it was my mother's idea that we buy our present house; actually she joined forces with Lady in urging me to buy it. She wanted to get me back to town.

I've never heard of another man whose bride maneuvered him into having a tonsillectomy on his honeymoon. She said she was being practical; it would save money. Well, perhaps it did. But it spoiled the trip. And Ava made trouble for me by not notifying my mother of the operation. When Lady finally got the news, she was so upset she had a heart attack. My nerves go haywire when I think I've caused my mother to get sick. I get a thick, choked feeling, I can't seem to breathe, and then I get a blinding headache.

A good many of Ava's criticisms of me are valid. I know there are times I am extravagant and behave as though I had a money machine in my basement. There are times I just can't seem to curb myself. I gave the best jigsaw puzzle I ever made to a neighbor's daughter. I gave my favorite record album to a hospital for shut-ins. Something drives me to pass along my possessions to others. When I see the smile on other people's faces, I feel repaid. For a few minutes, knowing others will enjoy things in the same way I've enjoyed them, I feel friendly and close with people. Afterward, of course, I feel foolish and like a show-off.

It is stupid of me to give away an expensive record collection out of sheer vanity, you might say. It is stupid of me to lend my good tools and let door-to-door salesmen talk me into buying things we don't need. But the salesmen are glib-spoken and seemingly friendly. I find myself listening and being convinced by their patter, despite the knowledge I will regret it later.

I have always wanted to be cordial and easy with people. It has always been hard for me to feel at ease with anybody. Unless I'm in exactly the right mood, people, particularly in a crowd, make me jittery. When I used to promise to take Ava to a party, she would hold me to the promise no matter how I might be feeling. If she and my mother put on one of their battles in the afternoon, I would be sure to be feeling rotten on the evening of the party. So I stopped accepting any invitations. I haven't been missed. A man like me adds nothing to a social gathering.

But in the present foul-up not all the faults are mine. I don't think it would have hurt Ava to show Lady a little consideration. And I don't think it would have hurt Lady to treat Ava with a little tact.

One of their worst rows occurred when my first son was born. I would have been glad to have Stephen named for my dad, but I thought Ava was entitled to name the baby, and I told my mother so. Still and all, I thought Lady was entitled to see her first grandson in the hospital. At the time Stephen was born Lady was visiting in Chicago, but she flew back to the Coast on receiving my telegram. Ava had chosen "rooming-in care," which meant the baby stayed in the room with her and that nobody was admitted except me. Lady was furious she wasn't allowed a peek at the new baby, and that same afternoon flew back to Chicago. That same afternoon, too, Ava suddenly decided she was tired of "rooming-in care," and Stephen was moved to a crib in the hospital nursery. Ava's mother did get to see her first grandson in the hospital. Lady has never forgotten it. To this day, Ava declares that sudden change of hospital arrangements was pure accident, but I've always been doubtful. Although Ava complains of my mother's fabrications, there are times she herself isn't strictly accurate.

As for this latest wrangle that sent Ava and the kids flying out of the house, Lady shouldn't have made up a tale about my mother-in-law, but I'm not wholly convinced of her guilt. Lady denied to me she'd done any gossiping. It was her contention that Ava had manufactured the story for the sake of creating a fuss. Ava's mother had a third version of what had happened. Helen—and I wish I knew why my wife buddies with an old girl friend of mine—produced a fourth version.

In the midst of the charges, countercharges, and contradictions, I got so confused I didn't know whom to believe. When women start disputing among themselves and the Supreme Court couldn't decide where the truth lies, I get a feeling of helplessness. I realize I will be pulled into the argument and maneuvered by somebody into doing something I don't want to do. I didn't want to push Ava into the bathtub. Lady's advice that wives respond to rough treatment—combined with a cold, hard note in Ava's voice—caused me to lose my head.

I had some rugged combat in the Army—I fought both at Tarawa and Okinawa—but I'd rather face combat than quarreling, arguing women. Actually the first thing I can remember from childhood is sitting with my sister in a stalled automobile, while my dad tried to change a tire, and my mother denounced him for having the puncture. My sister—Ruth was probably six or seven at the time—was also scolding away at him. I spoke up for my dad, and both Ruth and my mother then turned on me. I tried to jump out of the car and get away, but I was caught and got a spanking.

My sister and my mother, like my wife and her mother, are quick on the trigger—quick acting, quick thinking, machine-gun talkers. I take after my dad; I'm slow. Not only was I slow as a boy; I was sickly. Or so Lady says. I had severe whooping cough in the fourth grade—the grade they taught phonetics in my school—and I was kept at home for a year. I never did catch up with my reading. My memory of my boyhood Saturdays is other kids outside playing and my mother standing over me with a book insisting I read from it, when I didn't know how to read. Lady always managed to get me to obey her. My sister would rebel. I just couldn't. The times Ruth would skip out on the dishes, I was likely to do the dishes and run the vacuum cleaner to boot. Lady would make me feel sorry for her or . . . something.

Perhaps I tried extra hard to satisfy Lady because I early realized what a disappointment I was to her and my dad. When I was in the seventh grade my parents went to a PTA meeting where my teacher told them I wasn't college material. Both were badly cut up, though Dad attemped to hide it. Years later, tests I took in the Army indicated that the teacher had been too pessimistic. My I.Q. was high, and in music and math I scored exceptionally well. But my parents believed my seventh-grade teacher at the time.

I seem fated to disappoint those I would like best to please. Ava thinks I should earn more and be more stable in my business. I agree. But when my work is criticized or I'm criticized, I become unnerved and incapable. The only time I've ever *felt* I was a success was out on the desert. I had no trouble there getting up in the morning. If work was waiting, I practically leaped out of bed. I had no troubles with health and no trouble with quarreling women. I was blessed with quiet and serenity.

It is impossible for me to keep the peace between my wife and my mother or to find any personal peace. Much as I dislike to have Ava bring up our sons by herself—I'm afraid she will boss them around the way I was bossed around—I doubt I can persuade her to come back home. I came to this interview only because I was told Ava needed my help. It seems improbable Ava either needs or will take help from me. Long ago she stopped listening to any of my ideas or accepting any of my advice. She knows all the answers herself.

* *

Ava Russell did not know all the answers by any means. On the contrary, she was as badly mixed up and, in some respects, was as emotionally juvenile as Chad. Ava had committed her mind and emotions so thoroughly to the feud with her mother-in-law that she had lost sight of almost everything else. Ava's hardships as a small, fatherless girl had left her with a healthy distaste for divorce. Nevertheless, she seemed to be working almost deliberately to break up her marriage. She put far more time and energy into dreaming up plots against Chad's mother than she put into thinking about him or their tottering marriage.

When Chad took refuge from his dissatisfactions by constant playing of hi-fi or in childish fits of the sulks, a wiser, more patient wife would have tried to overlook his sulking unless she understood and could change his mood. Frustrated by Chad's obstinate silences and her inability "to get anything out of him," Ava retaliated with scenes. The scenes did not help her to "get at" her husband. Indeed, she succeeded in driving him deeper into himself and farther away from her. Both she and Chad needed to learn how to sense and respond to the other's *feelings* instead of blindly reacting to the other's exasperating behavior.

When Chad stubbornly refused to disclose the hour he would leave his office, it was useless for Ava to pay him off with anger and tears and thereby prolong the unpleasantness. As it happened, Chad's seemingly mysterious reticence on the subject of his working hours was not mysterious at all. He knew that if he told Ava he was leaving early, she would immediately take charge of his leisure and load him with errands to be performed on the way home; if she learned he was working late, she would arrange that his overtime earnings come under her control.

Any observant acquaintance could have told Ava that she was bossy and domineering, but she would not have believed it. Ava's answers to a test of temperament which is taken by all our clients indicated that in a random crowd of 100 people, including both men and women, she would rank at the top in aggressiveness. The result of an impersonal and scientific test disturbed and convinced her as no words from us could have done. Armed with this knowledge about herself, she reviewed and discussed her past history with fresh insight.

Before her marriage to Chad, Ava had been engaged to three other young men, and in each case she had done the original choosing and most of the subsequent chasing. (Although Chad covered thousands of miles during the courtship, her telephone calls prompted his journeys from the desert to the hospital.) No man whom she had ever attracted or who attracted her, Ava finally admitted, had been notable for either stability or strength. In fact none of her previous admirers had measured up to Chad in charm, integrity, and ability. There was a strong likelihood that, if she divorced Chad, she would drift into marriage with a man of the same type but less worthwhile. Once Ava recognized this probability, she was willing to make changes in herself to preserve the marriage.

Ava acknowledged that Chad's boyishness and need to be looked after had appealed to her, and that her maternal qualities—her interest in his comfort and welfare—must have appealed to him. For purely conventional reasons—"A man should be strong"—she had tossed away personality assets her husband treasured. On the evening she followed him into the park and was tempted to join him on the bench, Ava was operating on Chad's wave length. When she retreated, she took a wrong turn in her marriage.

Chad's major difficulties with his marriage, his career, the world, and himself dated back to his boyhood and relationship with his tyrannical mother. A child can react to the overdomination of a parent either with rebellion or submissiveness. Less lucky than his sister who rebelled, Chad was handicapped by the belief he was a disappointing son. It was easy for his mother to make him feel guilty when he did not obey her.

In his boyhood Chad had obeyed, but he acquired the habit of dealing with the sometimes intolerable pressures his mother applied by disappearing from the house or by withdrawing into long spells of sullen silence. He learned how to hold his tongue and suppress his natural resentment at the injustice that was his lot. In this way, without realizing it, Chad learned as a young boy how to be a lone wolf and gradually lost the knack of making contact with others. He did not enjoy his role as a lone wolf. His wild bursts of generosity, so irritating and baffling to Ava, reflected his longing to share the feelings of others, to make their feelings a part of his own life experience.

In his manhood Chad consistently repeated behavior patterns established years earlier in childish skirmishes with his mother. Treated unfairly, he repressed his feelings, sulked, and then retired from the situation exactly as he had done at the age of five when he felt abused by his mother. His feelings and reactions when he heard a harsh note in Ava's voice duplicated his boyish reaction to the harsh, commanding voice of his mother. His fearfulness aroused by quarreling, arguing women, his sensation of extreme helplessness, were echoes of old clashes with a mother and sister teamed against him.

With these revelations, Chad suddenly thrilled to the hope he could not only salvage his marriage, but that he might also learn to conquer his emotional blocking toward people in general. He had long been aware that many of his mother's illnesses were psychosomatic, and that he was too closely tied to her. But he did not know how to go about escaping from the bondage of habit.

It was obvious that Ava and Chad lived too near his mother. They rented their house and bought another place located a long way from the old neighborhood. With the move, many of their problems were eased.

Lady was no longer in a position to play on Chad's too-ready sympathies and summon him to her bedside with every minor illness. Stephen and Malcolm ceased to be a source of dissension. Lady was the sort of grandmother who complained that she saw too little of her grandsons, but when she saw them, she complained she was being used as a baby sitter. Ava and Chad's new home is located in a development populated by families with young children. Ava now trades off baby-sitting duties with other young wives, and everybody is satisfied. Ava also profited by breaking off her association with Helen. Chad's old girl friend was no true friend of hers and, in fact, was responsible for a goodly share of the gossip and tale bearing.

The couple's most important gains, however, should be credited to the change in Ava, which in turn brought about a striking change in Chad. When Ava began trusting and following her instincts and responding to Chad's inner needs and feelings, she did not weaken him. Instead she helped him to become more manly, more assured, more mature. Chad carried his new assurance into his business and benefited. With Ava's encouragement he began to stand up for his rights and defend his professional opinions. To his surprise and pleasure, his fellow workers were not angered and alienated, but were proud of him. Tentatively Chad began to express a little of the cordiality he had always felt and was able to establish a few friendships. His extravagant generosity then became unnecessary to him and soon disappeared.

Ava now knows that Chad's nature is, and will always be, less aggressive than her nature, that he is slower than she to reach a decision. She does her best to keep a tight rein on her tendency to manage and maneuver him, out of sheer impatience. She allows her husband sufficient time to think and make his own decisions. For she wants Chad to feel, as she now feels, that he is the head of the family.

* * *

In the matter of in-laws Ava Russell was harassed only by a mother-in-law. Henrietta Baldwin thought of her husband, Douglas, as the chieftain of a large, noisy clan standing together to challenge and threaten her marriage.

Douglas Baldwin's family consisted of his mother, father, sister, and brother. The brother and sister were both married with families of their own. His mother and father had been divorced for many years. Yet the personal responsibilities and financial obligations of the entire group fell on Douglas' shoulders. In Henrietta's opinion, Douglas welcomed the burden while he appeared to begrudge everything he spent on her and their children.

If thrift had been necessary, she would gladly have economized to help her husband. But Douglas was a top-flight, upper-bracket lawyer. He had been a confirmed bachelor of forty when she married him. Henrietta was ten years younger, a divorcée with one child, a boy of eight.

When she met Douglas, she was leading a fairly pleasant life with her boy. She was well established as a fashion model, was earning a good income, and had many friends. But she had about lost hope she would ever experience a deep, wholly absorbing love. In her first marriage—she eloped at nineteen—there had been sweetness and youth, but no depth and very little reality. From her first meeting with Douglas Baldwin, she believed she had found the real thing. Her feeling for him went far beyond sexual attraction. She loved his clever mind, his vitality and his strength, but she loved his weaknesses, too. For a short while, she thought he loved her in the same way.

Then even in the early months of the marriage the humiliating quarrels over finances began. Although Douglas was the only man she had ever truly cared for, Henrietta eventually decided she could not continue to live with him as his wife unless changes occurred. In the third year of her marriage she came to the Institute to see if we could help her.

She was a long-legged, slim-hipped woman, whose beauty, carriage, and high-style clothes at once suggested the fashion-modeling career she had formerly pursued. She continued to look down at her pretty, well-shaped hands after she took off her gloves and she sounded embarrassed as she said:

✿ ✿

It is so undignified to bicker over money. Before I married Douglas, I was earning fifty dollars a day as a model, and I seldom worked less than three or four days a week. I now have no household allowance. I have no joint checking account with Douglas or any other type of bank account. I do have "charge-a-plates" at several department stores. Douglas audits their monthly statements with the passionate zeal of a bank examiner hot on the trail of a suspected embezzler. I tint my hair, a matter I would prefer to keep private. Douglas inspects the bills I run at the beauty shop with equal care. I am supposed to apply on bended knee for every penny I receive from him. If I need cash, he almost always gives it to me—after an endless cross-examination. He then pinches my cheek or pats my head and informs me that I don't appreciate my luck, that he wishes somebody would hand him money whenever he asked for it. After such patronizing remarks, I don't want to touch his money. Douglas makes me feel like a whiny little girl begging for candy.

I have always hated to ask for money, but nearly all my life I've had to do it. As a child I lived with my grandfather, who was a prosperous small-town merchant, but I had to wheedle and turn on the charm to get school books and clothing and other necessities. I didn't attend my graduation exercises because I was too proud to ask for a new white dress.

Douglas' relatives have no such problem. He is fantastically gen-

erous with his mother, father, sister, and brother. Generous of his
money, his time, and himself. He shares his deepest thoughts not
with me, but with his brother, Tim. He sees more of his brother—
Douglas and Tim are in daily communication—than he sees of our
two small sons. He ignores my son by my first marriage, except to
complain about the cost of feeding and clothing an active eleven-
year-old. Any of the extras that make a growing boy happy—a pair
of skis, a tennis racket—opens up a degrading debate in our household. Usually I let my boy do without. At such times it's difficult for
me not to recall that Douglas virtually forced me to sign away the
youngster's rights to the support of his real father.

Unless Douglas is in a beneficent mood, our own little sons fare
poorly, too. When our second boy was born, Douglas did hire a
nurse. The amount of the nurse's wages is a regular and very tiresome feature of his conversation.

A year ago I had the nursery redecorated without obtaining
Douglas' permission, and he is still keening over the expense. Later,
at a bookstore sale I bought a set of the *Children's Encyclopedia*
for the room. Douglas assumed his most sarcastic air and wanted
to know what would be wrong with our sons using the public library
when they were old enough to read. At his insistence the nursery
walls were hung with examples of modern art, including two mediocre paintings done by his brother, Tim. Douglas refused to tell me
what he paid his brother for the paintings, but I'm sure the price was
staggering.

In our household only my purchases are subject to question.
Douglas is quick to side-step any questions of mine. Indeed, he
has done his best to keep the size of his practice and the amount
of his income a secret from me. He has a safe at his office, a strong
box at home. He has a special lock on the trunk of his car in case he
needs to transport canceled checks or other records that might be
illuminating to me.

I feel that I should be treated as a full partner in our marriage. If
Douglas is willing to trust me with the care of his two sons, he
should be willing to trust me with his confidence and a just share of

his income. Why should I be forced into the position of a mendicant?

Douglas' kinfolk have no hesitancy about asking him for what they want. They have ample opportunities to press their claims. Douglas and I don't entertain our friends; we entertain his family. Douglas doesn't belong to the professional organizations that normally would bring him into contact with other lawyers. He can't spare the time. We can't spare the time for theater, concerts, outings by ourselves.

We visit brother Tim at least three times a week, or Tim and his wife, Mimi, call on us. Every Saturday night there is a gathering of the entire clan. Douglas' divorced parents invariably appear with the light of battle in their eyes, determined to keep tabs on how much the other is getting from Douglas. Everybody in the clan shouts at each other and at me. I wilt under the combined attacks. Sometimes I burst into tears. Once I became hysterical and ran out of the house and threw myself on the grass and just lay there shuddering. Douglas and his family went on with their noisy wrangling, and I doubt they noticed I was gone. Not once at these gruesome gatherings has Douglas ever tried to protect me from the assaults of his kin or spoken up in my defense.

I didn't regard his family as my rivals until after we had become engaged. One Saturday Douglas took me to meet the clan. I could tell they distrusted and disliked me, but he laughed at my doubts and set a wedding date for us. I bought a beautiful summer dress wholesale, an Italian import. The month Douglas had selected was June.

In June he suggested a postponement and set a date in late July. By then I had cut myself off from my other friends—Douglas is a possessive, dominating man—and at his request, or rather at his command, I had given up modeling assignments. My son and I were living on my savings. I was disturbed by the postponement, since Douglas' excuse was very vague. However, I didn't protest. July came. When he suggested still another postponement and spoke in terms of September or October, I was obliged to acknowledge the truth. His family intended to break us up, and Douglas was allowing it to happen. It nearly broke my heart, but I told him our marriage was permanently postponed. I returned his ring. Douglas wouldn't accept the ring. He put it back on my finger. He then insisted we be married immediately.

We drove in wild haste to Las Vegas. I barely took the time to toss my beautiful imported dress in the car. In the end, I didn't wear it. Douglas and I joined a line of other couples waiting in a dusty Nevada street for a turn with the preacher. I had worn pedal pushers and a sunback blouse on the sweltering desert drive from Los Angeles, and I wore pedal pushers when I stood at the altar. I was so afraid my groom would change his mind again that I didn't dare leave him long enough to change into the proper clothing. Douglas thought my costume very amusing.

We got off to a bad start all around. We quarreled bitterly on our first day. Douglas wanted us to drive straight back to his home. At that time he shared a rented house with his father, his brother, and Mimi. I refused to share my honeymoon. We spent four days in Nevada, and then we stayed temporarily in my Los Angeles apartment. Douglas' next idea was that we should build two new houses on two adjoining lots—one house for Tim and Mimi, another house for us. I balked at that cosy arrangement. Fortunately for me, Mimi also balked.

During our first days together, Douglas and I established a plan of living that I've been fighting ever since. A plan where his family comes first in his affections and his thinking. I don't deny that some of Douglas' parents' claims on him are justified. He can well afford to support his mother and father. I begrudge the time he spends with them more than the money.

Over the past three years Douglas has lent his sister several thousand dollars. It is unlikely the loans will ever be repaid, but Eloise has five children, and it's been a struggle for her husband to get on his feet.

Tim is forty-one years old, and he will never be self-supporting. From time to time, he languidly accepts a job that somebody else finds for him but he soon grows bored, drops the job, and returns to what he fondly calls his painting. Tim has never sold a picture in his life—except to Douglas. Perhaps I'm not competent to judge the quality of Tim's work—his murky, gloomy style does not appeal to me—but I'm competent to judge the quantity. Tim paints only when the spirit moves him, which is seldom. Weeks pass when he doesn't touch a brush.

Tim and his wife, Mimi, fawn on Douglas sickeningly. Douglas repays their flattery handsomely and not just in a financial way. He proclaims Tim everywhere to be an unrecognized genius. He feels privileged, as he tells everybody, to be Tim's only patron. Ordinarily Douglas has a lively sense of his own worth and a high regard for his legal skill. At times he can be almost arrogant. In Tim's company Douglas becomes a diffident, obsequious sort of person, apparently overwhelmed by his brother's "brilliance." To see Douglas, my strong, clever husband, permit himself to be diminished in this fashion makes me feel almost ill.

Tim and Mimi seek Douglas' advice at every turn. The three of them talk over their most intimate affairs and my affairs, too. As soon as I told Douglas I was pregnant with our first child, he rushed to the phone and notified Tim. Immediately Tim and Mimi, who had been married for ten childless years, began to wonder whether they ought to start a baby. They automatically consulted Douglas. He approved. Their daughter was born four months after our first son. Douglas settled Mimi's hospital bills, he paid for their baby's layette, he bought nursery furniture that is a duplicate of ours. Whatever I do, Mimi is bound to copy. The moment she heard I had enrolled for a few college courses, she decided to go to college, too. Douglas is happily paying tuition for us both.

He is also paying their grocery bills, as I learned from the butcher the other day. Tim and Mimi have no rent worries. Douglas built a house for them, after we bought our house. He is half owner of the building where Tim has the studio he uses mainly as a recreation-lounging room. This studio is in the same block with Douglas' office; he and Tim manage to lunch together four or five times a week.

Whenever Tim feels the need of something special, he and Mimi go to work on Douglas. There is one important ground rule: the giving and receiving are supposed to be done behind my back. With practice I've grown expert at sensing a conspiracy in the making.

Two weeks ago Tim casually remarked that his car was in the repair shop. Mimi followed up by asking Douglas what he thought of this year's automobile models. Douglas obliged with his opinion. That was all—for then. Several days later Tim and Mimi drove over to our house in a new car. At once I knew the score, but Tim explained to me that he'd landed a new job; Douglas explained that the new job carried a tidy advance; Mimi explained that the tidy advance exactly covered the down payment on the car. I was cut to the heart, but too dispirited to pick holes in this flimsy tale.

Yesterday Douglas laid out several suits for me to send to the cleaner. He was in a hurry and less careful than usual. Checking through the pockets, I came across the key to his strong box. I used it. The registration papers for the new car, made out in Douglas' name, were in the box. He had made the down payment. Douglas' insurance policies were also there. When I examined them, I got a real shock. He has not transferred his policies since our marriage, as he has many times told me he had. Douglas' beneficiaries are not the children and myself. They are his mother, his father, his sister, and his brother.

I didn't hide the fact I'd found the key he has always kept hidden from me. When Douglas came home from the office, I let him walk in on me, looking at his private papers.

We had a terrible quarrel, the worst of our marriage. I screamed dreadful things at Douglas, and he denounced my prying in words I know originated with Tim and Mimi. Then he slammed out of the house. I suppose he spent the night with Tim and Mimi, but I don't know where he went. Nor do I care.

Douglas' mother, his father, his sister and her family, and their emergencies have been hard for me to take. But in time I believe I could have coped with them.

Tim and Mimi defeat me. For they threaten my integrity. Because of them I am poisoning my life with hatred, suspicion, venge-fulness. I'm not that kind of person. Tim and Mimi are changing me into the kind of woman I despise—a mean, suspicious shrew—a sneak and a snoop. I don't want to be like that. Although in many ways I still love Douglas dearly, I think I should take my three boys and leave my husband in order to save my self-respect.

*   *

Douglas Baldwin had blazing black eyes, was dynamic and com-manding in appearance. Obviously, he would be a hard man to argue down, once he had made up his mind. He looked scornfully around the counseling office as he said in challenging tones:

*   *

Most lawyers of my acquaintance would be very much surprised if they knew I was here. But I thought it only fair for you to hear the side of the story that I'm sure Henrietta forgot to tell. My side. My brother's side.

Henrietta and I would never have met except for Tim. She was modeling for a sculptor friend of his. Tim thought she was attractive and arranged for us to meet. My brother and his wife liked Henri-etta in the beginning, but they rapidly cooled to her. No doubt they sensed her antagonism to them. Henrietta is antagonistic to every-body in my family. She complains endlessly that I give too much to them. My parents, my sister, and my brother are more than entitled to anything they get from me. I owe them a debt that can never be paid in full.

A law degree isn't to be had at bargain-counter rates. Every mem-ber of my family owns a piece of me. I got my education during the depression years, and at their expense. I studied hard—I ranked third in my class—but my family's sacrifices made it possible for me to apply my whole mind to learning law. My sister clerked in the dime store, Tim washed dishes in a diner. My mother couldn't pro-vide cash, but no week passed when she didn't pick up and do my laundry, mend my socks, or turn the collars on my shirts. My father squeezed pennies out of a tiny business to buy expensive books for me. Eventually he sold the business and turned over the proceeds to me so I could equip and open a law office.

Tim, who is two years my junior, got no such break. I'm a fair enough lawyer, but there are plenty of others equally skilled. Tim is an outstanding artist with real talent. The only artistic training he ever received was by courtesy of the WPA. For two years he painted murals in small-town post offices. My parents are simple people, and Tim's artistic leanings were beyond their comprehension. My father wanted Tim to become a teacher. When Tim refused to knuckle under and enter a teachers' college, my father lost interest in him. Tim received neither financial assistance nor sympathy. Yet it didn't embitter him, and he never felt cold toward me.

In any sensibly organized society, Tim's talent would be recognized and richly rewarded. Tim can't earn a decent living. In this day and age, creative talent does not pay off. How many serious artists in this country—I'm not talking about the slick, commercial boys—are able to support themselves exclusively with art? Not many. Vincent Van Gogh, if you recall, was subsidized throughout his lifetime by his elder brother, Theodore. Who now remembers Theodore except as the patron of his brother?

My pride in Tim means nothing to Henrietta. She has no appreciation of his talent. Henrietta is like all women. She measures inspiration and enterprise by concrete results. For the past few years I'll admit Tim hasn't been too productive. How can anybody be creative without peace of mind? Tim can hardly enjoy peace of mind when he is keenly aware that Henrietta thinks him worthless and indolent, that she begrudges his family food and shelter.

My sister's husband, Frank, is more generous and far more understanding of Tim than Henrietta is. Frank has located several motion picture jobs—as a set designer—for Tim and has even lent him money. It wasn't Tim's fault the jobs didn't last. I have returned the money Tim borrowed from Frank, although Henrietta doesn't know it. My wife has made my relationship with my only brother so difficult I've learned to hold my tongue about anything I do for him.

Henrietta knew I had a family while she and I were courting. Yet she now behaves as though she expected my family to disappear after our marriage. Jealousy is Henrietta's complaint. Henrietta never knew the joys of family life as a child—the closeness, the giving and taking, the quarreling and the making up—and she is envious of the pleasure I find in my family.

I am convinced Henrietta's money worries date back to her childhood. She seems to feel chronically insecure. Henrietta wasn't mistreated or abused; she simply wasn't loved enough. Her widowed grandfather was too old, too tired, and too preoccupied with his business to feel responsive to a lonely child. Both her father and her mother—I gather that her mother buried herself in some odd sort of religious cult after the divorce—drifted from her life early. Her father was supposed to be responsible for her financial support, but he remarried and frequently neglected to send the checks he promised. I doubt her prosperous grandfather was greatly perturbed, but Henrietta suffered torments.

It's preposterous that Henrietta should object to the financial assistance my parents and Tim receive from me. She and the three boys get better than a third of my income; whatever Henrietta asks for I give her gladly. I do object to her spending money without my knowledge on things I may or may not approve. She had the boys' nursery redecorated without telling me. Those kids are *my* sons, too. I was entitled to a voice. She selected colors for the nursery that I particularly dislike; a banal pink-and-blue combination that throws Tim's pictures, especially painted for the boys, completely out of key.

She was astonished and irritated when I objected to paying taxi fares so her son, John, could ride in style to school. When John dawdles in the morning and misses the bus, Henrietta's solution is a taxicab. John's school is only twelve blocks away. If he got up when he was called, he wouldn't need either a bus or a taxi; he could walk the twelve blocks to school and profit by the exercise. In my college days I walked twice as far and rejoiced in the opportunity.

Henrietta spoils John outrageously. He left his expensive tennis racquet outside where it was ruined by rain. She bought him another without a word of reproach. To this day I've never owned a tennis racquet or a pair of skis. In Tim's boyhood and mine, our playground was a city street. Our sports equipment consisted of a crooked stick and an old tin can. Henrietta insists that I favor our sons above her son. It isn't true. Whenever I buy toys for our youngsters—I always choose something simple—I bring some trifle to John. But I don't want any of the three to be spoiled. It's a tough world they're growing up in.

In my opinion Henrietta herself is spoiled. She has everything any woman could want. Frequently when she asks for money I double the amount she says she needs. She doesn't thank me. Instead she is likely to flare up, bewail her loss of independence, and announce she wishes she had her old job back. In our circumstances, it would be ridiculous for my wife to work.

I've given Henrietta a beautiful home and beautiful furnishings. I've given her a car, and she can charge all the gasoline she wants. I give her beautiful clothes; I would give her jewelry if she would wear it. I've hired a nurse to look after the children so she can be free to fool around with college classes, run errands for me, and see those sparkling friends she is always urging me to meet.

Still she isn't satisfied. She is aggrieved by my family; she went into a frenzy when she found out I had overlooked transferring to her name insurance policies that had been in force for years. In this connection, I have a grievance, too. I strenuously object to my wife meddling in my business affairs and prying into my private papers, then offering me unsolicited and silly advice. Henrietta has no comprehension of money matters.

Henrietta talks constantly about her integrity. Yet she wants me to destroy my own integrity by ignoring all I owe to my people. My good fortune is not a personal possession. My financial success belongs to the family too. I have a moral obligation that Henrietta refuses to acknowledge. I love our sons and I love Henrietta. Weeks ago she moved out of our bedroom. I miss her, but I have no intention of humiliating myself by asking her to return. That will have to be her own decision. If she thinks she can pressure me into abandoning the loyal people who brought me up, she is wrong. I won't do it. I cannot do it.

Sometimes it seems to me that I married too late. But I know I married a girl quite different from the wife I have today. The Henrietta I married wasn't mean or ungenerous. I do wish she could be changed back into the lovely, loving girl I used to know.

✿   ✿

It was not easy for Henrietta Baldwin to persuade her husband to consult with us. Douglas Baldwin put little stock in marriage counselors. Although he finally consented to an interview, he refused to take our routine tests.

A financial success—Douglas' annual income from his law practice was around $50,000—he was not a successful or flexible personality. Since he had remained a bachelor until the age of forty, his habits of acting, feeling, and thinking were deeply ingrained. He saw no reason why he should change. In the rare moments when he expressed self-doubts, his family was usually available to burnish his ego.

To Douglas' mind, Henrietta alone was to blame for their marital difficulties. Why, he wanted to know, couldn't she get along with his people like a dutiful wife? Why must she object to the way he handled his own money? Why didn't she thank him for his gifts and acclaim his financial wisdom? To Douglas' way of thinking, Henrietta was naïve and inexperienced and required his guidance. He was ignoring the years she had earned her way in well-paid jobs.

Douglas was quick to spot the connection between Henrietta's adult feelings and her childhood environment. Yet he did not realize that his own youthful hardships and experiences had also left a mark. Short on spending money and leisure in his school days, Douglas concluded he was deficient in the social graces, unattractive to girls. This belief caused him to postpone thoughts of marriage, cling tightly to his place in the family circle, and strengthened even further his already strong sense of duty. Highly confident of his legal ability, Douglas' lack of confidence in himself as a person showed quite clearly in his jealous unwillingness to allow Henrietta's first husband to support and keep in contact with John. His emotional insecurity was also revealed by his reluctance to seek membership in the professional organizations to which most lawyers belong.

Only in the midst of his family, where he was admired and applauded, did Douglas feel safe and at ease. In the main, his family was content to seek his assistance in every trivial emergency and was delighted to accept his leadership. As a consequence Douglas acquired a vast appetite for keeping others under his thumb financially and for ordering and controlling the lives of others. Douglas did not recognize this quality in himself nor did he recognize that his largesse had quite possibly weakened his brother's initiative: Tim's stature as an artist was hardly increased by his indolence. Douglas' devotion to his brother, his overprotectiveness, was rooted in the guilty feeling that he had got all the breaks, that his success had been won at the cost of Tim's failure.

During his interviews—he had only two—Douglas vehemently denied that he wanted to dominate and keep both his brother and his wife financially dependent. In an effort to pacify Henrietta, he declared his willingness for her to be a full partner in their marriage. He also promised that the matter of Tim's support would be settled to her satisfaction.

Henrietta immediately proposed an eminently sensible plan: that Tim and Mimi figure out a definite budget and be allotted a generous but fixed proportion of Douglas' income each year. There were to be no more impulsive gifts from Douglas made without her knowledge. Douglas' outraged rejection of the plan did not surprise us. But Henrietta was so surprised and outraged that we thought the marriage was done for.

Henrietta gathered up her three sons, took them to the home of one of her relatives, and went job hunting. She did not find modeling assignments, but she landed a fairly lucrative job as a steward-

ess on an airline operating to Honolulu and Japan. She was out of
the country for several weeks. She worried about the welfare of her
children and found herself missing Douglas badly; upon her return
she was not pleased with the care her youngsters had received.

In the meanwhile, to Douglas' chagrin, three members of his
temperamental, unpredictable family—his mother, his father, and
his sister—placed the blame on him for the separation. In the family
sessions held during Henrietta's absence Douglas was roundly denounced for "driving away that sweet, beautiful girl" and for risking
the loss of "those fine sons." Henrietta was heartened by this un-
expected partisanship. Furthermore, she stepped off the plane in
a mood to acknowledge that independence comes more easily to
a girl in her twenties with one child to support than it comes to a
woman in her thirties who is the mother of three.

For his part, Douglas was somewhat chastened. He opened a
bank account in her name and promised to deposit $300 on the first
of each month, which she was free to spend on household and personal expenses without his supervision. He made Henrietta the
beneficiary of most of his insurance policies, but he continued to
maintain some of the policies for his brother. Henrietta made no
protest.

She now realized that any woman who married a bachelor of
forty must realistically expect to do a major share of the changing
and adjusting. There were some adjustments Douglas was incapable
of making. Henrietta knew that. She resigned herself to compro-
mises. When Douglas offered to go out with her friends at least one
evening a week if she would accompany him on two family visits a
week, she agreed. When Douglas broke his bargain, as he sometimes did, she tried not to fret about it.

After she acknowledged the impossibility of loosening Douglas'
family ties to any great extent, Henrietta perceived that some of her
unhappiness with the situation was of her own making. The product
of a lonely childhood, she had grown up ill-prepared to cope with
the noisy, argumentative gatherings that were the breath of life to
her in-laws. She had not tried very hard to fit herself into the group

or to look objectively at Douglas' relatives. An objective viewpoint helped her to realize that Douglas' family might sometimes cherish her, but at other times would regard her as an interloper.

During the months of counseling when Henrietta was developing objectivity and maturity, something very pleasant occurred. Douglas suggested on his own volition that he adopt his stepson, John. This had long been an unspoken hope of Henrietta. There *had* been a difference in Douglas' treatment of the three youngsters. After the adoption, he treated all three as his sons.

Not long ago Henrietta pleased Douglas by arranging a show for brother Tim; none of his pictures sold, but at the show Tim made contact with various motion picture executives, and it appeared a job was in the offing. John is active in Little League baseball, and Douglas has become such a fan that he has missed several sessions with the clan in order to drive his adopted son to games in other neighborhoods.

Henrietta, with a laugh, sums up the present situation with: "You might describe me as being like the woman whose husband used to keep an elephant in the parlor but now is satisfied just to keep a medium-sized bear."

*   *

Henrietta and Douglas Baldwin did not achieve unqualified success in straightening out their affairs. Both were vain and stubborn. Both clung to unrealistic notions of independence. However, each treasured and loved the other and really wanted to continue in the marriage. In the end, they accomplished a workable compromise.

They and the other couples struggling with in-law problems settled most of their differences by learning what made them personally tick—or not tick, as the case might be. It is doubtful their marriages would have run smoothly if the mothers, fathers, sisters, and brothers, who touched off so many explosions, had not existed. Once the husbands and wives learned to understand themselves and each other, they simultaneously learned to cope with their in-laws.

Section III: Growing Up Emiotonally

We have always known that people differ in physical development, that we cannot expect from a child what we expect from a man. We have long accepted the fact that people differ in intellectual development. In the matter of emotional development, however, we are continually perplexed, partly because there is no obvious relationship between either physical or intellectual development and emotional development. We say, "Why, he is a grown man and a college graduate. I don't see how he can behave in such a childish way." The answer is, of course, that he may be 6 feet tall, weigh 200 pounds, and have a string of degrees and academic honors, but still be a small child in handling his emotions.

Ability to get along in the adult world and in marriage depends more on emotional maturity than upon either physical or intellectual development. Many couples who seek our advice come from disorganized, undisciplined families and have had no contact with mature behavior. We suggest they learn to identify the patterns of maturity by cultivating the society of others who are happily married. Or we suggest they study and compare the appetites and actions of young children with their own.

A child, for example, likes to break things. Hand him a hammer and a glass bottle, and he will soon smash the bottle. Many of our clients try to win or end a domestic argument by hurling dishes on the floor or throwing things at each other. A child likes to make a noise. Give him a drum, and he'll keep on beating it until the neighbors complain. The child is not so different from adults who shout and scream insults and vituperation until the neighbors would vastly prefer the drum. And surely the drum-beating child is the emotional equal of the Sunday driver, caught in immovable traffic, who blows and blows his horn and irritates the ears of others in order to express his personal irritation.

The average child is wholly absorbed in loving himself and the mother who feeds and looks after him. Every day we talk to men who want their wives' attention devoted exclusively to feeding and caring for them and anticipating their smallest desires, to women who want the same amount of attention from their husbands. We try to show these people, who clamor for the impossible, that they are emotionally infantile.

The child has an active "hate life." He hates the chair because it was in his way and he fell on it. Later he recognizes that the chair in itself is guiltless and so instead of hating things, he hates people. He blames someone for leaving the chair in his way. Few of us completely outgrow this childish stage. But an emotional need for fixing blame, a slippery proposition at best, invariably makes for trouble in marriage. Nobody except children can afford the luxury. Marriage is an adult relationship and demands emotional maturity.

Judging from the unhappy couples we see at the Institute, the vast majority are plagued with emotional immaturity. We often refer to such people as "leaners." Thousands of our clients in bitter conflict with each other are attempting to live in an adult relationship with the emotional equipment appropriate only to a child—a child who learned at the age of six months that he could govern his mother by tantrums and now tries to rule his wife in the same way, or a child who learned at the age of five that when anything went wrong she needed only to call on her mother. Now thirty-five and the mother of two children herself, she still runs home to mother when anything goes wrong in her marriage.

To succeed in marriage is to grow up emotionally.

The mature person accepts responsibility for his own actions. The immature person, like the child, is always blaming somebody else or alleging that "I never had a chance."

The mature person gets along reasonably well with parents, friends, office associates. The immature person carries a chip on his shoulder, thinks "the boss has it in for me," and speaks of "getting even with so-and-so if it's the last thing I do."

The mature person accepts criticism calmly, profits by justified criticism, disregards unjustified criticism. The immature person sulks when criticized and mutters, "If you know so much more about it, you'd better do it yourself," or "Why does everybody pick on me?"

The mature person respects the customs of others as well as his own. The immature person continually flouts convention and makes trouble for himself (and others) to attract attention and show off.

The mature person realizes that life involves give-and-take, is capable of compromise, and is altruistic. The immature person wants to have his own way at all times, is bossy, ill-tempered, and stubborn.

No adult likes to admit that he is behaving like a self-centered child. A mulish husband will insist that his obstinate selfishness is merely "enlightened self-interest." An indolent wife will defend sloppy housekeeping on the grounds of poor health. Both shrink from acknowledging they are afraid to grow up. Our counselors can help such people see themselves more objectively and profit by reading and introspection.

Turning away from childish behavior and behaving like a responsible adult is a matter of practice and habit formation. Mutual consideration is essential in attaining emotional maturity in marriage. One of the best ways a wife can help her husband grow emotionally is to eliminate her own childishness. Significant evidence of maturity is the ability to compromise and adjust to a difficult or even a hopeless situation.

*   *   *

Jenny and Max Zimmerman were miles away from compromise and adjustment when they called at the Institute to discuss their bruised and battered marriage.

The Zimmermans came from different cultures, religions, and backgrounds. Max was Austrian-born. He had escaped from Vienna just before World War II. Much better educated than Jenny, he had a Ph.D. in European law, a degree in psychology, and now, aged thirty-eight, was studying for a degree in engineering. He spoke five languages and earned a mediocre living as a translator and tutor.

Jenny, eight years younger than her husband, had close-cropped, chestnut hair, a robust, but not-an-ounce-too-heavy figure, and smoldering, blue eyes that defied the world. At the time we saw her, she still spoke in the emphatic accents of western Oklahoma, where she grew up.

Jenny had not had a happy childhood. Her mother and father had been divorced, and her mother had remarried. The second marriage was not successful either. Jenny's mother and stepfather quarreled often, and the mother had tried to keep the quarrels a secret by locking her daughter and sons out of the house whenever a fight was in progress. It did not occur to the embattled adults that the children might peek through the windows, or that they might be miserable over being locked out of their home at all hours of the day and night.

It was after Jenny finished high school and was taking a business course that she met Max, who was serving his first Army hitch on the post in her home town. At first his very "foreignness" attracted her. Embittered as she was against Max twelve years later, she remembered how she had felt about him in those early days:

*   *

Max was different from anybody else I had ever known. He was a man of twenty-six, not a callow boy. Things had happened to him, real things. He could talk about Rome and London, Vienna and Paris, cities I had only read about. He had wit and polish. In those days, when Max was opening the world to me, his good manners and his sense of humor hid his arrogance and meanness.

Max and I met at a USO dance. Afterward we saw each other every day for three straight months. I couldn't get enough of his conversation. Max would tease me by pretending that he was a great ladies' man, but I didn't believe him. He didn't even kiss me until we had gone together for a month, and with every other boy I knew it was smack smack smack after fifteen minutes.

I quickly made up my mind I'd marry Max if he asked me. Possibly my mistakes began right there. I was too humble, too dazzled by him. Nowadays, in our quarrels, he reminds me of how I chased him and says he didn't want to marry. That isn't true. Max proposed to me. On a Saturday night we had dinner at the only decent restaurant in town. There were flowers on the table bought by Max. After I admired the flowers he suggested we exchange napkins. I was puzzled but I took his napkin. Out tumbled a diamond ring and a wedding license made out in both our names. "Marriage is what you want, isn't it?" asked Max. I gasped out that whether we married depended on what he wanted, too. Max replied that he thought marriage might be good for him. "Medicine might be good for you," I said, "but that doesn't necessarily mean you want to take it."

On Monday morning we married. I extracted only one condition from Max. That there would be children. He wanted none. To me a marriage without children is meaningless. Indeed, if I'd had the choice, Max and I wouldn't have stopped with a family of three boys. We would also have had a girl or two.

Max has always been an abominable father. When our oldest boy was born—Gus is now ten—Max wasn't proud and pleased. He sulked and refused to help me in my first difficult days at home. Home by then was a Quonset hut in northern California; Max had been transferred to the Pacific Coast. We were still in the Quonset hut when the other boys came along; I used to marvel that all of us weren't turtle-backed. Max hasn't ever slapped or cuffed our sons

—he wouldn't dare with me around—but he's never treated them as genuine members of the family, members of the family with rights and privileges as well as duties.

After his World War II discharge, Max was content to work at a piddling, poor-paying job while he acquired a second college degree under the G.I. bill. I thought he had ample education and that his learning should be turned to some practical advantage. But in those days I kept my sentiments to myself. Max continued his efforts to improve and educate me. I love to read, but I don't want to read philosophy every minute; I used to hide my paper-backed mystery novels under the mattress.

Then along came Korea, and Max, as a member of the Army reserve, was called back to duty. When Max sailed for the Orient he had spent ten successful years convincing me that I was too stupid to draw a breath without his advice. I was lonely at first, but I soon found out that other people didn't consider me a hopeless dumbbell. Within a few weeks I landed a defense job at high wages; I met another working wife at the factory with whom I could exchange baby-sitting hours, and I began to save money. When the bank account reached sizable proportions, I made a down payment on a decent house and moved my youngsters out of the Quonset hut.

For the first time—no thanks to Max—we had a pleasant place to live. Frankly, the boys and I enjoyed his absence. We enjoyed the blessed silence—no nagging, no complaining, no one to pick on us. But on the day Max returned, our peace was ended. He was fiercely critical of the house and the furnishings. He objected to my new friends and my new clothes. He jeered at my haircut. He demanded that I quit work, and I refused. He took a low-paid job himself and once again resumed the college study that leads nowhere.

Max can be generous at times—but always with a purpose. He gives me what *he* wants and with a smirk on his face like an emperor tossing an emerald at a slave girl. Three months ago he wiped out his bank account to buy me a mink cape when the fur I admired and wanted was squirrel, and squirrel is a whole lot cheaper.

I just don't get the point of his silly vanity. I cut our sons' hair, and I used to cut Max's hair, too, but he turns pale whenever I mention the fact in public. Some of our worst arguments have occurred over my barbering skill. Max doesn't like me to excel in such mundane things. Nobody will ever convince me it is smart pretending to be rich when you are not.

Max is an intellectual snob, but, despite his book learning, many of his ideas aren't too hot. He prides himself on the fact that he is a freethinker; he has borrowed some of his notions on sex from Bertrand Russell and theoretically he believes in polygamy. Yet he is shocked by my interest in sex. He regards me as too forward in both speech and behavior. He used to hurt my feelings by criticizing the ardor of my response to his love-making. We gave up love-making long ago. In his heart Max thinks there are good women and bad women—and I guess he can't decide which category to put me in.

In many ways he is an old-fashioned man. He can't afford to hire five servants to wait on me, as he would like. Lacking servants, he attempted to turn me into a built-in cookstove, pressing machine, and laundromat. He wants to wear two clean shirts a day and knife-creased trousers and eat three-course meals by candlelight—with no children in evidence. The end of the road came for us six months ago when I arrived home from my job one afternoon and found our three boys sitting forlornly on the doorstep. Their father had locked them out of the house—my house—so he could read a book in quiet. It was then I told Max to find living accommodations somewhere else.

We quarreled for two months before he finally took me at my word and went. But he is still a steady visitor in my house. When he stopped by last night, he and I at once became involved in one of our whing-ding disputes. Ordinarily Max is quiet-voiced—I'm the noisy one in the family—but he is a master of the taunting, sarcastic remark. He let fly with words to the effect I was a stupid, unculti-vated peasant who should be grateful to him for rescuing me from the backwoods. I answered with some choice and assorted words of my own. I should be ashamed to admit it but in a peculiar way that disgraceful scene was bracing and stimulating to me. It was as though I'd won some sort of victory over Max, proved he couldn't push me around any more. Yet I know my lack of control is harming our children, and my children mean everything to me.

The boys and I are better off without Max. Max and I are more civilized and worthwhile people when separated. Our marriage is finished. It's his fault, not mine. For twelve years he bullied and abused me and the boys.

*   *

Max Zimmerman did not look like a bully. He was slight in build. His face was sensitive, olive-skinned, and narrow. He sounded completely disillusioned as he told us:

*   *

My reward for serving my country in Korea was to lose my wife. For ten years Jenny and I were happy together except for minor differences of opinion. For ten years Jenny respected my wishes, conceded that my intelligence was superior to hers, and acknowledged that the man should be the master in his own home. While I was overseas she changed into a different woman—a woman I feel I hardly know at all.

Jenny now sports a man's haircut; she wears pants more often than she wears dresses. She has become a termagant and a shrew. She is determined to rule in everything. She tells our sons not to obey my orders. In their presence she shouts that I am an over-educated egghead. It's hardly surprising they, too, are unmannerly and undisciplined.

Jenny has forgotten the gratitude she used to feel at the pains I took to educate her. She now professes to be bored with Plato and Aristotle and the philosophers to whom I introduced her. In our honeymoon days she was fascinated by the world of ideas. She now complains I waste my time on books and refuses to admit she is corroding her good brain by reading scores of trashy novels on the sly. Furthermore, she wastes her time working for the telephone company when she should be at home caring for her family. She declares our boys need the money she earns. What they need is more of a mother's company, a mother who would teach them to pay heed to their father's wishes, a sweet and gentle mother who could still be firm and maintain control of them.

Jenny has become mercenary in spirit and intolerably penny-pinching. The two years I was in Korea I regularly sent back enough money to support her and our boys on a modest scale. She wasn't satisfied with that arrangement. She took a job without my permission and without my knowledge. She then proceeded to bank $200 a month until she had a sufficient sum to make the down payment on a house. I was overseas when she mentioned in one of her infrequent and misspelled letters that she was the owner of a seven-room house. None of the other G.I.'s I soldiered with had wives who invested in real estate without their knowledge. Naturally I didn't like it. Nor do I like the house. The construction is wretched. Nevertheless, it rather amuses me to hear Jenny grandly refer to "*my*" house. Surely, since I supported her and the boys during my absence, it would be graceful of her to speak of *our* house.

Nowadays it pleases Jenny to laugh at me because I respect spiritual and intellectual and, let us say, romantic values. I'm no money grubber, but it did appeal to my sense of pride a few months ago to give my wife a mink cape even though we were living apart. Jenny belittled my gift and humiliated me in the eyes of the saleswoman by announcing she preferred a cheaper fur, and then she stated bluntly that on my earnings I couldn't afford even the cheapest fur.

As a boy I never intended to marry at all, but once married I certainly did not intend to degrade myself by becoming involved in a divorce. There was too much divorce in my childhood, far too much. My father was responsible for it. On the surface he was an educated man, a cultivated man, a philosopher, a student, but his marital antics matched those of an international playboy. Before I was twelve years old I had five different stepmothers. I've never understood my father. All I know is that I despise him. In my boyhood, as I was shifted from one household to another, carried here, carried there, by his amorous peregrinations, I used to put myself to sleep by imagining new methods of torturing him to death.

My mother allowed my father custody rights because in those days in Europe a divorced woman of her class found it difficult to marry a second time and virtually impossible if she were burdened with a child. I never blamed my mother for giving me away, although long before I became a political refugee I knew what it meant to be lost and adrift. I was obliged to adapt to one stepmother after another—none was as harsh and unkind to me as my father—and very early I had to learn to accustom myself to hideous quarrels. My quarrels with Jenny are ugly, God knows, but the quarrels of my childhood were worse.

There was something pathologically askew in my father. I was the only child of his many marriages; yet he had no affection for me. My scholarship was always high, but never high enough to suit him. He delighted in calling me stupid. On two occasions when he abandoned a wife, he abandoned me with that wife. The humiliation, the fear, the lack of security was, I believe, harder on me than the ever-present threat of war that hung over the whole of my youth.

My father's conduct combined with my upbringing made me wary of women. Frankly, as a young man, I thought of sex as a commodity to be bought and paid for. As a young man I didn't dream of a wife and family. I didn't want to bring children into a world as troubled as the world I knew. I shrank from the idea of any permanent entanglement.

As a girl Jenny was amusing and original; she was the only person in the wretched, flea-ridden town where she was reared who was capable of speaking the king's English. Also she knew the whole world wasn't contained in the county where she was born.

Jenny now declares all twelve years of our marriage were a prolonged misery. It isn't true. I was a good husband to her and I am a far better father to my sons than *my* father was to me. Yet when I came home from Korea, she and the boys made it painfully clear there was no room for me. They greeted me as though I were a stranger. They scorned and ignored me. My sons talked back to me while Jenny hurled insults. Once again I had the same lost, sick feeling I used to have when I was shunted among the homes of my many stepmothers. Jenny didn't care.

I've made concessions to her. Jenny loves gardening. I hate it. But last Sunday I went to our house and planted a pear tree in the yard. Jenny promptly came storming out and told me there was no use bothering, that I would never live there to enjoy the shade.

I consider it most unfair of her to take away my sons and my house, but I don't see how to stop her from doing it. I've reached the point where I agree our marriage is done for. It's her fault, not mine.

* *

Jenny and Max Zimmerman, born of different cultures and with very different traditions, had both obstinately decided their own particular conceptions, notions, and values were 100 per cent correct. Both were what we call "angry people." They were long out of the habit of being at peace with each other and living in harmony with their children. Engaged in a struggle to dominate, they ate, slept, and breathed conflict. A prolonged feud between a married couple is wasting and damaging, but feuds can be fascinating, too.

Jenny and Max believed their flaming, destructive quarrels were ignited by differences over money, sex, tastes in clothes, how to bring up children to the best advantage, and so on. In actuality, the two were quarreling over who should be the boss.

A European upbringing had convinced Max that the female of the species is inferior to the male, a conviction that would handicap any husband in this country. In addition, Max was a seriously disturbed person. Back in childhood, he had acquired a perverse appetite for dissension and discord. In our opinion, some of the imaginary tortures he devised as a young boy to annihilate his detested father had left an imprint on his personality. It took Max a long while to perceive that even in the early days of his marriage, the days when an awed and browbeaten Jenny strove to please, there was not the faintest possibility she could satisfy him. For it was his peculiar joy to torment and demean his wife, and he battened upon her humiliations.

It was easier for Max to acknowledge the truth about his unsatisfactory relationship with his sons. It was not the perilous state of the world, as he professed, that made him a reluctant father. His personal history was responsible. Himself an unwanted child, Max wanted no children. Having acquired the family, Max endeavored to ensure that his three sons should fare no better than he had. Once Max recognized that he had molded himself into an autocratic father and husband—a father less cruel than his own but without tenderness and love—he became able to understand Jenny's fiery reaction to his treatment of their children. With her background, with her painful memories of shivering on the outside while her elders quarreled inside, she simply could not tolerate her children's being locked out of their home so her husband could read a book in quiet. Upon reflection, Max also acknowledged that some of her impatience at his constant studying with no definite objective might be justified.

Jenny's eventual revolt from the pressures to which Max subjected her was almost inevitable. It was only her timidity and lack of self-confidence that kept her under his thumb so long. In many ways, even in their early years together, she had subtly defied his wishes and played little feminine tricks to lessen the shaky self-esteem hidden behind his arrogance. Max's absence in Korea presented her with a perfect opportunity to stage an all-out rebellion. When Jenny bought the house, it seems likely she not only wanted to provide a good home for the boys, but she wanted to show Max how much better she could manage financially than he had done. Certainly he interpreted the purchase in that fashion.

Although emotionally infantile, both Max and Jenny ranked well above the average in intelligence. She readily recognized that in her childhood home, like Max in his many homes, she had become habituated to a pattern of quarreling. Then, too, as a small girl seeking individuality she had begun to take pride in her "frankness." Jenny's conception of frankness was explosive indeed. It was based on a maxim she had picked up from a Sunday-school teacher: "It is as bad to *think* something as to *say* it." By this reasoning, if you think your friend's new baby is homely, you may as well go ahead and tell her so.

We seldom offer concrete advice to our clients. We did tell Jenny that even if people cannot restrain themselves from thinking uncomplimentary thoughts, they can refrain from making cutting remarks without being insincere. We advised Jenny that the sooner she began to hold her tongue the better off she would be.

A year after the counseling began, Jenny and Max went back to living together again. Their troubles were by no means ended. It took them a long time to assess the damage of name-calling, to discover that vituperation may be an escape from problems, but is no solution to them. Slowly Jenny and Max learned that there are no bosses in successful marriages; there are only partners. Gradually they became able to explore their differences of opinion with gentleness and tact, instead of succumbing to a passion of rage and thus destroying any possibility of reaching a compromise and a solution. There is some anger in all people, but Jenny and Max were obliged to learn that for them anger was a warning to tread warily and cautiously.

In the end the Zimmermans achieved an unusually successful marriage. As they grew to understand themselves and each other, their personalities and attitudes changed startlingly. They found there was pleasure to be had in mutual appreciation and consideration. Max stopped mocking Jenny's native state and her fondness for paper-backed novels. For the first time he allowed a television set to be installed in the home. Watching some of the programs with his sons brought him closer to them and their interests.

For her part, Jenny allowed her hair to grow and wore more

feminine clothes. She also resigned from her job when Max stopped being a scholastic dilettante, permanently quit college with an engineering degree, and went to work as a well-paid engineer.

By means of calm discussion Jenny and Max eventually worked out their individual spheres of influence to the satisfaction of them both. Their reward was personal content and the realization that if they had not changed, it was highly probable they would have dissolved their marriage in the divorce courts and still have been burdened with the same unsolved problems within themselves.

*   *   *

Georgia and Terence Crawford had already taken that fateful step into the divorce court before they appeared at the Institute, but neither seemed to be enjoying their new-found freedom. It was understandable. Their divorce had followed, by only a few months, a deeper and an irrevocable tragedy: the death of their small daughter, Kathleen, who had been run over by a bakery truck in their own driveway.

Instead of bringing them closer together, the Crawfords' sorrow had pushed them further apart. Each blamed the other. Terence took the position that if Georgia had been at home tending to Kathleen, the accident would not have occurred. Georgia's answer to this accusation was that if Terence had earned enough money to support his family, she would not have been away from home working at the time.

The day after her daughter was buried, Georgia decided she could not bear another moment of the house where her daughter had died. She packed up eight-year-old Albert, her surviving child, and flew out to Nebraska to visit her father, a prosperous rancher. She and her son were not made welcome. They were regarded as consumers, not producers. With Georgia's father, work was everything.

A tough, pioneer type, the sixty-year-old rancher had fathered a big family by his first wife. Georgia was the only child of his second wife, a frail, submissive woman who, the neighbors whispered, had been driven to her grave by overwork. Georgia found she was just as miserable in Nebraska as she had been in California, and after a few weeks she flew back to Los Angeles. But she did not return to her home. She filed suit for the divorce she had been contemplating for years, got a job, and sublet an inexpensive apartment for herself and Albert. Terence sold their house and moved into a bachelor apartment.

The court awarded Georgia custody of her son but granted Terence week-end visitation rights. On these visits, the Crawfords continued to quarrel vigorously, mainly over how their boy should be reared.

Georgia's blond hair still retained its radiance; yet there was no sparkle, no confidence in her face when she first talked to us. Slumped in a chair in the counseling office, she looked older than thirty-one when she said:

❖   ❖

Terence considers himself a wonderful father, but he doesn't handle Albert any better than I do, if as well. Whenever Terence drops in, he thinks our boy should jump the minute he raps out an order. Terence's discipline is unfair and inconsistent; he hasn't an ounce of patience and he expects too much. He wants Albert to lead in everything—studies, music, athletics. When Albert is outside playing with the other kids, Terence nags at him to come in and do his homework. If Albert is busy with his lessons, Terence thinks he ought to go out and play and develop his muscles.

His attitude toward me is just as inconsistent. I didn't ask for alimony, partly out of pride and partly because I didn't think I could collect it. Terence himself proposed to the court that he pay $100 a month for child maintenance, but he is chronically behind with his payments. Since I count on the money, I'm always letting my bills pile up. Sometimes my father sends me a small check, probably to demonstrate his approval of my divorce, but I never know when to expect it.

Every time Terence comes to see Albert he trots out some fresh excuse for his latest delinquency. Or else he flares up and denounces me for managing so poorly that I need the money he promised to pay. Then when I am cool to his good-by kiss—it seems odd to me a divorced couple should be kissing—he flies into a rage.

Terence and I shouldn't have married in the first place, I guess. We only knew each other twenty-seven days. At that time we both belonged to the Air Force, but our meeting wasn't especially dramatic. The war was over, and I was feeling anxious about how I'd adjust to civilian life. We met aboard a war-weary C-47 on the way from New York to the West Coast. Engine trouble forced us down at Milwaukee. During the four days we were waiting for repair parts Terence and I got fairly well acquainted. He took me out to lunch and dinner all four days. I thought he was attractive. After we reached the Coast and went our separate ways, I found little slips of paper tucked in everything—my purse, my cigarette case, the pockets of my blouse, in my cap, in the fingers of my gloves. Each slip of paper gave Terence's name, serial number, and address and said, "I love you, darling. Please, please call."

In about three weeks we were married. My father was furious. He disapproved of the haste, and he disliked Terence before they even met. My father wanted me to go back to college—I joined the Air Force in my junior year—although he had complained of the cost of my tuition and sneered at my scholastic record. I wasn't in the top third of my class. I wasn't bid to a sorority. I wasn't an officer in any club. I wasn't a success in college. I've always failed at everything. It seems to me whatever I do is bound to be wrong.

My divorce has worked out poorly, too. When I got my decree, I had no idea the nights would be so long and lonely. Of course, I have Albert, but an eight-year-old boy isn't a very stimulating companion. Girls are usually closer to their mothers. I love my son, but he is as contentious as his father. When Albert doesn't get his way, he sulks and pulls his black, heavy eyebrows together and looks like a miniature Terence. Kathleen was fair and small-boned like me.

I can't afford a baby sitter more than once a week. Anyhow a movie by yourself hardly seems worth the expense and the effort of a long walk to the bus stop, a long ride to the theater, and the return trip with nobody to talk to. I have no friends. There is nothing special or unusual about me, and parties are built around couples. A week ago I heard a party going on a few doors down the block. I went out in the back yard, walked along the alley, and listened to the laughter and the talk. Then I climbed up on a trash box where I could see them dancing. In the dark I almost cried.

Evening after evening, I sit waiting for bedtime, eating out my heart with loneliness. Terence has been urging that we remarry, and I've seriously considered it. Last night he visited me, and again suggested marriage. I was so glad of company, I was tempted. But it was the same old thing.

When I turned on the hi-fi, I chose "Moonglow," which is quiet and soothing. I like soft music. Terence has a good musical education and an exceptionally true ear, but he likes his music loud. He changed the record to "Chinatown," and the noise practically blew off the roof. I demanded he take his record off.

Albert then jumped in the family fracas. He wanted to play a piece on the piano to show how his playing had improved. Terence is determined that Albert play the piano well, but right then Terence wanted to argue with me that "Chinatown" is a better pop tune than "Moonglow." He and Albert got into a dispute that wound up with Albert being sent out of the room. I felt sorry for the kid.

Later in the evening Terence explained I'd have to wait for the money he owes me, although my rent is overdue. Then he started to kiss me, and I pushed him away from me. He got mad and I got mad and we had another of our ugly quarrels. Terence was still in a towering rage when he left, but next week end he is bound to visit us again.

I'm not happy divorced. But I don't see how Terence and I can ever be happily married unless he agrees to cooperate in the rearing of Albert and stops criticizing me and losing his temper like a baby.

✦ ✦

Terence Crawford was also unhappy in the divorce. He was a handsome man, whose voice was brisk, but the breezy assurance seemed counterfeit. Underneath there was a defensive note, as though Terence wondered about the impression he was making on the counselor when he said:

✦ ✦

Albert needs a father, I need a wife, and Georgia needs a husband. Our divorce was a foolish mistake.

I'm willing to overlook Georgia's unkindness and take her back. I will try to forget her insults. When our little girl was killed, Georgia nearly broke my heart. She behaved as though Kathleen had belonged exclusively to her. "I've lost my daughter," she said to me that terrible day. "You still have your son."

Georgia has always been prejudiced against Albert. To cover up, she insists I was indifferent to our daughter. It isn't true. Many, many evenings, after I leave work, I stand in the hall at the door of my apartment thinking of Kathleen, overwhelmed by memories of other, better home-comings. I can recall so well the rush of Albert's footsteps when he heard my key, and then the second footsteps, lighter, slower, following his. . . . I used to call Kathleen "the little cow's tail." Often I have to lean my head against the wall before I can see the keyhole, turn my key, and go in.

Georgia would scorn such weakness as unmanly and play-actorish. She has no respect for my deep feelings, and she stifles her own. At the time of Kathleen's death, I allowed her to take Albert and visit her father—the old man despises me—because I feared for her reason. She had no comfort to give me, and she shrank from any comfort I offered her.

Yet I know Georgia loves me. There have been times I have been able to *feel* the love flowing between us. I'll admit the times were rare. Georgia is to blame. She should acquire an understanding of the nature of love, the tenderness, the abandonment, the escape from self, the freedom from embarrassment and shame. She should learn to understand me and my philosophy. Love is giving, that is certain.

I crave and need signs of affection. Yet Georgia won't slide her hand in mine when I stoop to kiss her. She won't run her fingers through my hair or caress my cheek. Nor will she put her arms around me, raise her eyes, and smile into my eyes. Georgia used to flinch if I brushed her shoulder when we sat down in a restaurant or if I touched her knee in the movies. She would protest that it wasn't necessary to show other people we loved each other. She should have been proud to receive an outward expression of our love at any time and place. In the Elizabethan Age, men who met friends on the street would embrace joyfully instead of coldly shaking hands as is the custom now. It isn't surprising there was a renaissance of painting, sculpture, music; in those days the human spirit wasn't oppressed and crushed, lonely. Everybody was up-lifted by the exuberance, the unself-consciousness, the general out-pouring of love. Georgia won't believe it. She just can't let go. From the beginning of our marriage she was undemonstrative. I wanted to be awakened every morning with a kiss. Georgia considered this nonsense. I always wake up feeling fine; she used to be gloomy and taciturn even after we'd breakfasted and I'd dropped her off at work.

The fact that she hung on to a job after our marriage didn't ever bother me. I'm not a stuffed shirt and I haven't any objection to women being financially independent. I was proud when Georgia went back to work shortly after each of our children was born. And I don't mind admitting we could use the double income. I've never been much of a money-maker.

These days Georgia is worried that I won't be able to pay the monthly allotment I offered her voluntarily. She deliberately pro-voked a quarrel last night when I visited Albert, but I gave her $50 on account, which means I'm only a month and a half in arrears.

Georgia is a crack secretary, and her salary is adequate to cover her household expenses. Moreover, I know she receives an occasional check from her father. It burns me that she lacks the pride to send back those checks. Georgia's father cares nothing for her, and she knows it but in a queer way she is emotionally dependent on him. Whenever he brings up the subject of his will—he likes to dangle the prospect of an inheritance before all his children—Georgia gets morose at the idea he won't be around forever.

My father died when I was a year old. I lived with my grandmother. My mother spent most of her time traveling with my stepfather; he was an oil prospector. As a young child I was taught to believe he was my father, and I would wonder why he was so different from other kids' fathers. Not that my stepfather was cruel or mean. He just ignored my existence. He didn't ever give me a birthday present, a Christmas present, or any other kind of present. Oh yes, my stepfather did give me a present once. I'd almost forgotten. He gave me an English bicycle, but it didn't cost him anything. He won it in a raffle. A favorite sport of my stepfather was to make fun of my ears because they were a little prominent. He called me "Sails" and would warn me the day was windy, and I'd better stay inside. For a long while I glued down my ears every night with adhesive tape; I wore the skin raw but I didn't improve the appearance of my ears.

It's a wonder I ranked near the top in school. Nobody in my family ever encouraged me. But they were mighty quick to find flaws. One time I brought home a report card that had four A's and one C. The A's were passed by in silence, but my grandmother and my mother took plenty of notice of the lone C. Nowadays I try and remember to praise Albert's achievements. Georgia won't even go to the PTA meetings at his school. That means a lot to a kid. I know.

Nobody in my family attended PTA meetings. Nobody went to my school to hear me in a recital or to admire a picture of mine on exhibit. In the sixth grade we had a play and I was the star, but nobody in my family saw me. My grandmother said school affairs were silly; my stepfather guffawed when I invited him; my mother said: "Next time, dear."

My mother loved me, I guess. I certainly loved her. There are occasions I still feel guilty because Georgia and I weren't married in my mother's church, although I wasn't baptized in it.

It was one week to the day after my mother's death when I saw Georgia for the first time. I was flying back to my post from the funeral. A sailor, hitching a ride, shared my seat on the plane. I was reading a book when Georgia came aboard. The sailor whistled and I looked up. I saw Georgia in the aisle. Sunshine was tangled in her wonderful blond hair, and her lips and eyes were smiling. It was as though an inner voice spoke to me. Anyhow I heard my voice speak to the sailor. "Take it easy, bud," I said. "That's the girl I'm going to marry."

Compared to Georgia, who is intensely practical, I suppose I sound like a dreamy-eyed dope. But I still believe it was destiny that forced down our plane and gave me four days to court her. I know Georgia and I were meant to love each other and be happy. If she will agree to make a few changes and improvements—I'll be glad to tell her how to be a better wife—we can be ideally mated.

*   *

Georgia and Terence Crawford's marriage collapsed under the stress of tragedy, but the foundations of the union were flimsy.

As children Georgia and Terence were not physically abused, but both were unusually sensitive. They reacted unfavorably to circumstances other youngsters might have taken in stride. Both Georgia and Terence *felt* neglected, lonely, and deprived of love.

Georgia's mother, we gathered from numerous discussions, was a pallid, dejected neurotic, too frightened of her dominating husband to press the claims of her only child, too overworked to spare time to show affection. Georgia grew up in the clamorous midst of her father's first family—three older girls and four older boys who seemed like unfriendly adults to a timid youngster. In Georgia's childish mind her father loomed as a giant of strength, a heroic but terrifying figure. One of her earliest memories is revealing and pathetic. As a rare treat—the only such occasion Georgia could recall—she spent part of one morning in her father's company while he supervised the digging of post holes. At midday dinner an older half-sister forgot to lay a place at the table for the three-year-old. Exhilarated by the morning's adventure, Georgia innocently borrowed from language she'd heard her father use, and asked: "Where is my dod-dam plate?" She was promptly sent to bed without her dinner.

Georgia early lost confidence in herself, learned to repress her feelings, and pessimistically concluded life was not likely to be very rewarding to her. If you do not expect much, she reasoned, you will not be disappointed. On the isolated ranch she had no playmates, but when she entered a town high school her good looks attracted masculine attention. Georgia sold herself so short—deprecate yourself and other people are likely to accept your underevaluation—that many of her admirers quickly fell away. She was dissatisfied with the others. Subconsciously, she was demanding two things of a husband. She wanted someone like her father, strong and dominant, but someone unselfishly and tenderly willing to build up her flabby ego.

She married a man whose emotional requirements and expectations of marriage were almost identical with her own. We sometimes describe couples like Terence and Georgia as "two clinging vines with nothing to cling to." In many ways Terence was spoiled by his grandmother and his mother, but his particular emotional needs were left unsatisfied. A boy of Terence's disposition needed a father on whom to model himself and from whom he could learn to be a man. Terence's stepfather did not meet the bill. Curiously enough, as Terence later acquired personal insight, he discovered he had been too harsh in his judgment of his stepfather. He nursed bitter grievances because his stepfather had not taken him to ball games, on fishing and camping trips. Many boys do not enjoy such pleasures with their fathers and are not harmed by it.

It seems quite possible that Terence was jealous of his mother, resented his stepfather's appearance on the scene, and that his sulky behavior might have prevented the newcomer to the family from being more paternal. A mistake was made in attempting to palm off the stepfather as Terence's natural father. During our consultations with him Terence remembered something long forgotten: he had not really been deceived. The mystery concerning the fate and whereabouts of his father (we did not solve this riddle) may have been an important factor in causing Terence to become too emotionally dependent upon his mother, who understood her son too little.

On the surface Georgia and Terence had responded very differently to environments with equally impoverished emotional climates. Georgia's inner fears and feelings of inadequacy were apparent in her outward attitudes, in her tiresome what-a-poor-creature-am-I line of talk. Terence endeavored to hide his inner anxieties with brag and bluster and bullying. For a short while Georgia was taken in. So long as she fancied she had married a handsome, romantic version of her father, she let Terence lead her around by the nose and was content to follow in her mother's meek footsteps.

But in reality Terence was fussy, picky, critical. Here, of course, he was instinctively imitating the two women who had reared him. When Georgia saw through his pose, she rebelled at being ordered around by a man as weak as herself. Long before Kathleen's death, she and Terence were quarreling over sex, finances, and child rearing.

It was clear that both Georgia and Terence would be obliged to effect some rigorous habit and personality changes before they could hope to succeed in a second try at marriage. Eventually they both perceived it was unlikely they could find happiness together unless they stopped expecting the other fellow to make all the changes and improvements.

An undisciplined man, Terence set himself a severe course of

self-discipline. When he grasped the causes of his nagging criticalness—this unpleasant trait was partly an echo of his grandmother
and partly a shield from his own fears—he was able to curb his
tongue. When he recognized he was a braggart and a bully, attempting to masquerade as a strong man, he modified his attitudes.

Neither Terence nor Georgia was competent at managing money.
Instead of pressing further budgetary advice on Georgia, Terence
assigned himself the task of sticking to a budget. For ten months
he kept track of every penny he spent, a record unparalleled in his
history. By then Terence had answered most of Georgia's complaints against him. His excitability and extravagant manner of ex-
pressing himself were too basic a part of his nature to allow much
alteration.

But Georgia was so impressed by his hard-won consideration for
her and his newly acquired sense of financial responsibility that she,
too, undertook to do some changing. Her most important struggle
concerned her handling of her son. It was difficult for her to admit
that in subtle, quite unconscious ways she was making small Albert
pay for his resemblance to his father and for the death of his sister.
Georgia finally acknowledged this unpalatable truth and acknowledged, too, the heedless, self-centered childishness of both herself
and Terence in their reactions to their children. Each had been
partial to the child who best reflected himself, a situation which is
not too uncommon with parents, but is tough on the children involved. When Georgia began regarding and treating Albert with
love, she was richly rewarded.

A year after their divorce, Georgia and Terence remarried. Nowadays Georgia has plenty of time to wrestle with domestic problems. She had long wanted to quit work and learn how to be a good
wife and mother. She did not know Terence felt too insecure as a
breadwinner to tolerate a stay-at-home wife. He lacked the confidence in his earning powers to risk the loss of her pay check. But
when Terence received a substantial raise, she quit her job, at his
suggestion.

Both Georgia and Terence feel that the loneliness of their divorce was almost worthwhile. During their separation they grew greatly in their knowledge of each other and of themselves. They now can face together the grief of the loss of their daughter. Their second marriage, they say, is far better than their first.

❋ ❋ ❋

Kate and Joe Mason, who were younger than the Crawfords, were even more emotionally immature. The Masons had been married for only three years when they came to the Institute; Kate was twenty-two; Joe was two years older. An unusually pretty girl, Kate seemed almost as unsure of herself as Georgia Crawford. And she, too, complained that her husband was a blowhard and a show-off. Her voice was tense as she launched upon her story:

❋ ❋

Last Saturday at a formal party, Joe nearly drove me out of my mind. The hosts were older people and only slight acquaintances of ours. As usual Joe breezed into their house on Cloud Seven. Just as the after-dinner coffee was served, there was a little lull in the conversation. Joe took care of it by demonstrating he could chin himself twenty times on the overhead beams. He dared the other men to try. Naturally, all of them refused. Joe then shook hands with himself like a circus strong man and took a lot of deep bows as though he'd performed a miracle. Everybody laughed at him. The other wives looked out of the corner of their eyes to see how I was reacting. I was so mortified I had to leave the room. Perhaps I am too sensitive and thin-skinned, but with Joe around I can't help it. For half an hour I stayed in an upstairs bedroom wishing I was single again.

Other girls' husbands don't act like mine. Everybody we know—although they're too polite to say so—thinks I'm married to a *character*. Some of them think Joe is a phony, which he isn't. Joe is talented at lots of things, but he blows his own horn and lets on he's twice as good.

Nowadays I feel nervous with Joe even when we're alone. He has embarrassed me in public too many times. Sports and excitement, his business and himself, are Joe's main concerns in life. He won't go to church with me because he'd rather watch TV on Sunday mornings. The only TV programs I care for are musical, but we never listen to any music. If I ask the neighbors in for a quiet evening, Joe does all the talking. Or he turns on the television set full blast and corrals the men around him to watch some hinky-dink sports event.

Joe thinks of our home only as a way station and a place to play the fool. He changes his clothes there so we can rush somewhere else. Every Monday I clean the house from top to bottom, polish our wedding silver, put flowers in all the vases—I've got nothing on my hands except a wedding ring and time—but Joe would be as well off in a skating rink. Five minutes after he bursts open the front door, our living room is a wreck. Joe's sample case and his newspaper are lying on the floor, his topcoat is lying there too, and he's spun his hat across the room to see if he can land it on a lamp.

Two Mondays ago he upset a vase of flowers shadow-boxing with his darned old hat. He caught the vase just before it hit the floor. Water splashed everywhere. Joe laughed fit to kill, and for a minute I had to laugh myself. I didn't laugh when I cleaned up the mess. Joe's gags and nonsense, his kidding with me and everybody else, his bragging and his showing off, don't add up to my idea of the way a husband should behave.

Maybe if Joe and I could have a baby we might hold our marriage together. He's crazy about children too. But we've been trying for that baby three years without success. I've had the Rubin test, the oil and iodine test, every other kind of test. There's nothing physically wrong. According to all the doctors—I've shopped around—the trouble is psychological. They say I probably never will become pregnant unless I get less tense and learn to relax.

Living with Joe is not relaxing. It's like being on a perpetual merry-go-round. I was born to be a homebody. My mother died when I was fourteen, but I'm a great deal like her. No enthusiasm for sports, poor muscular coordination. I can't even play a decent game of Ping-pong. Dancing is the only recreation which sends me —but Joe won't dance. My mother took me to dancing school and she taught me to cook. I can spend a whole afternoon preparing a snazzy meal straight from my French cookbook and discover when Joe arrives home that we are dining out that night. I've had no warning, although the Los Angeles telephone system still functions.

If we eat at home two evenings a week it's a wonder. And then we don't eat on time. I never know when to expect Joe. Last Thursday I made a cheese soufflé. It was perfect at 7 P.M. When Joe came home at nine-thirty we ate canned beans, and Joe was very funny about "Madame's Magical Manufactured" baked beans. I wasn't one bit amused.

To be honest, I must admit Joe is often delayed by business. He is a salesman—he's a knockout at that—and he has to run around town with customers. But Joe doesn't know what telephones or clocks are made for. His sense of time was left out of him at birth.

On his days off, he can go to the grocery on a fifteen-minute errand. Hours may pass, literally hours, before I see his face again. He gets to talking to somebody, loafing around, canvassing a new real estate development—Joe isn't in the real estate business— and his errand, his wife, and his home skid right out of his mind. Two weeks ago he went to buy a quart of milk I needed for a custard pie, and four hours later he came back with a full explanation of the merchandising methods of a dairy. He had forgotten the quart of milk.

Possibly Joe doesn't mean to be inconsiderate; he is sweet about apologizing. But he just doesn't grasp the things which drive me into a frenzy. After three years of marriage my reactions are a mystery to him. Sometimes, they are a mystery to me.

I know that I'm made sick by embarrassment and worry, but I don't know why. When Joe cuts up in public I agonize. When Joe is late I worry about him terribly. I picture traffic accidents and office-building fires and acute appendicitis. Soon I get frantic. My heart pounds, spots float in front of my eyes, my throat closes, I have stomach cramps. Then nausea sends me running for the bathroom. Joe doesn't understand that he is responsible for my being upset so much.

He and I are as different as two people can be. Joe will do anything to keep the center of the stage. I was meant by nature to stand in the wings. I like to watch people instead of having them watch me. Maybe Joe was meant by nature to hold the spotlight; anyway he assumes so. He and I are always the last guests to leave a party, the very last. When our hosts begin to empty the ash trays and ferry the glasses to the kitchen, I'm still pulling on his sleeve. Frequently he stops on the doorstep to repeat a corny wisecrack he's already made three times during the evening. Then he roars with laughter. Joe always laughs at his own jokes. That simply slays me.

Strange as it seems, our family backgrounds are similar. Joe's father is a well-known theatrical lawyer in Hollywood; my father is a successful lawyer, too. Joe and I and my brother went to the same university. My brother—you've probably heard of Butch Brown, the football star—introduced us. Joe was on the varsity, too. Both of his parents are darling, but, unfortunately, they encouraged Joe as a boy to excel at practically every game and sport. Personally I am convinced my husband's early training went to his head and gave him too much self-confidence, whereas I have too little. Joe wasn't quite as good at football as my brother, but then Butch was All-American two years running and is now playing in a professional league. Joe can beat the socks off Butch at tennis. Joe is also super at swimming, badminton, boxing, golf, softball, basketball.

Every Tuesday and every Friday he coaches a neighborhood basketball team in the high-school gym just for the fun of it. On Saturday mornings he coaches a kid softball team. He always yells louder than anybody else at the games. He says it's his "Will to Win" and a good thing. I say it's pure bad taste. Other people agree. At games I can sense them glancing in my direction, whispering about my husband. You can hear Joe cheering his team a mile away, and you can also hear him booing the other team. He calls them dopes and drips, and worse names than that. Once at a softball game he got into an argument with an umpire and was ruled off the field. Another time he had a fist fight. I don't go to games with Joe any more.

I do go to parties with him. We visit his parents every week. When they happen to be alone I get on fine. But my father-in-law knows half the celebrities in Hollywood. At first I was thrilled to be in the same room with a famous movie star or a famous director, although I wanted to keep my distance. Joe pushes me at the celebrity, the celebrity looks bored, I congeal, and Joe immediately begins to show off. He either talks about himself or rings in a play-by-play description of Butch's latest football exploit. In the three years of our marriage, Joe has never failed to introduce me as Butch Brown's little sister. I love my brother. But once in a while I'd like to be considered a person in my own right.

A great deal of our social activity is necessary. Part of Joe's job, the major part he says, is to entertain his customers in style. Since he's on an expense account, we frequently go to very glamorous places. I've reached the point where I dislike glamour almost as much as I dislike sports.

When we enter a restaurant or a nightclub, and everybody stares at us, an iron band seems to clamp around my throat, and my stomach ties in knots. I feel like a—a nothing. I feel as cold and lonesome as I felt when my mother died. My mother has been dead eight years now, but I still miss her. I often have dreams about her. Just the other night I dreamed I saw my mother riding away from me in an old-fashioned coach, and through the glass windows of the coach I could see my mother was crying. When I woke up, I was crying myself. I try to talk to Joe about my feelings, but he just looks blank.

I shouldn't have married a man like Joe. Probably I shouldn't be married to anybody. I know I'm too self-conscious and nervous for my own good. I have always longed for a home and children, but I intended to stay single until I was thirty. Even in college, I had sudden fits of nerves over nothing in particular. For no reason I would dodge across the street to keep from meeting somebody face to face. It might be a friend, but I would feel like running and hiding somewhere. I was uneasy about dating. Joe thought I was silly. When we fell in love—he swept me off my feet, wham—I wanted to postpone our marriage. He wouldn't hear of it. I was right. He was wrong.

I'll tell you something very personal. I can't bear to see Joe walking around our house in nothing but his shorts. I've bought him two bathrobes, which he won't wear. He thinks my modesty is absurd. When he is in the shower or the tub, he often yells to me to bring him a towel—and just because he knows I will open the door a little crack, look the other way, and toss the towel inside. The fact is that I like people—all people—better when they're wearing clothes.

Sex upsets me too. For Joe and me, sex is an ordeal. It always has been. Sex causes me pain, extreme pain. Joe is not to blame. It's all my fault. According to the doctors, my nervous system is responsible for the trouble. Apparently my muscles contract at the wrong time, and the contractions produce the pain. I just don't understand. I want a baby more than anything else in the world.

I have tried and tried. Even when I feel warm and loving—there are times I feel very loving toward Joe—the pain swoops down. Joe has done his best to help me, but finally I have given up the idea of ever enjoying sex. I have given up the hope of ever having a baby with Joe.

I think a divorce is the only fair way out for both him and me. Joe deserves a different kind of wife. He will soon find some girl who won't be unnerved by his temperament, and with whom he can start a family. Later on, years from now, perhaps when I'm thirty, I may find a quiet, dignified man with whom I can feel relaxed and easy. Then, with my nerves in order, I can get married again and have a baby and enjoy the peace and happiness of a real marriage.

❋   ❋

Joe Mason was an attractive young man who looked as if it
would be no trick at all for him to chin himself more than twenty
times on an overhead beam. However, when he entered the counseling office, he was unusually subdued. His merry blue eyes were
earnest and sober as he said:

❋   ❋

This divorce talk has certainly rocked me. My marriage isn't perfect. But I think Kate and I should keep on trying to improve it
instead of calling in the lawyers.

I don't want to lose her, and that's for sure. Why, I would walk
around the world for Kate. I love the girl. Everybody loves Kate,
although she can't believe it. She's beautiful, she's kindhearted,
she's a lady. She has a special little glow, all her own. In the crowd
of screwballs and prima donnas we operate among—I'm something
of a loud mouth myself and well I know it—she is like a breath of
spring air.

Kate is a hard girl to understand. She complains about me all
the time, but I don't let it bother me. My mother used to complain
about my father, and it didn't worry him. They're still married, and
what's more they're happy. When Kate starts riding herd on me I
try to kid her into a different frame of mind or else I think about
something else. Kate is moody. I'm not. Kate broods. I don't.

Kate thinks I'm the world's worst show-off. Occasionally at parties I probably do go a little haywire and give the impression I've
temporarily slipped my bonnet. Nobody minds. Nobody except
Kate. As I often tell her, we wouldn't be invited places if people
didn't enjoy our company. I get a charge out of an audience. I like
fun. I like people, all kinds of people.

It's a funny thing, but I can get along with everybody but my
wife. Up to now I've been shot with luck. I like my parents and
they like me. They saw to it I had real spending money as a kid.
We had a swimming pool and a backyard gym that were constantly

in use. I could lick any kid in the neighborhood and, to my dad's delight, I did. Just automatically I became boss of every gang I belonged to. I've got plenty of competitive spirit. My report cards at school—no fooling—used to say I was the "leader type."

I've got no worries now—except Kate. For a man my age, I'm climbing fast into the big time. I earn $9,000 at the moment. My interest in sports has been a definite help. I'm the head salesman for a line of Pacific Coast sporting equipment, a fact Kate may have neglected to mention. I've also been helped by the gags and wise-cracks that set Kate's teeth on edge. My customers expect a few laughs from me. If I didn't deliver, they'd think I was losing my grip. My boss, who is vice-president of our company, ribs me and I rib him right back. Not long ago at a dinner party my boss got talking about my ambitions and asked me what job in the company I eventually wanted. "Your job," I said, "and I don't mean eventually. I want *your* job at nine o'clock tomorrow." Kate had the vapors over that one. She thought my answer wasn't dignified.

It beats me that Butch Brown's sister would have practically no sense of humor and would be dead set against sports. Kate says I yell too loud at games and get into fights. Maybe I do like to win more than some—I sure hate to lose—but that's my disposition.

Kate claims she can't play games because she's poorly coordinated and awkward. That simply isn't true. She is a whiz at dancing. Her mother had the idea one athlete per family was enough. Consequently Kate wasn't taught any games. That doesn't matter to me. Female athletes have never raised my temperature. I would be perfectly satisfied just to have Kate watch me at games, but she won't even do that. I would gladly watch her dance at parties. She refuses to dance, since I can't dance with her. I don't know how to dance. I've always been too busy horsing around with the fellows to learn.

I went for Kate in the first place because she was shy and stand-offish and wasn't bowled over by my attractions. In college I got somewhat fed up with girls chasing me, and I was in the humor to do a little chasing myself. Kate's brother, who is my best friend, mentioned one time that Kate didn't particularly want to meet me. I got interested, very.

To meet Kate, I had to chase her thirty miles. The night Butch phoned her sorority house we were coming, Kate panicked. She ran outside and jumped in the first handy car. As we were arriving, we passed her racing in the opposite direction. We took out after her and finally ran her down in Long Beach, right on the edge of the Pacific Ocean. Then all three of us got together, and we got to laughing, and Kate let me drive her back to the sorority house. After we were married—I was all for marriage; she wasn't—I thought she would get over being so stiff and shy. She told me about her nervousness, but I thought marriage would be a sure cure. So far, it hasn't worked out that way.

Kate must have talked to you about our sexual problem. She doesn't blame me for it, and I don't exactly blame her. I just get baffled and discouraged and keep on hoping she will change. Or else I get disgusted with her and with myself, too. Kate isn't a cold girl, that I know. Very often she wants to be affectionate and loving with me, but it always turns out she can't be. When I take her in my arms she is sweet and responsive, very feminine. Then, suddenly, I can feel her tighten up. We both are interested in starting a family, but, dumb as it seems, Kate almost acts as though she was scared of being pregnant. She fights her tension. Sometimes I think she fights too much, concentrates too hard on bracing herself against pain. It makes us both self-conscious.

From working in athletics I've learned something about people's different pain thresholds, and I'm sure Kate's pain threshold is low. Still and all, she can be an awful baby. She howls to high heaven if she cuts her finger. I have to be Johnny-on-the-spot with the bandage and the sympathy. Any trifle upsets her stomach. Her mother used to let her stay out of school if she had a headache or stomach-ache, and she was babied in every other way. Kate didn't know how to comb her own hair when her mother died, and she was nearly fifteen years old. Maybe Kate's mother made her proud of her constant jitters. I just don't know.

Needless to say, the situation doesn't delight me. I've never been unfaithful to my wife although several times I've been tempted. Kate doesn't know that. When I'm tempted, I go and work off steam on the basketball court or a baseball diamond. I doubt Kate can enjoy sex or become pregnant until she gets control of her nervous system. I've told her so. The doctors have told her the same, but nobody has told her how to stop being the way she is. I keep hoping she will change when she gets a little older.

Since I'm willing to accept Kate's faults, it seems to me she should accept mine. However, if it will help her, I'm willing to string along, listen to suggestions and advice and change my own personality. I will try to be less of a Joe-Blow and if Kate will go to games with me again, I will prove I can keep out of fist fights. I can do anything I want to do. What I wish, of course, is that somebody could teach Kate how to stop being tense and nervous and how to relax. Then she could be happy, and that would make me happy.

*   *

Kate and Joe Mason were so-called Hollywood brats, products of an excitable town where sports, television, and the movies mix. They were an engaging pair who loved each other and were needlessly drifting apart. Kate's love for Joe was pretty clearly shown by her determination to make him comfortable in his home, by her desire to bear him a child, and, of course, by her anxious identification with his public behavior.

Kate's and Joe's upbringing was not nearly so similar as they fancied. With his family and in most of his boyhood ventures, Joe had placed first. She grew up overshadowed by her older brother, with her mother, so she believed, as her sole ally. Her mother was an Eastern-bred woman, who had vigorously disliked the easygoing manners of the West and was less than enthusiastic about the ways of her Western husband. In Kate's girlhood home, the sports-minded father and son went to the football or baseball game while the mother and daughter went to dancing school or to a concert or lecture. At a very impressionable age—fourteen—Kate lost her mother and her ally. It was small wonder she felt grief-stricken, alone.

Then she married Joe, a fun-loving, outgoing, self-assertive young man, who was noisy, exuberant, and, at times, too appreciative of his own virtues. Joe and his crowd of noisy friends, even his parents, swamped Kate. To be sure they liked and admired her, but they were too busy and self-absorbed to say so.

This situation partly explained Kate's exaggerated shyness and sensitivity, her prudishness masquerading as modesty. Her sexual rejection of Joe, even though it punished her too, could have been an unconscious expression of resentment at the inferior role she felt she played in their life together. And we thought it possible that she was using, also unconsciously, her frequent illnesses to gain the attention her ego craved and needed.

After our first interview Kate agreed, and very readily, to stick to the marriage. She was eager to become a better person and a better wife, although she was doubtful of success. Joe was the complete optimist. He was willing and supremely confident of his ability to make radical personality changes. The project interested him. He did not want to fail at marriage or at anything else.

Instead of blithely admitting his faults and letting it go at that, Joe went to work at self-improvement. For one thing, he adopted the habit of looking at his watch and acquired a husbandly sense of time. When he was held up by business, he telephoned Kate. When he left the house on a fifteen-minute errand, he did not disappear for hours. By his actions he demonstrated what was the fact —his wife and his home meant something to him. Obviously, this built up Kate. She soon reacted by becoming less critical on the occasions when he did slip. When Joe praised her—our prescription called for at least one compliment a day—Kate responded by praising him.

With the cooperation of his parents, Joe did his best to make Kate feel important and at ease in their circle. He dropped the tactless habit of introducing her as "Butch Brown's little sister."

That was one reason, a very natural one, for her hostility to Joe's preoccupation with sports. Her common sense told her, once she stopped to think, that sports were important to Joe's happiness and his business career. When he offered to teach her to play tennis, she accepted the offer. She did not become very proficient, but she gained more understanding and tolerance for her husband's interests. Joe took a few home lessons from Kate and thereafter began to dance with her at parties. He discovered he enjoyed dancing with his wife.

In the matter of sports in the home, the two arrived at a satisfactory compromise. They divided the use of the television set, with Joe sometimes listening to music for Kate's sake and Kate sometimes watching baseball and football for his sake. Small as it was, this mutual consideration brought them closer together and prevented many unnecessary arguments.

After Joe promised to harness his language and curb his "Will to Win," Kate started going to sports contests with him again. There, as well as at parties, she endeavored not to keep a sentinel eye on her husband every single minute. At our suggestion, before Kate went to parties with Joe, she decided upon five different topics to talk about. This helped her to be less self-conscious, to circulate at social gatherings.

For his part, Joe espoused a policy of moderation in monkey-shines. He made strenuous and reasonably successful efforts to channel his seemingly inexhaustible stream of wisecracks and gags into his business life, where his humor was appreciated. Frankly, there had been occasions when Joe had bored his after-hours friends as well as embarrassing his wife.

Within a couple of months, the Masons began having fun when they went out together. Kate was much more relaxed. She freely admitted that she valued her marriage and loved her husband. Nevertheless, the couple's sexual relationship remained unhappy.

By then it had become apparent that Kate was the victim of some hidden problem, that where sex was concerned she suffered from strong feelings of fear, shame, and guilt. Although she badly wanted a baby, she was *afraid* of sex. To find out why, she took a test devised here at the Institute to explore people's emotions. This test indicated not only that she did feel guilty, ashamed, and afraid, but that her crippling feelings dated back to her very early years.

While we were analyzing her answers to the test with her, a dramatic thing happened. Suddenly an unfortunate, frightening, long-forgotten experience came to the surface of her mind. As a child of four or five, Kate had been sexually molested by a teen-age boy, the son of close friends of her family.

This incident she had concealed from her mother and from everyone else. In a sense she kept the incident concealed from herself, for it had left her conscious memory and taken root deep in her subconscious. That "forgetfulness" had caused her to carry into her maturity a damaged, fear-ridden personality. A childish episode (important only because of its effect on her) explained the nervousness and tension which so long had caused sex to bring her pain instead of joy.

When Kate brought that buried memory out of its dark hiding place, she found release. Her tension and fear gradually melted away. Her feeling of guilt was gone. Inside a few weeks she found that sex was not only painless but was pleasant. Later on, we had an excited phone call. A miracle—or so Kate and Joe considered it— had occurred. She was pregnant.

The Masons' baby girl is now three months old. No young couple could be more pleased and proud. Kate finds herself "much too busy to be sick." These days Kate and Joe share the boasting, an agreeable form of boasting. The topic: Our Baby.

❊　❊　❊

When Patsy and Nils Knudsen married, they, like Kate and Joe Mason, hoped to have a family immediately. They too were disappointed, and the doctors could find no physical reason for their inability to have children. After seven childless years of marriage, the Knudsens adopted a little boy whom they named Kyle. Three years later, they were forced to conclude that their adopted son was not the answer to all their problems, some of which had been in existence long before he was.

Five years before the adoption, the Knudsens had almost split up over the issue of moving from Baltimore to Los Angeles. Characteristically Nils arranged for the shift from the East Coast to the West Coast without consulting or notifying Patsy or anybody else. Patsy told us she had always found Nils baffling and infuriating and to back up her statement related the circumstances of her abrupt change of residence:

*   *

I had suspected Nils was bored with living in the Baltimore neighborhood where my entire family lives—he has no more feeling for his own kinfolk than a fish—but it was only a suspicion. Both he and I were holding good jobs and after an interminable search we had landed in a charming apartment. Nils didn't hint he was dissatisfied with the East and was feeling restless. No, that isn't his style.

I will never forget the afternoon I learned of his intentions. I stopped by the place where he then worked so we could ride home together. His office building was a few doors from an airline ticket office, and I saw him turn in there. By the time I followed him inside he was already at a counter paying for one one-way ticket to California.

Nils didn't turn a hair when I stepped up. It seems he'd expected to take me to dinner at our favorite restaurant. At dinner he planned to announce that he personally was all set to fly away and begin a brand-new life. He had already quit his job. He had figured out I could quit mine—I'm a trained nurse—sell our furniture, dispose of our lease, travel 3000 miles across the continent, and join him as soon as he found work and another place for us to live.

It just didn't enter my husband's head that his plans should have been regarded as *our* plans, that I was entitled to a voice in such an important matter. I had never been separated by more than a hundred miles from my mother and father, my sister, and my three brothers, as he was well aware. I was so enraged by his callousness, I was so hurt that I burst into tears. Nils's sole concern, as I recall, was to get me to dry my eyes and to spare him embarrassment in a public place.

I guess I knew in my heart that if I let him go kiting off by himself, it was unlikely the two of us would ever get together again. Anyhow, I spent that night at my parents' home. Nils treats them abominably—he treats his own father even worse—but my mother and dad both stand up for him. My sister and my brothers were called into the conference at my parents' home that night. Everybody in my family agreed a wife's place was at her husband's side. I'm the oldest of the children and pretty much accustomed to getting my own way, but I couldn't hold out against the whole crowd.

Next morning I bought myself a ticket, and a few days later Nils and I flew West on the same plane. He wasn't overly pleased. If anything, he was provoked.

I resigned my hospital job, I sacrificed the companionship of my family and life-long friends because I loved Nils. No other reason. To this day I dislike California, although we haven't done badly financially since our move. A year ago we made the down payment on an attractive, three-bedroom house but our prosperity has brought no joy to me. I'm deeply grateful for our little boy, but even with a child in the house there are times I'm almost crazed with homesickness and loneliness.

Nils's selfishness, his lack of consideration, his coldness have worn my love for him to a shadow. He shows me no appreciation whatever. I regularly did private nursing out here—private nursing is highly paid but involves back-breaking labor—until he could establish himself in work he enjoys. He is now one of the top credit managers for a big finance company. Nine people work under him. His earnings average $10,000 a year. However, I am still obliged to take occasional nursing cases so we can pay for luxuries —his luxuries.

Nils glowers if I mail a birthday gift to my mother or send a pair of socks to one of my brothers. But when he visits a store the clerks probably mistake him for a movie star shopping incognito. Last month he ordered six ten-dollar neckties, six, mind you, and three monogrammed shirts. I returned the neckties, but the shirts couldn't be returned. When Nils first went to work for his present employers he needed a suit of clothes. One suit. He bought four suits; two were tailor-made. At the time the four suits were delivered I was going barelegged on the street to save money for the white stockings I had to wear at work.

If he had been brought up in the lap of luxury it might be easier for me to accept his silly, selfish buying habits. His father was harder hit by the depression than mine, and there were twelve children in that family to feed and clothe. Last summer I took our son back East so he could meet his grandparents on both sides. My parents, my sister, and my brothers showered Kyle with gifts and love exactly as though he had been born to us. Nils's mother had died a few months earlier. His father just grunted at our child, and I forgave because he seemed sad and lonesome. I suggested he return West with us for a three-weeks' visit. Kyle and I rode tourist class, and I used the savings to pay my father-in-law's fare. Although he had just sold the home place for a fair price he didn't offer to buy his own ticket, and he didn't stay with us three weeks. He stayed six months.

During that time my father-in-law had so much trouble with his teeth that he couldn't digest his food. I arranged for a dentist attached to a hospital where I'm on the registry to make a denture for him; I was allowed a courtesy rate, and the $500 denture was billed at $300. My father-in-law was delighted with his new teeth, but refused to pay for them, and my husband also refused. In order to maintain my reputation at the hospital I entered Kyle in a nursery boarding school, took on a twenty-four-hour private case, and finally, after several weeks of hard work, I paid the dentist in full. Neither Nils nor his father was grateful. Nils said I was a chump for letting his dad get the best of me; his father said I was foolish not to let the dentist whistle for his money.

For six months my father-in-law sat in our house and didn't buy Kyle a lollipop. On the way back East he visited his most prosperous son, a Minneapolis attorney. He bought their two children an outboard motor that would have more than covered the cost of his teeth.

I just can't understand people like Nils and his father. People who take and won't give, except for show. Nils has turned Christmas, once my favorite holiday, into a nightmare by howling over the gifts I buy with my own earnings for my family. He ignores the fact they always send him and me and Kyle fine presents. He thinks Christmas is a silly money-trap and that my devotion to my family is sentimental slop.

When Nils received his first promotion I was terribly thrilled and excited. I immediately telephoned the news to Baltimore, and my parents were equally thrilled. They telegraphed congratulations to Nils at the finance company. He was annoyed. I met him at the door that evening with loud huzzahs, a hug, and a great big kiss. He was disgusted with my enthusiasm.

I met Nils through his older sister; she was my hospital supervisor, and she frequently spoke about her kid brother. When Aline wrote to him I would sometimes add a gag postscript. And when we finally met I was attracted by his good looks. I even liked the fact he talked very little. I didn't know the time would come when I would deliberately smash a plate and scream at him to say something, say anything to me. Or that he would sit and stare at me in cold amazement, mum as an oyster. Perhaps I should have known. During our courtship his kisses were hurried and awkward. Perhaps I should have known he wasn't really affectionate.

I thought marriage would change Nils, that he would become gentle and sweet, less silent, more enthusiastic and demonstrative. We have now been married ten years, and he hasn't changed a particle. Weeks go by when he doesn't kiss me. I've got some spirit, too. If Nils won't kiss me, I can't see why I should share his bed. Last year when we moved into our new house, I moved into a separate bedroom.

Nils is a hero among the people he works with. Despite his man-handling of our finances—he paid $800 for the landscaping of our grounds to impress the neighbors, but we do not have a living room sofa for them to sit on—he is a wizard at talking other people into budgets and persuading them to settle accounts the company has labeled uncollectible. Quite a while ago he was placed in charge of borrowers seeking loans over $5000. Everybody says his rapid rise is due to his understanding of human nature. All day long he listens sympathetically to strangers' tales of woe. He won't listen to me for three minutes.

Nor will he talk to me, except in monosyllables. He is close-mouthed even in matters most men boast about. Not long ago, going through an old suitcase, I discovered he was decorated several times for bravery back in World War II. This was something he had never mentioned to me. When I asked him about his medals he just shrugged his shoulders.

Twice in two years he has taken Kyle to the circus. I wasn't asked to go with them. He seems to think it unmanly to share recreation with a wife. Many evenings he arrives home late, mumbling he's been held up at his office. At times this may be true. Other evenings I'm sure he goes to some movie he wants to see. He attends night football games and wrestling matches without me. On Saturdays he bowls with a male bowling team in city-wide competitions; I've never been invited to watch him.

Nils and I have practically no friends. In Baltimore my family's house boiled with friends and relatives. I've done my best to acquire a circle out here. Nils is not helpful. Last Saturday our nearest neighbors dropped in. When he stalked outside and began to clip a hedge that required no clipping, our neighbors took the hint and left. Sometimes his behavior with callers is just the opposite. On two occasions, he virtually forced money on acquaintances who didn't ask for loans and plainly had no way of repaying them. When the inevitable occurred, Nils got furious at the defalcations. Then he got furious with me when I asked why he didn't apply his public business judgments to our private affairs.

I know I complain of Nils too much and start too many fights. I used to be even-tempered, but it has become almost impossible for me to control myself. Nils's indifference to anything I say or do makes me feel as though I were married to a man of wood. I lose my temper all the time. I nag and scold but I never reach him.

I had hopes our adopting Kyle would draw us together. My hopes weren't fulfilled. A strange thing is that Nils objected vigorously to adopting a baby—he declared it was absurd to support somebody else's child—but he has turned into as soft a father as I've ever seen. Too soft, in fact. Our small boy seems to be the only human being in the world Nils is capable of loving. He spoils Kyle. Our son is three years and seven months old and still isn't toilet-trained because Nils read a book about the danger of repressing children and won't let me train him.

I feel a special obligation to provide Kyle with a normal home and not to rob him of his father. But right now I doubt that Nils and I can create a normal home. Although Kyle is very young, I think he already senses our disharmony. Nils confuses me and I suppose I confuse him. Possibly if he and I could understand each other we could hold our home together for the sake of our child.

* *

When Nils Knudsen visited the Institute, it was easy to see why Patsy had fallen in love with him. He was handsome as a Norse god, with blond hair and eyes the deep blue of a northern fjord. At thirty-six, his tall figure was as slim-hipped as a boy's. He and his wife made a striking couple. Patsy, two years younger, was an authentic beauty with dark-blue eyes and dark hair. Had she been unattractive, it would have been less surprising when Nils complained to us:

* *

My wife's tiresome chatter on the subject of romance and the ideal marriage puts me in mind of a disk jockey. After ten years, it seems to me she should be willing for us to act like a settled couple instead of a pair of moonstruck teen-agers. But Patsy is Irish—my family is of Scandinavian descent—and, boy, do the Irish go in for fireworks of every type and variety! They're either crying or laughing, and they're always celebrating some darn thing or the other. Believe it or not, a week ago Patsy had to rush out and buy a gift because a nephew of hers was graduating from a Baltimore junior high school. It was the month of May before we paid the last of the Christmas bills she piled up buying stuff her family didn't need. She sent her mother a sewing machine when she could use a sewing machine herself to make nice clothes for Kyle.

In my family Christmas was reserved for kids, and my father saw to it the twelve of us were promoted to adulthood early. Before the national depression he owned a machine shop, employed a dozen men, and felt like a big shot. Then everything fell apart, and he fell apart, too. Something happened to him when he lost his business. Our next-door neighbor rustled around and took any odd job available to feed his family. Not my dad. He had a skilled trade, but he wouldn't work at it. When people who remembered his skill came to our house to offer him day work, he wouldn't answer the door. He would lie in bed and holler at my mother, "Tell them I'm not here."

Pretty soon we were on relief. In a big family somebody is always caught in the middle, and that's where I was. The younger kids had to be fed because they were babies, and the older ones had to be fed because they were occasional wage earners. I can recall a good many days when I was hungry, my only food a bowl of oatmeal. I guess my mother did her best. But at times I would feel kind of desperate trying to get her to take notice of me in some special way. What way didn't matter.

Once I stole a bicycle from another boy and hid it in a junk yard until I threw away the siren, which I hated to do, and painted the green frame red. When I rode the red bike home my mother was hanging up a wash in the back yard. She noticed me riding up and down and asked where the bicycle had come from. I told her my friend, Billy, had given it to me—a thing she must have known wasn't true. I had no friend named Billy, and boys don't give away good bicycles. "Oh, that was nice of Billy," my mother said and went on hanging up the wash. What I wanted from her was a lecture on honesty or even a beating. To me it seemed my mother didn't care whether I was a thief or not.

When I started high school I had a morning paper route, and the ten dollars a month I earned was contributed to the family. My allowance from my father was ten cents a week. We were living in the Pennsylvania coal country, and us kids were supposed to put in the late afternoons along the railroad tracks picking up the anthracite that dropped off the coal cars. I was a good athlete and planned to be a professional baseball player. I was determined enough to stay after school for sports practice, and this kept me in constant hot water with the family.

In my junior year I participated in a three-state track meet. I broke a broad-jump record that had stood for seventeen years. I got praise from the coach, and I was interviewed by the local newspaper. I was awarded a little silver cup and carried it home to my mother. She looked at the cup and said: "You should have been picking coal this afternoon with the others. My stove is empty."

I didn't finish high school. It was a relief to join the Civilian Conservation Corps and eat three square meals a day and wear a good pair of shoes. I kept eight dollars of my earnings every month, and that was wonderful. By the rules twenty-two dollars were sent home, and, among the family, only my sister Aline ever thanked me. For some reason she and I were always fond of each other.

Some people have called the CCC a boondoggling enterprise and a waste of the government's money, but my gang and I were shipped to Arizona where we cleared and made all of the trails around the Carlsbad Caverns. Building up national parks is something, don't you think? There was one handicap to the CCC from my point of view. After a six-months' hitch you had to get out so other guys could join up and get the three square meals a day. I liked the West, and I wanted to stay.

My buddy and I worked out an angle to serve a second hitch in the CCC. We lifted our service records from the filing room in Arizona and rode the rods to the state of Washington. We joined the CCC there and spent six months clearing the forests around Mount Hood. In the middle of our third hitch—we were then near San Francisco—the CCC caught up with us and we were done.

I enlisted in the Army Air Force and was with them six years. I was based in England when I flew my first combat mission. I flew my last combat mission out in the Pacific theater after the European war was over. At last I came home on a furlough. I had been gone about eight years. When I walked in the door, two of my brothers were playing checkers in the living room. They looked up and said, "Hello." Then my mother came in from the grocery store. She also said, "Hello." She didn't even put down her packages and pat me on the shoulder. I cut my furlough short.

Then I met Patsy. I was stationed near Washington, D. C., and waiting for my discharge. One afternoon my sister Aline telephoned that she was coming to Washington and bringing Patsy along; I was to meet them at the station. I was annoyed and I was nervous. I knew Aline thought it was high time I became acquainted with some nice girl and got married. I had lived in a realm of men for a long time, and I wasn't sure I'd know how to act with a nice girl.

The only girls I knew were the kind who let you stay all night. In fact, my buddy, Sam, and I already had dates for the evening with a couple of that kind of girls. I telephoned them to expect us late and notified Sam he was elected to be my sister's dinner escort.

More to please my sister than Patsy, I picked a super restaurant. Patsy has a high regard for herself, but I can tell you on that particular date she was a dud—pretty to look at, but she offered no compliments on the expensive entertainment I had arranged for her. She was outraged by a joke Sam told and said so. She refused me a good-night kiss after I'd spent at least thirty dollars on her. I blew up and told her I was acquainted with a hundred girls who were better looking and better company than she was. I exaggerated, of course. Patsy blew up, too. She called me an egotistical buffoon and wondered out loud how Aline could possibly have a brother as poor-mannered, crude, and ignorant as I was.

Her cutting words put me in such a sore, sorry mood I canceled my later date, left the explanations up to Sam, and went back to the barracks by myself. I didn't suppose I would ever see Patsy again. But she had made an impression on me. Up until then I'd known a lot of women, and I'd heard a lot of sweet speeches. But I'd always had the feeling every woman I ever knew was trying to fool me and take me in for some ulterior purpose. In thinking about Patsy I realized that for the first time in my life I knew exactly where I stood with a girl, knew what the girl really thought of me. Patsy's honesty wasn't flattering, but I found a comfort in it, after admitting to myself I probably deserved some of her harsh remarks.

Three months later my sister wrote that Patsy planned to spend her vacation in Washington, D. C. Although I didn't hear from Patsy directly, it struck me there were other places she could have vacationed, that maybe she didn't downright hate me, and it might be safe to call her. We had a fine time and a lot of laughs those two weeks. Patsy used to be fun in the days she wasn't nagging, blazing mad at everything, and out to manage my affairs in every particular.

The afternoon I got my discharge from the Air Corps I went to a jewelry store, paid a $100 deposit on a $700 diamond and took the train to Baltimore to ask Patsy to marry me. I found Patsy and her whole family, none of whom I had met, in the midst of celebrating her father's fiftieth birthday. Easily a hundred people were swarming in and out of the house when I pulled Patsy out in the yard and proposed. She accepted me and dashed back inside the house before I could stop her and announced our engagement to the crowd. You never heard such an uproar; my back was pounded black and blue by people congratulating me. Then the noise stopped. Up popped an uncle of Patsy's, who owns a jewelry store, and he offered to provide us with an engagement ring at a wholesale price. Everybody clapped and cheered. Patsy threw her arms around her uncle and made me thank him for his generosity, while in my pocket was the ring I had bought for her.

Next day we picked out a diamond at her uncle's store. It wasn't exactly a bargain. I returned the ring I'd bought to the Washington jeweler but I didn't get back my $100 deposit. To this day Patsy wonders why I've never admired her engagement ring. I saw no reason at the time to go into lengthy explanations with her and her uncle and start up an argument. I dislike arguments, despite the numerous arguments I've had in marriage. A talking woman tires me and that's the truth. Jabber, jabber, jabber is Patsy's way. On my job I listen to people talk eight hours daily, and when evening comes I'm in the mood to rest my ears.

My family didn't chatter and spread goose grease all the time, as Patsy and her folks do. Frankly, I consider my wife's family insincere. My father-in-law habitually touts me as his "banker son," whereas I'm his son-in-law and employed by a finance company. Originally I believed my in-laws were fond of me, and I could tolerate their gush. But they hardly let Patsy and me have a minute to ourselves, and I quickly got the feeling they were teaming up with her against me. I felt we needed to move far away from them and fast.

Patsy and I have prospered in California. Most wives would be more than satisfied, but my wife yearns for Baltimore and runs back there every year. She prefers her blood kin to me and our son. The truth is she cares nothing for me. She has left my bed on the pretext I don't kiss her often enough. Hugging and kissing are for kids. I just can't feature myself holding hands with a woman I'm married to. The mere idea makes me feel—well—uncomfortable, foolish. I never saw my father kiss my mother.

Nor can I feature myself allowing a woman to lead me around by the nose as Patsy continuously attempts to do. She still carps about four suits I bought four years ago that I still wear. The most expensive was priced at $175, two of them were only $60. I like good clothes. I was twenty-five years old before I owned a regular suit of clothes. Up until then I wore blue jeans, work shirts, and government issue uniforms. I shot my wad on my first suit and why not? The suit cost $350, and I considered it worth the price. But I was a bachelor then. Bachelors don't know how well off they are.

Patsy complains our landscaping cost too much—as a boy picking coal I used to think of some day owning a yard full of flowering plants—and she objects our furniture is too scanty. If she wants fine furniture to impress the neighbors, why doesn't she buy it? She wasted enough money on my father to buy a sofa, although he never did a thing to help me. I had no interest in entertaining him, and I don't care to get involved in entertaining the neighbors. I've been stung by so-called friends as often as I wish to be.

Patsy clamors constantly for me to take her to the movies, to a bowling alley, or elsewhere. I doubt my mother ever saw a movie in her life. She stayed home and kept house and cooked and tended her kids.

Patsy has a son herself. Adopting Kyle was her idea, not mine, but his welfare now means more to me than it does to her. I'm determined our boy shall have a better break than I got. He needs and deserves two parents. For Kyle's sake, I think Patsy should behave herself and start acting like a good mother and a good wife.

* *

In childhood, Nils Knudsen fought hard to win individual praise and attention but was lost in the traffic jam of youngsters in the household. His spontaneous loving feelings, like his natural yearning for personal recognition, were crushed by the fierce competition offered by seven brothers and four sisters. Similarly, the loving feelings of his overburdened parents may have been buried under the weight of financial failure and poverty. In Nils's home affectionate consideration for others was not the approved and applauded form of behavior. For the most part the individual members of the large family were hard-working, cold, self-contained, and self-centered. The family motto might well have been "dog eat dog," or perhaps, "let the devil take the hindmost."

Except for his much older sister Aline, Nils had no special comrade, no sponsor. Exceptionally intelligent and ambitious, he was acutely sensitive to his brothers' jeers at him for being a sissy and a stupe if he undertook to be extra helpful and loving with his mother. He cringed from their derisive comments on the occasions he earned high marks at school. In his early boyhood he learned to repress his inner feelings rigidly, to keep his mouth shut about his private triumphs, disappointments, inner thoughts. He became a lone wolf, a man's man, a typical dyed-in-the-wool bachelor.

Patsy had no conception of the kind of man she was marrying. Dazzled by Nils's good looks and his intelligence, obvious despite his lack of formal education, she yielded to romantic imaginings. Unrealistically, she pictured her reserved, quiet fiancé as quickly making the necessary personality changes and assuming an important role in her gregarious, noisy, emotional family.

Nils balked. He was accustomed to writing off generosity as a sign of weakness; undue exuberance made him uneasy; he was very likely to interpret an impulsive compliment as calculated flattery. As a general rule he reacted to other people with mistrust. Occasionally, however, his deeply buried natural warmth would burst through, and he then attempted to buy a friend by a favor or with a money loan. This maneuver is common among young children who say, in effect, to another child, "I will lend you this toy and then you will *have* to like me." When Nils's friendship-buying attempts proved abortive, he decided that he and Patsy could dispense with neighborly social friendships.

After ten years of marriage Nils remained, essentially, a bachelor. He was leading what amounted to a bachelor existence. His marriage and home were distinctly secondary with him. When he married, he had no memories of warm, congenial family life on which to draw. Long practiced in repressing affection to avoid the sting of mockery, he was inclined to be standoffish and wary of affection expressed by others. Only with his small son, too young to represent a threat, was Nils able to be relaxed and warm, to be—himself.

To him marriage was an institution designed to provide a man with a place to hang his hat. Marriage was supposed to satisfy his physical needs but meant little else. He expected to find his comradeship and fun among other men. As for stimulating conversation, that was available at his office. Nils wasn't basically a cold personality, he was merely thwarted. His work, which fascinated him, offered a fine outlet for these thwarted feelings. His work day consisted of a parade of human problems. The sympathetic hearing he gave every prospective borrower, the key of his success, was truly representative of his nature.

Patsy was not entirely guiltless in the trouble. She was headstrong. It was not very bright of her to encumber herself with her father-in-law, when she knew how her husband disliked his parent. She was endeavoring futilely to enforce a family pattern familiar and dear to her—everybody adored Patsy's father—upon a pair of people with different ground rules.

To relieve her personal frustration, Patsy tried to shove around a man who resented and did not respond to feminine prodding. She had allowed herself to fall into whining and nagging; she mourned the beauties of Baltimore while overlooking the beauties of California. Some of the gifts Patsy was showering on her family were too extravagant for the Knudsens' income, just as Nils's clothing bills were too high. The origin of the thriftlessness of each seems too clear to require comment. Patsy and Nils have curbed their extravagance to some degree. Both are capable of commanding good salaries. Wastefulness was less a problem with them than their criticalness of each other's purchases.

Patsy and Nils had got off to a poor start together. In their first year of marriage, Patsy nursed on the night shift, and sports-minded Nils had the opportunity to continue his merry bachelor way. In the evenings he coached a basketball team, went bowling with his buddies, whiled away pleasant hours at a YMCA swimming pool. It did not occur to him that his wife was entitled to diversion and in his company. On Patsy's free evenings he did not suggest that the two of them share some amusement. She was too proud to protest in her honeymoon days. Later, she protested too much.

The years Nils spent almost exclusively in a masculine society had shut him off from gaining any worthwhile knowledge of women. This fact he recognized and admitted. Ignorant of the nature of femininity, he was unacquainted with the ways of tenderness, and the deep joy to be found in a satisfying sexual relationship. When he recognized the reasons he had found it difficult to show his love for Patsy by small outward signs of affection, he became able to change. Admitting his wife's need for recreation and variety, he dropped some of his sessions with the boys and discovered that domesticity can be pleasant.

For Patsy changed, too. To her a good-by and a hello kiss, a warm handclasp, were all-important. She returned to the double bed she had never really desired to leave. Her quarreling and nagging were silenced. As Patsy talked less, Nils talked more and found that conversations held with women are not necessarily tedious. One day, sheepishly, he actually quoted Patsy to us.

Six months ago Nils and Patsy adopted a baby girl, and Nils is as doting of little Clara as of Kyle. Nils is now a changed person indeed. Not long ago he went to considerable trouble to collect the scattered ribbons and decorations he had acquired in World War II. The medals Nils was ashamed to discuss even with his wife, for fear of seeming boastful, are now on display in the family game room. Nils collected the medals and ribbons, Patsy told us, because he wanted his children to be proud of their father. Patsy is very pleased. She knows that Nils is no longer ashamed to show and express his feelings. He admits he is human.

*   *   *

Ina Willard's problem was a sharp contrast to that of Nils Knudsen, the taciturn Scandinavian who did not know how to express his feelings. Ina showed and expressed her feelings much too freely. At the time we counseled the Willards, she was a beautiful young woman of twenty-three, with flaming red hair that fell to her shoulders and shadowed her face. Her first husband had been killed in Korea, leaving her with a baby girl. Her second husband, Nick Willard, was twelve years her senior. Although Nick was a physician, he was unable to help his young wife control her emotions and he urged her to seek our advice.

Almost from the beginning of the Willard marriage in Detroit four years earlier, Ina told us, she and her husband had quarrels for which she felt her nature was to blame:

* *

According to Nick, I'm too materialistic, and he may be right. But I can't help the way I am. When I can't have the things other wives have, I go crazy.

All through our courtship and in our first few months together, Nick seemed to be generous. But when the honeymoon ended I learned that he dislikes to buy anything. Whatever we need he automatically decides we can't afford, and an argument starts that may last weeks.

During those weeks, I forget Nick's good qualities. He has many. Actually, I should be grateful to him for marrying me. When we met I was an unemployed widow with a one-year-old daughter. Nick is as patient with my little girl as with our baby boy. I get impatient with both youngsters, particularly with Marie.

I'm not a very good mother or wife. I'm not efficient or well organized. I enjoy cooking, especially turning out fancy hors d'oeuvres and such, but it takes me forever to put together a meal. Somehow, I don't get started in time. I'm restless and moody, and I gloom around a lot. When I'm alone with the children after dark, I become frightened—terribly frightened. The other night Nick was out on a late call, and suddenly I woke. I thought I heard the sounds of a burglar walking in the kitchen.

For a while I lay listening, and then I forced myself to jump up and rush to the kitchen. I flashed on the light. There was nobody there. The noises kept on. It was the ticking of the kitchen clock. By

the time Nick got in I was hysterical and begging for a new clock—
a silent electric clock—and he was really disgusted. Frequently I
myself think I'm a little wacky.

In company I'm stupid, tongue-tied, and self-conscious. Unless I
feel well dressed, as well dressed and pretty as the other girls, a
wave of cold embarrassment sweeps over me. I clutch for Nick's
hand and fight my desire to run away. Afterward, senselessly, I
often get angry at him. I would like to be poised and gay and sweet-
tempered. Nick's criticisms only seem to make me worse.

Some of his criticisms are unjust. I know it isn't wrong for a wife
to want a pleasant home. Back in Detroit we lived in dreary apartments. Since our move to California, we have camped out like gyp-
sies in an almost empty house. Nick won't buy the necessary furniture. Our place is a ranch-type rambler—it's the first real house
either of us has ever lived in—and I wish we'd had the sense to
choose a split-level model. The people across the street have a split-
level house, and it's nicer. I haven't met the people yet, but they
must have lovely furnishings. Yesterday I saw a spinet piano arrive.
They've finished their landscaping. Five months ago, a truckload of
flowering shrubs was delivered. The garden across the street is now
a beauty spot. In the evenings I watch the woman and her husband
working together, and they seem so happy and content. How I envy
them!

To date, Nick and I have planted three spindly little trees, and
one of them has already given up the ghost. Our garden is minus
shrubs, minus flowers. Inside, we are minus practically everything.
Our living-dining area, which is huge, is about as cozy as an iceberg.
It's furnished with a sofa, an easy chair that seems to float in space
a mile away, and my Swedish-modern dresser that belongs in the
master bedroom. The dresser is the one good piece we own.

There is nothing in our den except a television set, a table-model
sewing machine I was talked into buying—I can't sew—and three
wrought-iron chairs originally intended for the patio. Our patio is
bare. In the room Marie shares with the baby, there is a youth bed
and a crib from which David has chewed the paint. The children

have no chest, no rug, no pictures, no toy box. Marie is nearly six and old enough to be taught good taste and tidiness. Yet when I proposed a cabinet for her doll collection, Nick and I had another argument. Consequently her dolls lie around on the floor. Nick won't even buy a playpen for the baby.

I keep the door of the children's room closed. I'm determined the grocery boy shan't get a glimpse of it; he serves all the houses in the block, and he's a dreadful gossip. The other day, out of sheer spite, he told me the woman next door had received a fur coat as a birthday present from her husband. I've never had a fur coat in my life. The Christmas I was seven—the Christmas we were in St. Louis and my brothers got English bicycles—my parents did give me a beaver muff and scarf. Another time—the summer I had to stay with an aunt in Canada because my parents were moving their shop again—they sent a quilted taffeta bedspread and taffeta draperies for my room there. My mother didn't want her sister to know how hard up our family was.

Nick and I have no curtains anywhere, just cheap shades. Our picture window is the only picture window in the whole development that doesn't have draperies. Last Thursday when Marie got home from kindergarten, I combed her hair and changed her dress and put on my best silk suit. Marie and the baby and I went walking, and we casually examined everybody else's picture windows. I counted twenty windows that had been draped by professional decorators. You can always tell the difference.

People passing our house on the sidewalk can look straight in on us. Most of them must wonder why, if my husband loves me, he doesn't get around to providing draperies and rugs. Several weeks ago the woman across the street spoke to me and I hurried by, pretending I didn't hear. I was afraid I might get involved in a conversation about our dismal furnishings and that she would notice I was wearing a bargain-basement cotton dress.

The other day the woman next door caught me in the back yard. She opened the gate and in she came. She asked me over to share a cup of coffee and to see her new wall-to-wall carpeting. I imagine she intended to show off her fur coat, too. Much as I wanted to become acquainted, I declined the invitation since I couldn't possibly return her hospitality. I hope she wasn't offended.

Nick is just establishing his practice in California, and it does seem he should understand the importance to a young physician of putting his best foot forward. I try to keep up appearances, but he won't cooperate. If I had the right kind of background and the right kind of clothes, I could entertain his patients and make friends for him in the community. Perhaps, too, I might make a few friends for myself. Most people just don't take to me. I can read dislike in their eyes. I wear sun glasses most of the time to keep the expression in my own eyes hidden and to hide from their dislike. Except for collecting occasional compliments on my looks or clothes, I'm a washout socially. Women invariably shy away from me.

I've only had one girl friend in my life. The winter I was nine or ten and parked with Wisconsin relatives for some reason, another girl about my age visited in the house for several days. We slept in the same room and every afternoon we played together on a snowy hill not far off. We would coast down the hill and clasp hands and walk up again. After she was gone I went to our hill each afternoon and looked at her footprints in the snow until finally they melted in the sun. I have forgotten my friend's name but I often wonder where she is. I felt close to her—close and friendly.

When Nick and I moved to the development, I imagined myself as hospitable and gracious. With our place the way it is, I'm ashamed to have my own mother visit us—my parents now have a store in California—although she comes seldom. Every time Mother does appear she comments on the barrenness of our rooms, and when she leaves I usually have a crying spell.

Way back in January I selected the material—a Finnish hand-blocked print—that would be perfect for our window. I made a deposit, too. Nick refuses to let me pay the balance or to start a charge account. I beg and plead, and he puts me off. Some day, Nick says, but he doesn't name the day. He tries to turn my thoughts to something else. He kids and says we're no worse off than goldfish in a bowl. Or he becomes affectionate and suggests we go in the bedroom, turn off the lights, and pretend we're honeymooning at the Ritz.

I want to be warm and affectionate with Nick. Too often I can't be. I hunger for his love, but our unfurnished house seems to rise like a wall between us. It makes me doubt he really cares for me. In my opinion, loving husbands are generous with their wives.

I've never lived any place where I could feel at ease and proud. My parents were always moving, always hunting a better location for the store. Both of them were wrapped up in making money, although they didn't ever make much. During their prosperous spurts, they gave my brothers the nicest gifts, the nicest clothes. In our family I was at the bottom. Mother thought my brothers would carry on with the store—it's a specialty shop—but neither did. So far as I know, she was never interested in what I might do or want to do.

Sometimes we lived behind the store, sometimes over the store, and sometimes we had rooms in a boardinghouse. Naturally I couldn't get acquainted with the other girls; I had no place to bring them. I wasn't ever asked to join a club or anything. One time I pleased my mother in some way—I don't recall how—and she gave me twenty dollars to throw a big party. I didn't know anybody to invite. I spent the money on a dress.

After I started dating—I was popular with boys because I was pretty—I learned for sure how little my parents cared for me. Twelve o'clock was my curfew hour. One Saturday night my date and I ran into heavy traffic, and I was twenty minutes late. My mother locked me out. We rang and rang, we pounded on the door, but nobody answered.

I was fifteen years old at the time and scared to death. My boy friend was scared, too. Finally he took me to his house and got his mother out of bed, and she telephoned my parents. They wouldn't answer the phone. So she sent me in a taxi to a hotel and paid the bill herself. Next morning when the store opened my father argued my mother into taking me back. Sometimes he was on my side. She never was.

A few months later I married my first husband. I was overjoyed to escape my parents. But when Alan was killed I was pregnant with Marie, and I had to go back to the family. Much as I dislike my mother, there are times I seem to need to be around her.

I wish I could turn into a peaceful, confident person. I know I'm making Nick miserable. I'm miserable myself. Why can't we be contented and stop quarreling?

❖   ❖

Nick Willard's face was haggard when he came in to talk to us. After he sat down he passed his hand wearily over his forehead, then he said:

❖   ❖

I am supporting three children: a five-year-old stepdaughter, a twenty-month-old son, and a beautiful wife who is as irresponsible as either of them. Because of the lunatic way we've lived, I am in debt for the first time in my life. That fact would mean nothing to Ina, even if I told her, which I shan't. Given free rein, Ina would cheerfully destroy my precarious credit standing inside a week. So far, I've tried to satisfy the most pressing of her insatiable demands with cash. I've bought myself no peace and her no happiness.

I love my wife. It was love at first sight with me. I met her on Christmas Eve five years ago. I'd played Santa Claus to my sister's youngsters, and then I realized my sister and her family might prefer to be alone. At loose ends, I dropped into the largest public ballroom in Detroit—a place accommodating hundreds. Christmas Eve—what a night to be in a dance hall! There were nineteen people present. Among the nineteen was Ina.

She was standing half-concealed by a post, hiding in the way she does. Her red hair was like a bonfire. I thought she was the most exciting-looking girl I'd ever seen. I still do. For some minutes I admired her at a distance. I turned to go. She smiled at me. Her smile was beautiful and it was frightened. I guessed the obvious. She was lonely, too.

I was thirty years old but I'd known no girls except my sisters. Too much responsibility, too little opportunity. My father was an unsuccessful traveling salesman, and in my teens we were always changing our address with the sheriff usually in hot pursuit. From the age of thirteen, I helped out financially. I worked my way through college and medical school against the active opposition of both my parents, who wanted me to take a full-time job. During the period I was acquiring my education I was unable to send them very much, although I continued to clothe my sisters. In my second year of practice, I bought my father a small business. My parents are proud of me now. My wife is not.

Since that Christmas Eve, Ina has never left my thoughts. Very soon I learned she was restless and undisciplined, a greedy, unthinking child. I blamed her mother's cruelty, her father's indifference and weakness. I didn't want to marry Ina. I thought she was too young and no wife for a doctor. For months I struggled to put her from my mind. I could have forgotten her beauty I think, but I could not forget her loneliness and need. Somehow I felt responsible for her and for Marie, too. They seemed so helpless.

Eventually I convinced myself I could change Ina, care for her, and make her happy. We began our married life in a furnished apartment, just three rooms, but better than any place she or I or little Marie had ever lived. Our sexual adjustment was fine. At least, I thought so at the time. Nothing else was fine. First, the curtains displeased Ina. I dipped into my savings—I then had a healthy bank account—and she replaced the curtains. Next, the rugs were unsatisfactory. I rolled up and stored the landlord's rugs in the basement, and she bought rugs. Then the furniture was too shabby. We'd hardly bought the furniture when Ina decided the neighborhood was unsuitable. We moved to a more expensive apartment.

Meanwhile Ina was demanding to be as well dressed as my patients' wives, or better dressed. I fought and argued but I paid for the clothes she thought she needed. When Ina is pleased, she can be very sweet. On the numerous occasions she isn't pleased, we are both in torment. Everywhere we went, so Ina said, the other women snubbed her. Snubs and cuts and slights—illusions most of them—are a part of her daily life.

When Ina became pregnant, I hoped she would settle down. Instead she began to clamor for me to buy a house. By then I had discovered she was extremely untidy. Since she couldn't keep an apartment in order—Marie's clothes and my clothes were strung from one end of the place to the other—I refused to buy the house.

At that point Ina cut me to the heart. She left me flat to follow her parents, who'd moved their business to California. They hadn't written her a friendly line. Yet she walked out on me and went to them. They had no room for her and Marie. She telegraphed me for money, and I sent it.

I told myself my marriage was ended. I tried desperately to put Ina from my mind and failed. I was haunted by the fear of what might happen to her and Marie. I couldn't tolerate the idea of her bearing my child in a strange city, friendless and alone. One night she telephoned asking me to come to her, and she was crying. By the end of the month I had sold my practice and virtually given away the furniture on which we had spent so much.

Until David was born there was an interval of calm. It was short. While I was establishing a new legal residence and studying to pass the tough California exams so I could practice medicine here, I worked at anything I could get. Pants pressing, painting white lines on the county roads, a three-months' stretch as a short-order cook. To me the jobs I held, my emigration halfway across the continent, seemed to be solid proof of my love for Ina. To her mind my odd jobs were peculiar work for a "professional man." I'm sure she'd have preferred we whoop away all the cash I'd salvaged from the Detroit fiasco.

I used that cash to buy into a practice the week I got my license. Even so, I had to take on a heavy load of debt. I'm also paying off commitments back in Michigan. To explain my financial position to

Ina would be like explaining it to little Marie. For a newcomer, I'm doing fairly well on paper. I am earning around $8,000 a year and expect to earn more, but I'm paying out $3,600 a year to settle past obligations.

Eight months ago we were living in a tourist camp, and Ina's laments were unceasing. Maybe, I decided, her longing for a house was an adult desire. Maybe she was right and I was wrong. At any rate I borrowed the down payment, as I informed Ina, and bought the house for her. I thought we had a deal. She promised to wait for furniture and to decorate on a modest scale, choosing things we could afford. How has that turned out?

Well, we own a Swedish-modern dresser, and the cost of it would have furnished the youngsters' room. We have handsome iron chairs for the patio, and they are in the den. Our windows are naked and our floors are bare. Ina is holding out for draperies costing nineteen dollars a yard and for wool-cut pile carpeting. Daily she confronts me with demands for household luxuries far beyond our price range. Her taste is gauged by the possessions of others. She wants the same thing, only better.

Our neighbors buy inexpensive shrubs and plants, and we buy expensive palm trees. Neither of us knows how to garden. Ina hears another woman has a fur coat—actually it was a fur neckpiece— and immediately succumbs to a crazy whim. She spends the money set aside for a dining table and chairs on a hat and three dresses to wear to parties. We don't go to parties. We have no friends in California. Ina is the original impulse buyer. We do need stuff in our house, I'll admit. But I've got to the stage where I won't give Ina money, even when I have it. For I know she is not to be satisfied.

Ina is emotional. So am I. We've had countless scenes. David sleeps on, but our caterwauling wakes Marie. When Ina loses her temper she hurts Marie's feelings just as she hurts mine. Or she frightens the child with hysterics—hysteria is a regular boarder at our house—and then she rushes out and buys Marie a new doll. Time after time I've spelled out to Ina the meaning of maturity. She can't seem to understand.

At this point, I don't care whether our house is ever furnished. I do care for the children and for Ina, too. Her extravagances and her pretenses are not normal. There is something sick in the way she thinks and feels. It's something deeper than just keeping up with the Joneses. I'm licked. Is there any way you can help me to help Ina?

* *

Nick Willard had a problem wife. Ina's unfortunate background accounted for many of her difficulties. As is sometimes the case, Nick's rather similar background had a different effect upon him. A strong personality, he reacted to his early hardships by becoming a responsible and self-respecting human being. Undiscouraged by parental objections to his ambitions, he steamed ahead and developed an unusual degree of responsibility. Without this, it seems unlikely Ina could have held him through five such hectic years despite her powerful sexual attraction for him.

Ina grew up filled with fears. After two marriages and two children, she was still in restless search of the emotional security her parents had denied her. Why Ina's mother rejected her daughter we do not know; it seems likely she may have taken out on a helpless youngster the rancor of her own financial frustrations. On the few occasions Ina pleased her mother, a gift—something tangible and costing money—resulted. A gift, preferably expensive, became Ina's definition of love. She carried this unsound notion into marriage. Her first marriage—she and Alan spent only seven weeks together before he went to Korea—was too brief to be a test. The test came with Nick.

During his courtship and the honeymoon, Nick was generous. To Ina that meant he loved her. Later when he balked at her extravagance and refused to buy the things she desired, her "feelings" immediately suggested he did not love her. And her feelings ruled her head. Ina would have been wretched in a palace, for always over the hill she would have glimpsed a finer palace occupied by a richer princess.

Before Ina's marriage could be mended, it was necessary for her to look at herself objectively and to understand the true sources of her chronic dissatisfaction. Her greed, her envy, were a heritage from her mother; her shabby code was a carbon copy of her mother's code. Ina had many consultations with us. Finally there came the time when she could look at herself and ask herself what she really wanted from life. What she really wanted, she at last acknowledged, was to be confident of Nick's love. She wanted the approval and liking of others. And she wanted these things more than she wanted money or material possessions.

It was obvious she had to change drastically. With pain and struggle she began to free herself from the fetters of self-absorption. She gave consideration to Nick and her children, and by a deliberate effort of will placed their needs ahead of her own desires. In giving, she gradually found a warmth and joy that were new to her.

On the practical side, the marriage improved rather quickly. Once she admitted that Nick and the children were entitled to a tidy house, however sparsely furnished, and punctual meals, Ina picked up some skills in homemaking. As youngsters, she and Nick had eaten at helter-skelter hours and often slept in unmade beds. By sticking to a schedule—previously it had been her habit to start cooking dinner long after Nick's arrival home—Ina achieved some valuable discipline and a sense of personal accomplishment. The whole family benefited.

Nick made some changes, too. Eager to help his wife and hold his marriage together, he readily perceived and rectified some of his mistakes. He had not been helping Ina to grow up. He had been *telling* her to grow up. Nick was proud of his battles with poverty—indeed he was inclined to be a little boastful in relating the details of his rise—but no amount of talking on his part had instilled a similar pride in Ina. She was too insecure.

Nick's numerous lectures on her failings—natural enough in the circumstances—consistently failed of their object. Lecturing only served to undermine Ina's already meager stock of self-confidence. Furthermore, his criticisms covered too wide a range. It was unfair of him to blame her for the disasters of the move from Detroit. After all, he had chosen to follow her.

Nick was unrealistic in expecting Ina to become financially mature while he continued to treat her as a child. From their honeymoon days on, he had kept a firm grip on the purse strings. The furnishing of the house was a constant source of strife. Since so many of Ina's demands were unreasonable and capricious, he had fallen into a routine of the steady, sullen, protective "no."

One night Nick sat down and outlined to Ina just what his income from a growing medical practice amounted to, what his burden of debt was, how thin was the line to which they must adhere until he was more solidly established. Together, he and Ina worked out a sensible plan to obtain the house furnishings they could afford, and piecemeal. They studied interior-decoration pages in the magazines, visited budget shops in the department stores, selected the tables, chairs, lamps of the future. In the process, they enjoyed themselves and grew closer. Ina bought monk's cloth draperies for the picture window at $1.50 a yard instead of imported material at $19 and was thrilled by Nick's respect for her judgment. Pleasing, too, was her discovery that when her mother came to call, the maternal sniffs of disapproval no longer had the power to trouble her.

Ina now has feminine friends in her neighborhood. Honesty and candor have brought her the companionship for which she longed. She made her first woman friend when she crossed the street, asked her neighbor's advice about gardening, and frankly announced that, for financial reasons, she and Nick would have to proceed slowly.

Through thought and effort, Ina has changed most of her standards. At times she relapses into fits of the blues and moments of envy, but she always comes back to the battle. With Nick's support she is standing on her own feet, as an adult. And she is sure in her own mind now that she has value in the world as a person. She and Nick are bringing up their children in an atmosphere more emotionally stable than either of them ever knew as children.

Section IV: Making Marriage a Success

We see all kinds of people at the Institute. We see gamblers and alcoholics and their wretched wives. We see women who find it necessary to diet and exercise and believe their marriages are foundering under the weight of excess pounds. Clergymen serve on our staff as counselors, but we have counseled the wives of clergymen who are certain their husbands are more truly wedded to the church than to themselves. And during every holiday season we hear about that insidious creator of marital discord, the office party.

Many studies have been made to determine the leading cause for divorce in this country, but no satisfactory answer has ever been reached. Men and women who file suit for divorce seldom put their real reasons on record and very often do not know why their marriages have failed. Our records show that most of our clients report a number of overlapping grievances and rarely isolate a single, primary source of conflict from their multitudinous woes.

✿ ✿ ✿

When American wives are canvassed about their husbands' commonest fault, they almost always complain of "conceited selfishness"; but they frequently mention excessive drinking. Excessive drinking would have topped the list of complaints on any poll presented to thirty-six-year-old Lucy Randolph. In discussing her impending divorce with us, Lucy said:

❋ ❋

Drunkenness and cruelty are my grounds. After nineteen years of marriage to Dan Randolph I've reached my breaking point. The five years since our son was born have been a nightmare. For the past three months Peter and I have been living with an elderly aunt of mine. Presumably Dan is liquidating his business to meet his community-property obligations. A reconciliation is out of the question; this time I'm in earnest.

I've gone through disgraceful brawls in the past and have forgiven him. On other occasions I have left home and then been bullied or persuaded into going back. Twice—Dan was drunk, of course—he tracked me to my aunt's apartment and dragged me and Peter home. This time I've asked for police protection, and I've got it. This time I've refused to see him or speak to him on the telephone.

Dan is possessive, jealous, secretive. He is supersensitive and yet insensitive to the feelings of others. The slightest thing provokes him into a terrible rage which leaves me limp and sends him to the nearest bar in search of further stimulation. He eats excitement. He is as restless and changeable as the winds. For a while he will be in the clouds, and then he will sink into a black depression.

There's a lot of gamble connected with Dan's business—he is a speculative builder—and I've sometimes wondered whether business worries might be responsible for bringing on some of his depressions. One thing is sure. His depressions usually lead him to the whisky bottle.

I don't pretend to understand why Dan drinks. Dan himself—and this is characteristic—lays the blame for his drinking on me. He blames my failings as a wife. The fact is Dan has failed as a husband and a father. From the beginning he had the wrong conception of what a marriage should mean. To Dan no woman, much less a wife, can be a friend, a confidante, an equal. Liquor brings to the surface

his belief that women aren't human beings, individuals in themselves. To Dan's way of thinking, I'm not a person at all. His version
of love is to treat me like a pet dog, patted one minute, kicked the
next.

Our last scene—the last I will endure—took place on Decoration
Day. Hank and Irene Smith, who used to be our best friends, invited us to spend the week end at their fishing lodge. Dan bought
me a new dress for the occasion. The dress was expensive and becoming, but the lodge was chilly. Irene was wearing woolen slacks,
and she offered to lend me a pair. As it happens, Dan loathes slacks
on women; it's a phobia with him. I didn't know how to explain this
to Irene without seeming ridiculous, and I didn't know Dan was
drinking. He had promised to stay sober. So I put on the slacks.
When the two men came up from the trout stream, Dan was roaring
drunk. The reason was plain. Hank had caught all the fish that
afternoon. Irene giggled and said something about fishermen's luck,
and maybe out of sheer nervousness, I giggled too. Anyway, Dan
suddenly noticed I was wearing slacks. He didn't stop to think. He
just reacted. His face turned red, then white. He bounced across the
room. He tore Irene's slacks off me, threw them in the fire, and left
me huddled on the sofa in my underwear. Immediately he was
sorry, but being sorry wasn't good enough. The week end and my
marriage ended right there.

I cannot imagine why Dan is fighting the divorce and seems to
want me back. Unless it's because he misses his household slave, his
echo, his audience. He abuses me in private and insults me in public. Our sexual relationship long ago became too dreary to describe.
I used to be as loving as any other wife. I'm naturally affectionate.
My affection for Dan was drowned in alcohol.

I can't bear to have him touch me when he drinks. For then he
loses all his inhibitions. Two years ago I put a lock on my bedroom
door. The lock did no good. Dan kicked down the door. I put on a
second lock, a third. The same thing happened. Afterward, Dan's
regret was undoubtedly sincere. He would beg for my forgiveness.
His apologies did not restore my self-respect.

I loved Dan once. When we were married, he was perfect in my eyes. I was only seventeen at the time, childish, inexperienced. Other people warned me Dan was difficult, that he was moody, arrogant, domineering. I didn't see it that way. I was attracted by his masculinity, his ambition—the self-assertiveness I mistook for strength. At first I was thrilled by his determination to shut out the world and keep me to himself. Afterward I began to feel stifled—as though my individuality were being smothered.

In our early years together, Dan drank little. We didn't have the money to pay for liquor. We were married during the depression, and although Dan had an engineering degree, the best job he could find was in a filling station. Typically enough, he gave me the impression he owned the station. Later on, when he established his own business, it was months before I was told. Perhaps Dan thought he would fail, I don't know. My whole marriage has been a guessing game. It was only by accident I learned Dan had borrowed the money to finance our honeymoon and buy me a huge engagement diamond. I would have gladly skipped the honeymoon and done without the ring. I would have preferred to receive his faith and confidence. That is something Dan cannot understand.

Since I'm a woman, he is unalterably convinced I'm mercenary and grabby, that he can buy my admiration and my love. I'm handed the frosting on the cake, but I would rather share a loaf of bread. I'm treated like a child or a gold-digging mistress.

The story of my diamond bracelet may be enlightening. One night about a year ago Dan went on a talking jag that lasted for hours. He painted rainbow pictures of our future, promised me a ten-room mansion and a swimming pool. In the middle of his monologue, he got amorous. I managed to escape upstairs. A few minutes later he passed out on the sofa with a lighted cigarette in his hand and set fire to the cushions. Oh, it wasn't a serious fire; by the time I got downstairs, he had it out. But I complained. At once he flew into a senseless, destructive rage. He smashed my favorite lamp and several ash trays. Peter waked up and started to cry. I ran upstairs to comfort him.

Dan left the house. He was gone all night and most of the following day. Next evening at dinnertime he reappeared. He looked fairly well, and he was carrying the bracelet which he had bought that afternoon. I think he expected me to fall into his arms in delight and gratitude. I was neither grateful nor forgiving. I had poured out all the liquor on the premises, but Dan produced a quart of bourbon from his overcoat. He poured a drink for me. When I refused it—as he knew I would—he threatened to drink the quart by himself. I ignored the threat. He took four straight drinks. He then informed me of an appointment he had made for both of us. Waiting at a downtown night club was a group of prospective business investors. Dan shaved and showered, hustled me into a strapless evening dress. At the night club my bracelet and I were introduced to a dozen people. What the other women thought of me, I don't know. The men in the party, who were drinking, too, were amused and seemed to be impressed by Dan. Everybody was impressed by the diamond bracelet. But I was miserably uncomfortable and embarrassed.

I'm easygoing by disposition and inclined to take the path of least resistance. I went into marriage with my whole mind and heart. For years I let Dan have his way in everything. Whatever he demanded, I gave him. When he wanted to make love, we made love. If Dan wanted to rush off to the movies instead of eating dinner, I put the food in the oven and went with him. When I suggested a household budget, he vetoed the idea. So we had no budget.

Dan decided where we were to live and how long we were to live there. In nineteen years I've lived in fourteen different houses, but I've never had a home. Once we lived in a house only seven weeks. By the time I would get to like a place, Dan would sell it to make a profit and move us somewhere else. Usually we moved into a bigger house, which was no consolation since I had no sense of permanence. I couldn't even plan a decorating scheme or plant a garden.

I like to plan ahead. Dan likes to act impulsively. For thirteen years I followed his impulses. I wasn't working, and we had no children. I could devote all my thoughts to pleasing him. I wanted a baby from the first, but he wasn't interested in acquiring a family. At last I talked him around.

From the day of Peter's birth, Dan showed he wasn't fond of our son. He was selfish, unreasonable. He took the position a baby could be introduced into a home without fuss, without bother, without change. I had much less time to spend with him, but he wanted more of my time. His sexual demands increased, although my interest in sex was diminished both by fatigue and by his indifference to our child.

During those days, his drinking became intolerable. He'd got drunk before, but in a less objectionable way. Busy as I was with Peter, I noticed he was throwing all control to the winds. I begged him to stop drinking. Several times he went on the wagon. Invariably he fell off. Once he made a public scene because I took Peter with us on a two-day automobile trip instead of leaving him with my aunt. Dan has always wanted to leave Peter behind, while I have wanted to take him along.

Peter and I both need peace and regularity in our lives. Dan should realize that. He should stop fighting the divorce and settle the matter of our financial support. I dislike asking him for money. I must. The amount of alimony I've requested seems reasonable to me. According to my lawyer, I'm entitled to a property division. For three months Dan has kept stalling. I doubt he has taken any steps to liquidate his business. If I could support Peter and myself, I would. But I've never held a job. I've looked everywhere and found no openings. Obviously we can't continue camping out in a single room with my aunt. She owes two-months' rent herself. Dan used to pay it. But since I left him, I haven't received a penny in cash and neither has Aunt Sara.

I don't hate Dan. Indeed I pity him. But I'm not going back to him. I can no longer cope with the problems of living with a problem drinker. I'm worn out with problems, sick to death of problems. I want to live in peace and harmony.

*   *

Dan Randolph was a handsome man in his middle forties with broad muscular shoulders and powerful hands. Although he was opposed to the divorce, he admitted to us that his marital situation was bad:

* *

Lucy and I are so far apart this time that you could drive six trucks between us. But I see no point in financing a separation I don't want.

I don't say Lucy hasn't got her grievances. When I get too much liquor under my belt—it seems to creep up on me, particularly of late years—I'm not myself. Lucy should make allowances. I don't intend to behave the way I sometimes do. I didn't want to humiliate her on that week-end trip with the Smiths. I apologized, but she wouldn't even try to understand.

She knew my opinion of women in pants. I was crazy with worry about a vital loan extension hanging fire at the bank. Hank Smith had been needling me all afternoon because the trout were hopping out of the water to strike his flies and were giving mine the go-by. Then Irene Smith—with Lucy joining in—laughed at me, and I blew my top. But it wasn't the loan extension or the bad fishing luck that really stirred me up. It wasn't even the slacks. It was Lucy's attitude. The fact that she didn't stick with me, I guess, was the thing.

Lucy used to be so different. Let me tell you about the first time I ever saw her. It was nineteen years ago, but the picture is stamped on my brain as though a die press had put it there. Lucy was on the beach, wearing a green-and-white sunsuit, and she was very shy. She looked like a little girl who needed to be protected and looked after. "She's what I want," I thought; "there's my girl, there's my wife."

I brushed aside the fact that I was in no position to marry. I'm always willing to gamble, provided the odds are right. Financially I was nowhere. Just a cocky ambitious kid, with a hard-won education of no value at that time.

The depression was tough on lots of people, including me. My father's business in Chicago was wiped out, and I was jerked out of an expensive prep school to spend my teens on a run-down farm in northern Illinois. My father went to pieces when he lost his business —my mother wouldn't let him forget his failure—and I had to work on the farm to see my two sisters through high school. Those days I lived in terror I would miss out on college, and I didn't get there until I was twenty-one. My engineering degree—the scrap of paper for which I'd sweated blood—eventually got me picked for a filling-station job from among two hundred other scared and hungry applicants.

When I married Lucy, I was earning fifteen dollars a week. I wore a pair of borrowed shoes on our honeymoon, and after I returned those shoes I stuffed paper in the only pair I owned to keep out the weather. Lucy never knew. Why should she? I was the man, the breadwinner.

To shield and protect Lucy, to take care of her, has always been a major objective of mine. I'm too well acquainted with the rough stuff of competition to be willing to let her in on any part of it. I enjoy my present business, but it is a speculative business. I manufacture prefabs and trailers and promote housing developments. Any speculative business is a rat race. You either swim or you sink, and you sink mighty fast.

Lucy complains about my drinking. Sure, she has a right to. But she knows nothing of the tensions I undergo. They're partly incidental to my personal make-up, of course. One day I feel fine, and the next day—bang—I feel as though the world had me by the throat. Perhaps I've just bought a carload of material at a bargain, but suddenly I don't believe it's a bargain any more. I'm skeptical—the deal was too easy. I need a drink. I see an absolutely secure option slip away from me. I see myself a failure like my father. I need another drink.

Everybody in my crowd drinks. I drop in a bar of an afternoon to pick up the news and trade lies with the next fellow; I maneuver to sell him 500 prefabs and he deploys to sell me 10,000 tires, and life takes on a little glitter. False glitter, maybe, but nevertheless—glitter. Then I go home, and Lucy greets me like Carrie Nation in person. Sometimes, with luck, I can get her to take a cocktail. Nowadays the only time she's sexually responsive is when she's had a few drinks. Otherwise she pushes me away.

Lucy used to be warm and tender, understanding. In the years before Peter came along I was bulwarked by a marriage anybody would envy. Lucy measured up to nearly all my dreams. She wasn't much of a cook or housekeeper, but that didn't matter to me. She gave me everything else. What I wanted, she wanted. Now when I move her into a bigger, better house—I want the best for Lucy—she acts offended. She now turns up her nose at a diamond bracelet, and objects because I like to show her off to my friends and associates. Lucy doesn't appreciate the necessity of putting up a front at certain times. At one single party—of which she has complained bitterly because I had too many drinks—I arranged the financing for my biggest prefab development to date. I drank to keep up my courage. Dutch courage, I guess you call it. For months I'd been secretly shaking in my boots while I contemplated selling myself and my idea, my good idea, to that particular group of men.

For many years I was the head man in my home. Lucy thought I was wonderful and made it plain. She listened to everything I said. She used to quote me constantly. She now quotes Peter.

I guess I'm not the paternal type. I haven't much in common with a five-year-old youngster. Anyhow, Peter cares nothing about me. It seems that in gaining a son I lost my wife. I was demoted to the doghouse. Everything was Peter, Peter, Peter. Lucy dragged Peter everywhere we went. She refused to hire a nurse. So she could hear Peter crying—or that was her excuse—she moved out of our double bed to a cot beside his crib. Ever since, she's insisted on separate bedrooms.

I know myself. I'm practical. I know my assets, my liabilities. I'm not a big shot yet, though I can be. I'm almost there. If Lucy will just be patient—if she will come back to me—in about two years I can and will put her in a mansion with a swimming pool.

But at the moment I'm overextended. Lucy couldn't have chosen a poorer time to walk out on me. The divorce laws in California, as you probably know, put men behind the eight ball. If Lucy forces this divorce and we have to divide our property, my creditors will jump on my back and clean me. Then I'll have no business to liquidate. It will melt away. Sure as shooting, there will be practically nothing left to divide. My reputation as an honest builder will vanish. So will my connections, my friendships, my credit standing. I'll be a commercial has-been. And where will that leave Lucy? She can't support herself, a five-year-old son, and a sixty-seven-year-old aunt.

* *

Lucy and Dan Randolph were as intertwined as the roots of a tree. In her justified outrage and hurt, Lucy was ignoring the practical aspects of her situation. She, her child, and her elderly aunt were financially dependent on Dan. In turn Dan was dependent on her for virtually all his emotional satisfactions. Without Lucy, he had small incentive to work. Without Dan, she was financially marooned.

The Randolphs were a difficult couple to advise. Obviously, their situation could not be resolved by lectures on sobriety. For years Lucy had lectured and scolded in vain. But if she and Dan could be assisted to some understanding of themselves and each other, it seemed to us they might be able to remedy mistakes of the present that were rooted in the past.

Lucy was malleable and gentle, the youngest in a large family. Two of her earliest memories of her childhood were interesting. She remembered herself being *pulled* in a small wagon by an older brother, recalled herself being *pushed* downhill on a sled. When she married, Lucy slavishly followed her husband's lead. She permitted Dan to move her in and out of houses without warning, to make all domestic decisions, to swallow up her life. Lucy felt stifled, but until the birth of her child she made few protests.

Apparently Dan's character had been warped by the haunting fears of his imaginative boyhood and the hard facts of the national depression. Financial success dominated his thinking, since he felt trapped and cheated by his father's financial reverses. When he was obliged to help his sisters through high school, a not uncommon circumstance, he suffered agonizing terror that he would miss college. To him a good education meant money, and money meant he could win back lost prestige. Less able than most men to tolerate the thought of failure, he entered a speculative business. At home he demanded, and for a long while received, an overwhelming amount of affection and consideration. Any hint of coolness or disapproval on Lucy's part he interpreted as failure. He carried a crushing burden of inner anxiety, acquired in his formative years. It seems clear he drank to escape.

Dan was an intelligent man. During our consultations with him he surveyed his own personality objectively—something he had never done previously. He had thought of himself as the average good fellow, a loving and generous husband whose lapses should be forgiven because he meant well. He perceived that his demands on Lucy had been excessive, that she was far more yielding and submissive than the average wife. He admitted to a need of reform in himself. He promised to modify his drinking, which he still believed he could handle, and to make strenuous efforts to control his temper.

Lucy then returned to him. Economic necessity was by no means the only factor involved. Lucy had more ties to Dan than she realized. Her love for him was battered, but it still existed. She wanted to help him. After Peter's birth, she had relegated her husband to a secondary place in her thoughts and in the home. Upon her return, she stopped keeping Peter on constant parade. In an effort to compensate for Dan's indifference, she had been spoiling the child. She soft-pedaled her praise of Peter and once again found virtues in Dan to praise. Dan badly needed praise, appreciation, admiration, love—much more than do most men. Lucy restored him to first place in her life. She moved back into the double bed, and their sexual relationship was resumed.

There was an interval of calm. This was followed by another storm. Finally Dan decided he must stop drinking for his *own* sake, that liquor was not for him. Of his own accord, he joined Alcoholics

Anonymous. He became an active member. Dan is still engaged in a highly competitive business, with no quarter given and none asked —a nerve-racking business. By his own decision—nobody else's—he is living with the tensions of his business and his personal make-up without alcohol.

For more than a year now he has stuck on a bone-dry regime. It has been a struggle all the way. But he and Lucy have salvaged a peaceful year, and Dan tells us his struggles become easier each month, each week, each day.

Even more remarkable is the change in his whole philosophy of life. The man who was completely absorbed in getting his own way and getting ahead now gives voluntary help, hours of voluntary help, to other people. It's a commonplace for Dan to be summoned from bed at 3 A.M. to respond to the appeal of some total stranger, in torment and longing to take a drink. Often the battle continues all night, and then, without sleep, Dan goes to his business. He has developed assets of which he was unaware, spiritual assets.

The Randolphs' marriage is far from ideal. Lucy and Dan still have many problems. Life itself is a problem, as both now realize. Dan's depressions continue; for days he sees a sober world through yellow glasses. He endeavors to bear this temperamental handicap with fortitude but often becomes surly and irritable. Lucy tries to be patient and understanding and usually manages.

Dan still finds it difficult to allow her a reasonable amount of freedom. At the Institute we compare a good marriage to a three-ringed circus—with the big ring representing shared interests and the two small rings representing the individual interests of the husband and the wife. Dan had many interests outside his home, and Lucy none. Painting was suggested to her, and she enjoyed the creative outlet, the thrill of personal accomplishment. Similarly, she enjoyed a session of swimming each Friday morning at the Y. Her absences from home so distressed Dan, who liked to find her there when he telephoned or, unexpectedly, dropped in that she has abandoned both activities—for the present. "Let's take our changes a little more slowly," Dan suggested, and she agreed.

Dan no longer regards Lucy as an extension of himself, an embellishment of his personality. He used to do all the talking for them both, a hard habit to break. These days, in company, he asks Lucy to express her opinions. And he does not expect her opinions to be a carbon copy of his. Mutual engagements are discussed in advance and are arranged to suit the convenience of both. Their friendships are shared. When Dan joined Alcoholics Anonymous, their circle of friends changed too. Most of their social life revolves around A.A. gatherings.

The mansion and the swimming pool are still around the next corner, but Lucy is well content. The family is living in a pleasant home where Dan has promised to remain until the ultimate move of his dreams is made. She has planted a garden. Incidentally—and this shows another marked change in Dan's thinking—he now talks of the future swimming pool in terms of its advantages to Peter. Dan began to give his son attention when Lucy stopped giving the boy so much. When Dan gave his son love, naturally he received love. He is now very proud of his child.

※　※　※

Lucy and Dan Randolph by their own efforts achieved a marriage that had value and meaning for them both. Such mutual effort was sorely needed in the strife-ridden household of Elsa and Josh Gifford.

Elsa was a pale, slim young woman of twenty-seven when we saw her first. Josh, five years older, worked in a big bank in Los Angeles. Married eight years and the parents of three, the Giffords had battled for years. They appealed to the Institute for help as a direct result of Josh's office party.

The party was staged on the twenty-third of December, a hectic day for Elsa as it is for most mothers with young children. In the morning she trimmed the house with tinsel and holly, baked cookies and made candy, allowing her two small daughters to help, which doubled the work. In the afternoon she went to the market, picked out a Christmas tree, and lugged it home on a crowded bus by herself.

Elsa was understandably bitter as she told us how her husband behaved when he came home that evening to a house full of happy holiday hustle-bustle.

* *

Josh barely glanced at the tree. The girls tried to show off the cookies they had baked, but he was in such wild haste to bathe and dress he hardly spoke to any of us. While we ate a supper of frankfurters and beans he put on his best suit, changed his necktie three times before he was satisfied with the effect, stuck a flower in his buttonhole, and then went off in a cloud of dust to attend his fancy office party.

Josh and I haven't an extra penny to spend on recreation and entertainment for ourselves. No expense was spared to make the office party a bang-up success. It was held at a country club that I have yet to enter. Only wealthy people belong. An orchestra was hired. There were favors for the girls. A wonderful dinner, including cocktails and imported champagne, was served. I haven't tasted champagne since Josh and I were married eight years ago. At our wedding we had one bottle of domestic champagne for six people.

Back in November when I first heard the bank was throwing a Christmas party I was thrilled and excited. Until quite recently we lived in a small town, and perhaps I have small-town ideas. I assumed that since I was Josh's wife I would be welcome at the party. I knew we couldn't afford a new dress for me. I scrimped on our food and bought a new fake-fur stole and made over an old dress. It wasn't until I modeled the dress for Josh that I learned I had wasted my time. He hemmed and hawed, but finally blurted out that the party was limited to bank employees. Wives and husbands weren't invited. It seems the employees had got together and decided they would have a jollier time by themselves. Josh insisted he and most of the other men had voted in favor of inviting their wives, which may be possible. The married women at the bank, he said, had voted against inviting their husbands. That should give you some idea of the nature of the party.

Josh declared it was his duty as a bank official to appear. Three months ago he became an assistant cashier, but I don't consider him a real official since he got the title instead of a richly deserved raise. At any rate, I thought a truly loving husband wouldn't choose to mingle socially with a lot of man-crazy, young subordinates. Josh supervises a group of twenty teen-agers who specialize in tight sweaters and plunging necklines. The bleached-blond siren whose desk is beside his—her name is Marilyn, and she is fluttering around Josh every time I stop in at the bank—spends her entire salary on clothes and in beauty shops. I can't compete with her, but I prefer not to share Josh's company with Marilyn in the evening as well as in the daytime. I lowered my pride, a hard thing for me, and asked him to stay away from the party to demonstrate his loyalty. He refused. We argued the matter for weeks. Eventually we compromised.

Josh agreed to eat dinner at the country club, take two drinks at the most, dance once, and come home by 10 P.M. After he left the house and the children were in bed, I put up their Christmas tree by myself. It wasn't any fun. Ten o'clock came and went, but Josh didn't come. By half-past ten I had begun to worry. At eleven o'clock I was frantic; one minute I would imagine a terrible traffic accident, the next minute I would picture Josh complimenting Marilyn or some other girl on her glamorous evening dress.

At eleven-fifteen I telephoned the country club. The bank party was still in full swing. In the distance I could hear music and singing and people laughing. It took forever, but finally Josh came to the phone. In a cold, curt voice he said he had been unavoidably delayed but would be home in fifteen minutes.

He broke that promise, too. It was half-past twelve before he arrived. The moment he came weaving in I discovered the cause of the unavoidable delay. His face was plastered with lipstick; there was lipstick on his collar, there was lipstick in his hair. His hair was tousled where some girl had been running her fingers through it.

His necktie was hanging out. There was lipstick on his necktie, too.

Josh had drunk so much he was incoherent. He mumbled something about the lipstick being a joke, but the joke was not hilarious to me. I thought his behavior was a disgrace and I said so. I started off to bed, and he grabbed my arm. I pulled loose. He lost his temper and hit me. Both our daughters—Lillian is seven, Jane six—were awakened by the noise and came running in. Their reaction was pitiful. Lillian threw herself in my arms and began to sob. Jane joined in. It took me hours to get them back to sleep.

The next night was Christmas Eve. Josh and I decorated the tree together, but we were hardly speaking. He refused to apologize for his conduct or to admit he was in the wrong in any way. On Christmas afternoon we drove the children to see his mother, a trip of ninety miles, without exchanging a word. By New Year's Day the strain in our house was terrific. The situation has now become unbearable. Lillian and Jane are creeping around like little mice, afraid of their own shadows. Even three-year-old Kenneth is affected.

If the office party were an isolated incident I suppose I could file and forget it, although it is difficult for me to forget an injury. Unfortunately I have just about exhausted my capacity to forgive and forget. This latest quarrel is typical of my dismal, unsatisfying marriage. Josh and I were wrangling and arguing even before our oldest daughter was born.

We had serious trouble in the town where we lived before we moved to Los Angeles a year ago. There was a woman in the bank there—another bleached blond, incidentally—who pushed us to the brink of divorce. Josh got romantically involved with her, and he confessed as much. I halfway thought he was deliberately trying to upset me—and I halfway thought he really preferred Irene, the other woman, to me. Although I was deeply wounded I didn't create a big dramatic scene. I simply told Josh that unless he broke off the acquaintanceship permanently I would sue for a divorce. He took me at my word and broke with Irene. However, he complained bitterly at my very natural jealousy.

Josh is twice as jealous as I am and without reason. I have never given him the slightest cause. He feels affronted if I attend a PTA meeting. He is jealous of my women friends. I try to confine visits to neighbors to the daytime, although daytime visiting is very little pleasure. All of us have small children, and we spend our time bobbing our heads and our eyes to see what the youngsters are doing.

Just last week I ran next door and stayed a while, and in a jealous rage Josh locked me out of the house. It wasn't the first time. I hate being humiliated in that way but I have to escape for a few minutes occasionally. We go practically nowhere. A drive-in movie once a month is big-time stuff for us.

Josh thinks his companionship should satisfy and stimulate me. Yet he talks of nothing but his job and the bank, and I've grown to detest the whole subject. There may be prestige in his job, but prestige won't support a family of five. After eleven years of working in banks Josh earns $380 a month; that's no bonanza. He has to wear good clothes, too. We can't afford to own our home. We rent a small, cramped house on an inconvenient street. Josh disapproves of installment buying which means we do without nearly everything that other couples take for granted. We don't even own a washing machine. An electric iron is my most expensive piece of equipment. I'm still nursing along a pop-up toaster I bought when I was single. Our rattletrap car is ten years old, and Josh needs it virtually all the time. Banking hours sound like a snap to the public, but he puts in endless overtime without extra pay, and his irregular schedule won't allow him to join a car pool.

I believe I could take the financial sacrifices in my stride—economizing is no new thing to me—if Josh would treat me with dignity and consideration. When he abuses me in the presence of our children, when he shames me before the neighbors, I want to curl up and die. There is an ache deep in my chest, in my heart. I just can't understand what happened to Josh and me.

When he and I started out together, it appeared we had everything in our favor. Our backgrounds were similar. We were engaged for six months; we had plenty of time to talk over our hopes and our dreams. Both of us seemed to want the same things. We wanted a home and children. We wanted security and standing in the community. I wanted desperately to belong to somebody.

After my mother's death when I was nine I didn't seem to belong anywhere. One day I had a home and a place in the world. Then my mother died of a heart attack, and in two-weeks' time our family fell apart. My brother and my sisters, who were older, scattered, and my father couldn't take care of me. I stayed with four different aunts in succession. I adjusted my ways to their ways, but none of them wanted to keep me. At sixteen I was sent to the Pacific Coast to live with my oldest sister. She was newly married, and her husband objected to my coming. My bed was in the living room, but the walls were so thin that night after night I could hear them in the bedroom arguing about me, and my heart would nearly break. I finally moved in with a high-school classmate, whose parents operated a greenhouse. I earned my keep by working in the greenhouse. Nobody was unkind to me, but it wasn't *my* family, and I didn't feel I belonged there.

When I met Josh I was nineteen and had my own one-room apartment. There was a peanut-sized kitchenette, and I bought a big second-hand refrigerator just for the pleasure of seeing my own food on the shelves. I was working as a secretary and attending college in the evenings and cooking two meals a day as well. Josh, who shared a bedroom with another boy, proposed to me in that apartment. I had baked a meat loaf for him. As I set the meat loaf on the card table and began lighting the candles, he asked me.

I was too awed and impressed at marrying a banker—as I thought of Josh in those days—to be curious about his prospects and the exact amount of his income. I didn't know Josh's salary at the time was $180 a month, less than mine, and that after banking hours he was working part-time as an usher in a motion picture house. He wiped out his saving account to buy my engagement ring, which was sweet of him but was foolish, too.

I held my job out of sheer necessity until Lillian was born. I was disillusioned with marriage before my honeymoon was over, although I did my best to conceal it. In my girlhood I learned not to air my feelings and to conceal my emotions. Josh is the opposite. He has no self-control whatever. When Lillian was born, he carried on at the hospital as though he were the mother. At the same time he plainly showed his disappointment that the baby wasn't a boy, something I will never forget. When the baby and I came home and I stayed in bed and let him prepare his own breakfast, he was outraged and yelled so furiously all the neighbors heard him. He never has been fair to our girls.

The other morning Jane meddled in the tooth paste, and he exploded and threw the child into such a nervous state she couldn't go to school. When Kenneth misbehaves, Josh thinks it is cute. His partiality to our son is hard on all three youngsters.

At best Josh has a hair-trigger temper. One evening last month he came home very late—I'd already dished up supper—and I didn't offer a word of comment on his tardiness. Not one word. I did ask him to carry out the trash; merely that, nothing more. His response was to aim a blow at me. I jumped aside, and Lillian burst into tears. Jane rushed at her father and started beating at him with her little fists. Josh spanked and put both girls to bed without their supper.

That night I cried for hours. Josh and I don't seem to be capable of achieving companionship, tenderness, harmony. Living with him is killing my self-respect.

✿ ✿

Josh Gifford was a tall, handsome man. In his conservative, pin-striped suit, he looked every inch the rising young executive as he recounted to us his troubles at home and at the bank:

✿ ✿

All day long I work under tension trying to get an honest day's work out of a bunch of stupid, inefficient kids who couldn't care less about their jobs. Our bank doesn't seem to attract conscientious, efficient girls. We get the drifters and the clock-watchers. I bawl them out constantly, but it does no good. They mock and laugh at me behind my back. They ignore my orders for the fun of seeing me lose my temper.

My average working day runs from 8 A.M. until half-past four. Not long ago I had to stay until 9 P.M. tracking down a shortage of $1.85 that resulted from the sloppy bookkeeping of a youngster named Marilyn. Next morning when I confronted Marilyn with the error, she turned her back on me and sailed into the rest room to smoke a cigarette. The other kids laughed like zanies and for the balance of the day flouted my authority in every conceivable way. Marilyn is their ringleader. Because she spends hours of time varnishing her fingernails and combing her hair, the rest follow suit. The other day my immediate boss dropped in, and my department looked like a beauty parlor. I would like to fire Marilyn, but firing her would convince my superiors that I can't control my own staff.

When I come home in the evening after a day of battling subordinates and bucking traffic—it takes me an hour to cover eighteen miles—I'm dead beat. All I want is to change into slacks and play with Kenneth or maybe relax a little over television before supper. What Elsa wants is to hurry me through a list of chores she's been saving up all day—it seems to me she could dispose of the trash herself—and then rush me through my meal.

I've got to the place where I need a little help and sympathy at home. I don't receive it. Elsa neither admires nor respects me. Last week she went over to a neighbor's house on the pretext of discussing a meeting of the PTA. I felt sure what she and the neighbor—a woman I particularly dislike—wanted to discuss was my failings as a husband.

I waited an hour for Elsa to return, getting angrier by the minute. Then I locked the doors to teach her a lesson. My daughter Lillian happened to be awake, and she and her sister take their mother's part in everything. Lillian slipped out of bed and unlocked the back door. I heard her fooling with the latch and went to the kitchen just as Elsa stepped on the back porch. I snapped on the light. Lillian screamed in fear—fear of me, her father—and Elsa flew inside and took the child in her arms. She held Lillian close and gave me a contemptuous look. Elsa's scorn either makes me mad or makes me feel like crawling. Last week I felt like crawling.

I wish Elsa would try just once to see my side of things. It shouldn't be hard for her to understand I was obliged to attend our office party. My boss specifically ordered me to go and keep my staff in line. Elsa's telephone call to the country club made me look ridiculous. It lowered me in the estimation of my superiors and, in my opinion, jeopardized a raise I've been sweating out since September. As I was leaving the phone booth I ran smack into a bank vice-president, and he cocked an eyebrow and cracked: "Domestic trouble? Wife wants you home, I suppose." I told him, "No." Promotions seldom go to men tied to apron strings.

The vice-president stayed on at the party and I did, too. I was so miserable and disgusted I drank twice as much as I had intended. I can barely recall the kids ganging up and plastering me with lip-sticky kisses, but I can distinctly recall Elsa's reaction later—the contempt in her eyes, the flat, unloving note in her voice. I'm sorry I hit her, as I've told her repeatedly, but I just couldn't help myself.

I'll admit I didn't distinguish myself at the office party, but Elsa has been paying me off ever since. She doesn't say much, but she keeps on the pressure. She lets me know in dozens of oblique, left-handed ways that she is clinging to her grudge. On Christmas afternoon she maneuvered me into visiting my mother, although my mother and I have no fondness for each other. The visit was meant to punish me.

All things considered, I don't think I've done so badly in life. I climbed from the bottom with nobody's help. When my mother was sixteen her parents, ignorant people, married her to an old man of sixty on the mistaken theory he had money. My mother had to go to work to support him and us five children. In those days I was terribly ashamed of my dad; the other youngsters in the neighborhood called him grandpop and I did, too. I'm sorry now. He died when I was ten and my kid brother nine. We then found out how he had shielded us from my mother. She had a fiery temper and a great fear we children would wind up as juvenile delinquents. Many a night my kid brother and I would wake in bed to find her beating us for practically no reason. One time he and I ran out of the house in our underclothes with her after us and climbed up in the rafters of a big barn. She poked us out with a broomstick and then whaled away at us until the broomstick broke.

I was a big kid for my age, and at twelve I got my first paying job —singing birthday messages for the telegraph company. About the same time I was put in charge of our school bank and was allowed to deposit the funds in the real bank. My mother was excited by the honor, but she had no real understanding of what it meant to me. When I told her I intended to be a banker when I grew up, she laughed. In our circumstances my ambition seemed as distant as the moon.

I can still remember the store where we traded when I was little. My mother would send my brother and me to buy the cheapest foods, and we always had to cool our heels until the store was empty before we were waited on. One day I noticed a number of spoiled bananas in a garbage barrel in the back alley. I asked a clerk—he was a smart-alecky young fellow—if my brother and I could have them. He said I could take a spoiled banana for every red pepper I would chew and swallow without a drink of water. I can still see the clerk laughing as I ate the peppers and hopped from one foot to the other, tears streaming from my eyes. I finally quit with six overripe bananas for my kid brother and myself.

It never occurred to me to break the bargain and swipe the bananas from the alley when nobody was looking. Honesty is a cardinal rule with me to this day. Another rule is paying my bills on the dot and staying out of debt. Elsa thinks we should buy a house—instead of renting. To me a mortgage is debt, and I would rather camp out than assume an obligation I can't liquidate promptly.

When Elsa attacks my principles I can defend myself. But I am cut to the quick by the way she belittles my job. Three months ago at a big general meeting of all the bank officials I was named an assistant cashier as a reward for devising a more effective method of keeping our records. The president of the bank congratulated me personally. That evening when I tried to describe the meeting to Elsa, a glazed look came in her eyes. After I finished talking she asked who had sat next to me at the meeting, whether it was a man or a woman. Then she asked why my promotion to assistant cashier didn't carry an automatic raise. She never did congratulate me on my new title. She takes no pride in it.

It is true many men of my age make more money. A bank job is no quick way to big pay. But I am doing what I want to do and what I am qualified to do. Preferment is slow, but, if she'll help, I think I can go places. So far she hasn't helped me—she has handicapped me. She has never been cordial to any of my associates, even when she pops unexpectedly into the bank. A few months ago I introduced her to my boss, and at once she began hinting around I should have a raise. That didn't boost my stock.

I started in a small-town bank in Oregon. I was doing well and I was getting promotions. We left because Elsa was jealous of a woman who worked beside me. I negotiated to get the job here, resigned from the Oregon bank, and, of course, lost my seniority. Frankly, I was a fool throughout. The woman in question, Irene, was very little interested in me, and I was little interested in her. Irene's main object was to make her husband jealous. My object was to alarm Elsa into paying some notice to me. I was hungry for attention and warmth.

When I was courting Elsa I thought we were ideally matched. I fell in love with her almost at first sight. I was going to college in Oregon, studying economics and banking. I heard about Elsa from mutual friends and, even before we met, admired her courage in carrying a full-time job along with college courses. Then one evening we were both invited to dinner at the last minute. Elsa had just washed her hair. Most girls would have excused themselves. Not Elsa. She wound a scarf around her wet hair and walked into the restaurant beside me with her head held regally high. I knew I loved her then.

Our six-months' courtship only made me love her more. We used to eat by candlelight in her apartment. Nobody had ever asked me what foods I preferred to eat. Elsa did. I shopped, and she prepared the dishes. She was a good cook and an excellent housekeeper. She was thrifty and clever in the handling of money, and she still is. But somewhere after marriage a change set in. I can't tell you exactly when or why.

But happiness for us was a long time ago. If Elsa wasn't sniping away at me because of the office party, she'd be at me for something else. At times, my temper boils over, and I literally don't know what I'm doing. Afterward I am ashamed—which I suppose is no help. I realize I should have more self-control, but I haven't much incentive to mend my ways.

Kenneth is the only member of my family who is impressed by me. When I leave the house in the morning Elsa doesn't kiss me and say good-by—she is usually still in bed—and in the evening I can be sure she and the girls won't smile at me and say hello. When I come through the door Kenneth is the one who smiles.

Our marriage is unsatisfactory to me, and I am sure is unsatisfactory to Elsa, too. However, I believe we should stay together for the children's sake. To do so, we will have to stop our incessant quarreling.

*   *

At the Institute we are not enthusiastic about office parties that exclude the husbands and wives of employees. The Christmas office party—happily now losing in popularity—we regard as a menace. We have seen too many of these celebrations mar the joy of the holidays for families. A good many times the participants themselves, like Josh Gifford, neither enjoy the party nor the aftermath. Particularly the aftermath.

In this case, the office party contributed to difficulties that had been accumulating for years. In analyzing the Giffords' unhappiness with them, we traced their association back to their courtship. At that time Elsa decided her background and Josh's were similar. It is true they had poverty in common. But she did not take into account the difference in their environments and in their temperaments, a difference as striking as that between Patsy and Nils Knudsen.

Josh, like Patsy, wanted warmth, attention, appreciation. When he felt he received too little from his reticent, inhibited bride, he reacted with outbursts of rage worthy of his violent-tempered mother. These outbursts, often occurring in public, humiliated Elsa and drove her even further into herself. Josh's undisciplined behavior, as Elsa saw it, robbed her of what she most wanted from marriage—a stable home and a solid position in the community.

Elsa was jolted and shocked when we told her she was partly at fault, that if she wanted a serene family life, she should learn to give Josh what he wanted from their marriage and thereby help him control his temper. She needed to be more outgoing, more appreciative, more demonstrative in love; she was so inarticulate emotionally that even when she had warm words in her mind for Josh, they stuck in her throat.

After her counseling began, Elsa forced herself in many small ways to prove to Josh her inward affection and good will. Instead of lying abed in the morning, she got up and cooked his breakfast and kissed him warmly before he went to work. She welcomed him with a smile and a kiss on his return in the evening. She taught her daughters to do the same. Josh's response to the change—it was an easy change for the little girls, difficult for Elsa—was immediate. He found virtues in his daughters as well as in his baby son. Josh had been jealous of Lillian and Jane and their partiality for Elsa. The little girls were delighted to be affectionate with him when he showed affection for them.

Elsa cut down on the dull array of evening chores she was accustomed to assign Josh at the very moment he stepped in his door. She set the dinner hour thirty minutes later, so he would have a chance to relax. Josh was appreciative of her thoughtfulness. Previously his wife had made him feel like an insignificant handy man, not the breadwinner and head of a family. Nowadays if Elsa happens to forget her new resolutions and does break into his period of relaxation with some tedious request, he usually is able to keep his temper in hand instead of flaring up at once. To Elsa's pleased amazement, he often volunteers to take out the trash.

When Elsa began to stop and think and express her feelings on every possible occasion, Josh learned to stop and think and repress some of his feelings. He studied and familiarized himself with Elsa's reactions. He now knows if he succumbs to sudden rage and roars at her, the result may be that she will remain glumly silent for the evening. His anger is not worth that to him.

Josh had no insight into his relationship with others. If everybody in his department at the bank was behaving badly, as he reported to us, it seemed fairly clear that his personality and his methods as an executive must be to blame. It developed that he was expecting too much of his staff. As a boy, he had struggled fiercely, and with a constant sense of failure, to satisfy a mother who expected too much of him. As an adult he instinctively expected and demanded that his giddy young subordinates struggle just as hard.

Although Josh was abnormally sensitive, it did not occur to him that the youngsters he supervised also had feelings, self-esteem, vanity. We suggested he put himself in the place of his subordinates, praise them when they deserved praise, and refrain from bawling them out for minor infractions. After he grasped the fact that his attitude as an executive was a legacy from his frustrating childhood, Josh followed this quite obvious advice. The morale of his staff quickly improved as did office efficiency. Taking his courage in hand, he discharged Marilyn, a clock-watcher to the end, and was gratified to discover that neither his staff nor his superiors protested his decision. In fact, Josh soon received his long-awaited raise.

Elsa deserved more consideration in the matter of the family budget. It was all very well for Josh to have principles against debt, but in the case of his family a modest amount of installment buying was sensible. He and Elsa bought an automatic washing machine, something she long had yearned for. They made the down payment by saving all their two-dollar bills for seven months. They have postponed buying a house, but Elsa has hopes they will own a home in the not-too-distant future. In the meantime she has the pleasure of driving around every Sunday with Josh and the children to explore current housing developments and to plan the kind of house she wants.

The Giffords' recreation picture is greatly improved. Elsa had been cooped up far too much. Now that Josh has less strain to cope with during his business day, he comes home less exhausted. He and Elsa occasionally entertain their neighbors at a simple back yard cook-out, and Josh has learned to enjoy the company of people he previously thought of as Elsa's friends and his enemies. The two regularly trade off baby sitting with neighbors, and once a week they go square dancing.

If Elsa had not been so housebound and deprived of the normal pleasures of the young, doubtless she would not have been so outraged by Josh's office party. The plans for this year's office party are already in progress. Josh intends to go to the party, once again by himself. Elsa is resigned, if not enthusiastic. Both she and Josh now feel too secure in themselves, too sure in their mutual love and understanding, to anticipate a renewed quarrel. Indeed both of them believe this Christmas will be the happiest they have ever shared.

❋   ❋   ❋

Christmas was never a happy time in the home of Carol and Martin Montgomery, but not because of office parties. Martin Montgomery was a clergyman. At the Christmas season, the church always required even more of his time than usual.

When we met the Montgomerys, they had been married for fifteen years and were the parents of two small boys, Anthony and Chuck. Thirty-three-year-old Carol was attractive and slender, with beautiful brown hair, but her manner was dispirited and her voice fretful as she said:

❋   ❋

You can't conceive what it's like to be a clergyman's wife. I can never induce Martin to make a definite promise—something might come up at the church and interfere—but two weeks ago he told me he thought he could take the boys and me to an ice-skating exhibition in the next town. For two weeks he repeatedly postponed the trip. The activities that kept him so frantically occupied were typical—three weddings, two funerals, his daily round of visiting at the local hospitals, several meetings with the Finance Board, hours getting out the weekly bulletin on a mimeographing machine that's antique enough to be a museum piece. Then there were conferences with the Red Cross, conferences with the Community Chest officials, a young people's dance to supervise, a short talk before the Lions Club, a full-dress speech at the Chamber of Commerce banquet.

Yesterday was the last day of the ice show, and Martin came home unusually early, around 6 P.M. I'm optimistic by disposition— or I used to be. With a heart full of hope, I hurried supper and called the boys. As we sat down I thanked their father for managing to give over an evening to us. I knew at once by Martin's expression that the whole matter had slipped his mind. With our boys sitting there all eyes, I begged him not to disappoint us again. I should have known better.

It turned out Martin's evening was filled until 11 P.M. He was scheduled to hold meetings with three committees—our church is in the midst of its annual building and fund-raising drive—and the architect was already waiting in his study to discuss the Sunday school addition. With two-weeks' notice Martin couldn't find time to drive his own sons fifteen miles, although he averages 1500 miles a month making church calls. We have only the one car, which he considers his exclusive property. I offered to take the youngsters to the ice show and drop him at the church on the way. This plan was vetoed. Martin had arranged to pick up one of the committee chairwomen at her home. Her car was in the repair shop, and her husband and her seventeen-year-old daughter were using *their* cars.

When I protested that a woman from a three-car family could afford to hire a taxi, Martin informed me he couldn't afford to supply gasoline for fifteen miles of "needless" driving and the money to buy tickets to "needless" entertainment. At that point I broke down and began to cry. It wasn't that I minded missing the ice show. It was something deeper. What I minded, what I couldn't bear, was the feeling I'd missed everything a woman values in life. I'd missed gaiety and romance and glamour as a bride; I'd missed being cherished and spoiled as a young wife; I'd missed novelty and excitement—I have yet to enter a night club or a regular theater—and in my thirties it was increasingly clear I was missing out on companionship and content.

The children are being deprived too. On the Saturday our older boy starred in a Little League baseball game, Martin wasn't at the school ground. Other busy fathers were there. It was no consolation to Anthony to hear that his father couldn't attend the game because of a previous commitment to help organize Cub Scout dens in our community. Anthony is an outgoing youngster, a born joiner—Chuck is our shy, sensitive child—but Anthony has no interest in becoming a Cub Scout. I don't blame him. I have no interest in volunteering to be a den mother.

I am tired of running second. With Martin the church always comes first. When my father suffered a fatal stroke I went back to Ohio on the bus by myself. Martin sits up with the dying and comforts the bereaved; my mother and I dried our own tears. Anthony was born in my girlhood home town, and my parents saw me through the difficult birth. Martin was attending his eastern seminary and did not get there until I was out of danger, and our son was two weeks old. Throughout our marriage whenever I've felt weak and depressed and in need of masculine strength, somebody else has had first call on Martin's strength. As I cried out my heart last night, it seemed to me that if I lived to be as old as Methuselah I would never have a warm, satisfying marriage. It seemed to me my sons were half orphans and that they deserved a concerned, affectionate father.

After Martin left the house last night, I finally pulled myself together, cleared the table, settled the boys in their room, and read them a story. By then I was started on a migraine attack—a bad one. This morning it was all I could do to crawl out of bed. According to our doctor, my migraine headaches are psychological in origin. Martin has no patience with any psychological ailment, unless some member of his congregation is the victim. He thinks I should conquer my attacks by the sheer power of will. I have tried, but my headaches have grown steadily and frighteningly worse. Just two weeks ago I dressed the boys and myself for church. A block before we reached there, I recalled Martin's text and wondered how I could sit and listen quietly to a sermon about love and charity delivered by a man who has love and charity for everybody—except his own flesh and blood. I became so ill I had to ask the boys to walk on by themselves; I turned around, went back home, pulled down the shades, and collapsed.

I blame Martin's church for my ill health and wretchedness. I'm a comparatively young woman. I don't want to drag on until I'm middle-aged, miserably unhappy all the time. Martin is capable of earning a livelihood outside the ministry. As soon as he finishes writing his thesis—it is nearly complete—he will get his Ph.D. and will be qualified to teach on a college level. The wives and families of college instructors are permitted to have private lives, private interests, a little freedom.

Martin's congregation refuses to think of me as a human being. As the minister's wife I am regarded as a sort of bloodless symbol, a woman with no normal desires, no preferences, no tastes, no individuality. I can't stand it any longer. For that matter, I burn at the way Martin himself is treated. Not one of his congregations has ever appreciated his sacrifices. His present church is still small—approximately 300 members—but is growing rapidly, and the credit belongs to Martin. During the three years of his pastorate he has doubled the membership by working from eighty to ninety hours a week, which means he is away from home *every* evening. Martin's overtime hours occasion no comment, and it is assumed he will gladly perform menial chores. Not long ago the head of the Board of Trustees requested him to drive posthaste to the hardware store, buy a box of washers, and repair a leaky faucet in the church kitchen. Every faucet in our home leaks, has leaked for months, and will continue to leak. Martin has no mechanical ability whatever. But he interrupted his scheduled appointments without grumbling and eventually put the church sink in apple-pie order.

As a result of Martin's unceasing labors, his church has been painted and landscaped, and a new organ has been installed. There is a new carpet, the altar has been improved, and now a Sunday school addition is being built. Nobody has said, "Thank you." His salary remains the same as it was three years ago—$3,800. The janitor's wages have tripled.

It hasn't occurred to the congregation that inflation affects a clergyman's family, too. Our utility bills have climbed, but the church hasn't increased our utility allotment. Martin's solution is to snap off every light the instant he leaves a room. It's the same story with gasoline and car upkeep. Martin spends between fifty and sixty dollars of his own money every month to drive the automobile which he seldom uses except on church business. The kitchen stove in the parsonage is a disgrace, and the wallpaper is hanging in tatters, but he makes no protest. Yet he fought like a saber-toothed tiger to raise $1,200 for painting the church.

We are obliged to economize rigidly on everything we eat and wear. Martin has to have two good suits, but in the house he wears patches and rags. My mother clothes our youngsters, and for the most part I either do without or make over dresses that are years old. On the rare occasions when I buy a new dress, the women in the congregation eye it as though doubtful I'd got good value for their Sunday contributions and by keeping a string on my dress, so to speak, make me hate it. Or else Martin makes me hate it by going along to the store to ensure I get a bargain. I'm anything but extravagant, but Martin considers himself a wiser shopper. He does all our grocery buying. He buys dull, thrifty staples in quantity— flour, bread, hamburger, lard, oatmeal, potatoes, canned vegetables, canned fruit and juices, powdered milk—but never a handful of raisins, a jar of sour cream, an exotic spice to lift an ordinary recipe out of the rut. And then, if it happens to occur to him, he complains because I've lost my interest in cooking.

Left to himself, I'm sure Martin would complain little of my cooking and housekeeping. He is too unobservant, too uninterested in everyday affairs. However, he is sensitive to the opinion of parishioners. This means the boys and I are at the mercy of 300 prospective critics, represented by one critic-in-chief, Martin. If Chuck clatters down the church aisle and somebody frowns, Martin later calls the child to task. If somebody feels my red hat is too gay, Martin suggests I wear my black hat. If a women's committee meets at the parsonage, he wants me to serve tea with real cream and nice little cakes—whatever the state of our finances. If the refreshments are skimpy or the cake is scorched, I hear about it.

Several years ago my mother shipped me the baby grand piano my sister and I played on as young girls. One cantankerous lady parishioner hinted that it was too elegant an instrument to be owned by a minister's family. The piano in her home was an upright. Martin took her mean-spirited attitude seriously. Seemingly he is unable to be loyal and stand up for me in anything. One day the church organist dropped by the parsonage and spied a pile of dirty dishes in the sink. Next morning Martin gave me a lecture on my inefficient housekeeping and insisted I wash the breakfast things promptly. I knew he was echoing the organist; ordinarily Martin is blind to his surroundings—I can scrub our place spotless without attracting his notice or his praise—and oblivious of the food on his plate. By choice he would read straight through his meals.

In the brief time Martin does spend at home he contributes nothing except his physical presence. He feels no obligation to talk to or listen to the boys and me. If I make a comment on his work at the church, if I speak of Anthony's troubles at school or Chuck's latest crying spell, my remarks fall on deaf ears. Martin is already deep in some book. He uses our home as a library, a boardinghouse, and a place to sleep.

Martin and I have no recreation as I understand the term. When we do go out for an evening we attend some church affair, and he has to work at making it a success. Perhaps the other young married couples enjoy themselves, but I feel as though I have no escort. We haven't gone on a family vacation in years.

Martin is everybody's friend. He is too self-sufficient and preoccupied with his work to require intimate friendships. I'm not that way. Often, on the lonesome evenings when the boys are asleep and he is off somewhere listening to the troubles of other people, I feel literally starved by the need of a real friend. I can't choose a friend— somebody I can trust and with whom I can be myself—from the congregation. Once when Martin was serving an eastern church I confided to a woman I considered a friend that I wasn't enthusiastic about the Sunday school superintendent. Within a week the superintendent resigned, and the church was engaged in a row that haunts Martin to this day.

I believe it was then I began to dislike his profession. When I fell in love with Martin, I felt very different about his church—our church. I was only eighteen and just beginning music school when we met at a sorority dance. Martin was twenty-four and still five years from his ordination—family obligations had interrupted his education—and I was impressed by his maturity, his strength, his manliness. I admired his idealism and his sense of purpose. I quit music school and took a $25-a-week stenographic job so we could be married while he was still a student.

I soon discovered what it meant to become the wife of a dedicated man. I'd had romantic visions of meeting my husband at the door every evening with a kiss, handing him his robe and slippers, and then feeding him a delicious hot meal. Martin was carrying a full-time, underpaid job at the Student Union as well as a full-time college course. He invariably arrived home hours late, so dazed with fatigue he often responded to my kiss with a peck on the cheek and sometimes didn't respond at all. Often he was too tired to eat, but he was never too tired to study.

Our marriage put an immediate end to dancing, fun, movies. For the two years Martin was completing his undergraduate work, we saved every extra penny toward his seminary expenses in New York.

During the three years we lived there I used to beg Martin to take me to a night club for a special treat, to celebrate a birthday or anniversary, say, so I could see a big-time floor show and hear a top-flight orchestra. He never felt we could spare the time and money—although I was working, too. Occasionally I bought a ticket to a concert, but I went alone and felt guilty at squandering money he always seemed to need to buy books. He thought I should satisfy my hunger for music by listening to the radio.

I became pregnant during Martin's last term at the seminary. At that time he was attending classes sixteen hours a week and was studying twice as many hours to win straight-A marks. He was a part-time minister, preaching two Sundays a month. He worked as a lunchroom checker to pay for his meals and held still another part-time job in a slum hotel to cover the cost of our lodgings there. The hotel—we had one cramped, grimy room without bath—wasn't suitable for children. I gave up my job in December and went back to Ohio to bear my first son. I was in no hurry to return.

When Martin was ordained the following June, he convinced me that at last we would have the chance to spend some time together, share each other's interests and activities, and become loving companions. That was ten years ago. In ten years Martin has served four different churches, and each church has absorbed all of his time and attention and left nothing for me and the boys. I thought the West Coast might be an improvement on the East Coast. I was mistaken.

Martin and I have now drifted far apart. I am sure he won't leave the church. Consequently I feel that a permanent separation is the answer for us. I would like to divorce my husband with as little damage to his career as possible.

❋   ❋

Her tall, lean husband had fair hair blurred with gray. When the Reverend Martin Montgomery strode into the counseling office, his proud yet ascetic face proclaimed that he would tolerate no weakness in himself. He soon made clear that he tolerated little, if any, weakness in his wife:

❀   ❀

Carol was more mature as a bride than she is now. Or maybe it just seems that way in retrospect. I'm now inclined to wonder whether Carol wasn't in search of a doting protector rather than a fallible, average husband when she married me. Her father, only moderately prosperous, indulged both his daughters to a ridiculous extent.

My father died when I was eleven years old, just as the national depression was beginning. He left a sizable estate, around $200,000. Inside a few months his investments were wiped out, and my mother was faced with the problem of providing food, clothing, and shelter for me and my three small sisters. She supported us by brutally hard work—harder work than Carol can conceive of—with very little help from me. Overnight, you might say, I was pitchforked from childhood into becoming the man of the family. Until my father died, I, too, was indulged. Possibly because I was outnumbered by the girls, my father treated me as his special companion. We often went hunting and fishing together; he thought nothing of traveling several hundred miles over a week end. As I look back, it seems as though one Saturday my father and I were riding off somewhere in a sporty, expensive car, and the next Saturday I was walking to save streetcar fare. I should be ashamed to admit it, but I still dream of owning a high-powered automobile some day, although I don't suppose I ever will.

I went to work in a grocery store. I unloaded fresh produce in the early mornings before school opened and in the evenings I delivered groceries at five cents a delivery. Each payday I handed my earnings, four or five dollars, to my mother. She offered to return an allowance to me but I wouldn't take it, preferring to hear her praise my unselfishness.

Although I was always pressed for time to study, I was expected to set a good example for my sisters and keep my school grades high. I will never forget my mother's shock, the look on her face, the day I brought home a report card with a C in arithmetic. I didn't like arithmetic, but the next term I saw to it I got an A. Throughout my schooling I've consistently outranked students more gifted than myself. I have my mother to thank for my scholastic record. She taught me self-discipline and industry, the importance of making use of minutes as well as hours.

My mother is a remarkable woman. When I finished high school at sixteen—I was class valedictorian—she had worked up from stock girl to assistant buyer in a large department store. She offered to finance my college education, but we both knew my three sisters needed her assistance more than I did. So I went to work and began a program of systematic saving. It took me six years to acquire the money for college.

During those years I debated my choice of career. Piling up money didn't interest me. Stocks and bonds could vanish; fine houses could be foreclosed; fine furniture could be repossessed. I was determined to use my life to accomplish something. I met a man, a clergyman, who was establishing boys' clubs among the underprivileged kids, the hungry kids, of depression days. After working hours I did voluntary work with him. I discovered his life had meaning and value and, I suppose, I chose him for my model.

When I met Carol I was an overage college junior with the long pull toward the ministry still ahead of me. I didn't intend to marry until I was ordained. In one evening Carol changed my mind. In those days she was sweet and uncomplaining, an eager sharer of my ideas and my ideals.

Again and again Carol assured me that she was prepared for struggle and hardship, that she was willing to undertake the obligations involved in becoming a clergyman's wife. At that time she didn't mind living on a modest scale. But she soon began to object whenever I hit the books. If she called from the stove while I was studying at the kitchen table, and I was too absorbed to hear her, she was annoyed and would try to provoke a quarrel. One evening I was concentrating on a particularly tough assignment, and she went out and borrowed a camera and came back and stood in front of me and took a time exposure. The fact that I didn't raise my eyes from my textbook or notice the camera until she shouted at me made her extremely angry. At the end of our first year I moved my textbooks out of our room and thereafter did all my studying in the college library. Carol then complained that we spent too little time together.

Except for her dissatisfaction, I would have been ideally happy in my three years at the seminary. Hard work had no terrors for me. Despite fatigue—I averaged five hours of sleep a night—every morning I awoke full of energy and to the knowledge I had drawn one day closer to my goal. Carol couldn't seem to share in the joy of our common achievement. In fact while she was pregnant with our first child, she proposed that I quit the ministry. The result of my refusal —how could I not refuse?—was that she packed and left me and went back to her parents. My term examinations were coming up, and I was in no position to stop her.

I thought her condition explained her attitude, that motherhood would help her grow up. When Anthony was born, she telegraphed and asked for a divorce. On the day I completed the last of my examinations I took to the road and hitchhiked to see her and the baby, arriving so exhausted that my mother-in-law bundled me off to bed where I slept for thirty-six hours. My mother-in-law showed me far more sympathy than did Carol. She refused to return for my ordination.

I was preaching in my first church before I was able to induce her to bring the baby and join me. It would be pointless to list Carol's complaints of the various places I have served. She complained that our first parsonage—it had fourteen rooms—was too large, too drafty, too hard to heat. She complains the present parsonage is too small. She complained that my first salary was inadequate, ignoring the fact that all new clergymen receive inadequate incomes. She complained we had no car as she now complains she has too little opportunity to drive our car.

I deliberately sought out and applied for my present post in the hope she would be more content in California. Carol takes no pride in the tremendous growth of our church; she merely complains that I'm away too much, don't earn enough, and that our living accommodations are poor. If she will only be patient, my salary is certain to be raised; the parsonage will be refurbished when the more urgent needs of the church are met.

I have tried to be patient and understanding with Carol, as has the congregation. She does practically no work for the church; she is musically talented, but she doesn't assist with our music programs. Two Sundays out of four she doesn't attend the morning services, explaining that to listen to my sermons makes her feel like a hypocrite. It doesn't occur to her that I might feel hypocritical when I excuse her frequent absences on the grounds of illness and refrain from adding that the illnesses are psychosomatic.

In my opinion the time has come for Carol to master her nervous system, assume responsibility, shoulder her share of the burden. It is time for her to behave like a grown woman, a wife, and a mother. Although she loves our children she neglects them. Since I'm unable to be with my sons as much as I would like—there are only twenty-four hours in a day—I feel she should give them extra attention. While she lies abed nursing a headache, Anthony needs her assistance with his home work, and Chuck needs her encouragement to be friendly with other youngsters. Anthony is falling behind in his studies, and Chuck is too shy and withdrawn for his age. When the boys are older and I'm less harried and driven, I expect to get closer to them.

I've had training in psychology—I've done marital counseling myself—but my own marriage and my own wife mystify me. Sometimes I'm afraid Carol may do something to cause an open scandal. Sometimes in her uncontrollable rages she is actually irrational. I love my wife and sons. I will do anything within reason to help Carol. But I cannot give up my life work or consider a divorce.

❉   ❉

Most people are aware of the tremendous rebirth of religious interest in this country. Few people are aware of the burdens placed upon clergymen—and their families. Preparing and preaching a sermon on Sunday is the smallest part of the average clergyman's duties.

The modern-day clergyman is expected to be an expert in many fields. He must organize and operate fund-raising drives with triumphant success. He is an administrator, responsible for the financial health and physical upkeep of the church. He has to be a force for good in the community, supporting and donating time to numerous civic activities only remotely connected with the church. He calls on and welcomes newcomers, gives psychological counseling to the troubled, marries the living, and buries the dead.

Martin Montgomery possessed unusual energy and determination. In his boyhood he acquired the habit of sleeping considerably less than the average and working far harder to accomplish an objective. The training given him by his mother, who asked for and received more emotional support and financial assistance from a young boy than is usual, imbued him with a remarkable indifference to hardships. At times, as we talked to him, he seemed almost to embrace hardship, perhaps as a test of his own strength.

When Martin married, he forgot the old saying: Many men receive a "call" to the ministry; few women feel they have been "called" to become the wife of a minister. Carol fell in love with and married a man, not his job. To her Martin's talk of his future was thrilling and romantic, but removed from reality. As a bride of eighteen—remember, he was a serious-minded man of twenty-four —she retained a natural interest in gaiety and fun. Then, too, she had much less stamina and endurance than her husband.

For a while she deferred to Martin's superiority in age and intelligence—she was originally drawn to him by his protectiveness and a fancied resemblance to her father—and meekly accepted a Spartan regime on his say-so. Before the birth of their first son, however, the seeds of rebellion were sprouting. Martin's hard work had purpose and meaning to him while her hard work, she thought, was slavery.

Martin studied psychology but expended little of his knowledge on a study of his wife. Because he felt fulfilled, joyfully adequate to the drudgery incidental to his life work, he assumed Carol shared his feelings and he insisted upon believing that *his* goals were *her* goals. A stubborn as well as a dedicated man, he ignored strong evidence to the contrary and brushed aside her desires as childish. In some ways Carol was inclined to be childish, but her yearning for some measure of personal self-expression was not childish.

The welfare of their young sons became another bone of contention. Carol believed boys should be the responsibility of a father. Martin believed Carol should be both mother and father; he felt his paternal negligence was justified by the good works he was accomplishing. He did not see that Carol's frustrations were undermining her nervous system and health to such an extent it was becoming impossible for her to be an adequate wife, mother, or human being.

It was inconceivable to Martin that Carol might carry out her threats and divorce him. Clergymen simply did not appear in the divorce court. It took us six weeks to convince him that his wife was in earnest, that he must make adjustments if he wished to hold her. We then tried to show him how the marriage looked from Carol's point of view. Eventually he conceded that the fifteen years which had contained great satisfactions for him had held few for her.

In moving to California, it was true he had been unselfishly inspired by the wish to please Carol with a change of scene. Yet to him the tumble-down, poorly attended, impoverished church represented a fruitful field of service. He felt richly rewarded for three years of unflagging labor by his success in meeting and surmounting difficulties. Carol felt no such reward. When Martin pushed the congregation to pay for sprucing up the church instead of pushing for an increase in his salary, Carol felt the plaster and paint had been bought at the expense of the children and herself. In a way, she was right.

We advised Martin to spend one day a week with his family, regardless of the pressure of his pastoral duties. This meant a movie, a hike, a picnic, an outing to the beach was to be planned and carried out, no matter what. He followed our advice. On one of the weekly expeditions, remindful of a childish but often expressed dream of

Carol's, he took her to a night club in Los Angeles. That was Martin's own idea. Once was enough; as soon as Carol's dream was realized, her appetite for garish glamour was sated.

We also advised that Martin devote his *exclusive* attention to his wife and sons for a minimum of one hour every evening, which seemed fair enough in view of the fact he was putting in an eleven- or twelve-hour day for the church. While Carol was cooking and serving the meal, he was to talk to and listen to her or play with his boys. He was not to thumb through a church report in need of revisions; most particularly he was not to pick up and read a book. This practice had irritated Carol to the point of hysteria for it indicated her husband felt himself too busy to spend a few minutes on her and the youngsters.

Martin had to *will* himself to overcome habit. When he came home in the evening his hands automatically groped for a book and then, a few moments later, groped again. Carol, too, had a lesson to master. She had to learn to *allow* Martin to cure himself of his bad habit, a more difficult trick than you might imagine. When she saw Martin unthinkingly reach toward a book, her body unconsciously stiffened, and she had an instantaneous impulse to utter a sharp, unpleasant remark. It was after she learned to stifle the sharp remarks that Martin freed himself of the habit of picking up a book to occupy every spare moment. Frequently, with married couples, it takes two to break a habit.

In time the evening family hour became agreeable and rewarding to duty-bound Martin. He and his boys discovered the pleasure of companionship, and the tensions between him and Carol began to lift.

Their financial problem remained. There just was not money enough to meet expenses. The family was steadily sinking into debt. Carol located a woman to care for the youngsters in the afternoon when they were out of school and took a well-paid secretarial job. For the first time in years she enjoyed a feeling of independence and freedom. She bought a dress or two that appealed to her taste, without dreading the congregation's criticism. She bought Anthony a bicycle and Chuck a toy fire engine with her own earnings. She took over the marketing; Martin conceded that she should be permitted to select the food she was expected to cook, even though an occasional bargain might be missed.

From the Montgomerys' first weeks in California, their automobile had caused dissension. Martin's parish was a sprawling one, and a parsimonious, unthinking congregation allowed him for official expenses roughly half of the amount he spent on driving. And Carol had almost no use of the family car. It seemed to us that she was entitled to a more equitable arrangement; at our suggestion Martin agreed to turn over the car to her regularly every Saturday. This concession from him had a curious but satisfactory repercussion. A member of the Board of Trustees asked him to run a ten-mile errand on a Saturday. When Martin explained why his automobile was unavailable, the whole story of the church's niggardliness in buying gasoline reached an influential member. He called a meeting of the trustees, and the car budget was set at a realistic level. Later on, this same board member saw to it that Martin's salary was raised to $4,400. This is hardly munificent, but it enabled Carol to quit a job that had already served its purpose.

In a town adjoining Martin's church is one of California's excellent small colleges. Carol enrolled there, resumed the musical studies interrupted by her youthful marriage, and the grand piano in the parsonage took on meaning again. Carol had regarded the church as a personal enemy, and it struck us as evidence of a sound personal readjustment when she volunteered to direct the choir's musical programs. She now attends church every Sunday. She has not had a migraine attack in four months. Carol still is not the ideal minister's wife, but Martin is conscious of her problems and she understands his. The Montgomerys and their boys will always live in a floodlight. They belong to their congregation, as all clergymen's families do. It may be unfair, but it is inevitable.

*   *   *

Whether or not it is unfair, it is also inevitable that people who eat more food than they need are likely to gain too much weight. This sad fact had been proved to twenty-six-year-old Abby Johnson long before the December day when she first called at the Institute. The counseling office was warm, but Abby sat through our opening interview huddled in a shapeless, bulky coat that further increased her size. In telling us what she thought was wrong with her marriage she obviously was still in love with her husband and blamed their difficulties on her undisciplined appetite:

* *

I'm five feet seven. I weigh 195 pounds and should weigh 80 pounds less. Yet last night I broke my latest diet again. I ate six eggs, four pieces of bread, and half a cake, topped off with two quarts of milk. I just couldn't stop eating.

With me it is apparently a matter of all or nothing. I can live for weeks skipping breakfast, having a grapefruit for lunch and two lamb chops or a small steak for dinner. Our sons seem to be eating every waking minute—our oldest boy must bang the refrigerator door a hundred times a day—and by 6 p.m. I usually feel as though I were starving and am so irritable I could scream. However, I can steel myself and resist the daily temptation of watching the three boys gobble peanut butter, jelly sandwiches, cookies, and the kind of sweets I adore.

But then suddenly I get upset over something and go on an eating binge. I get upset easily—too easily. I've always been supersensitive.

My husband is a C.P.A. who does a great deal of work in the evenings, but yesterday Clark was free and he suggested we do our major marketing for the week and then take in a movie. A drive-in was what I supposed he had in mind. The last time he and I entered a regular motion picture theater we both heard an usher remark to the cashier that a man had gone by with a woman who looked like a bale of hay.

Clark and I have no baby-sitting problems. We dropped off the youngsters with my parents, as is customary on our evenings out. I'm an only child myself, and there is nothing my parents won't do for me. They are wild about our three boys. When our gang trooped in on them last night, both my mother and I noticed that Dean—he is our oldest—was wearing a badly torn pair of pants. I was humiliated and furious. While I was helping the little boys with their buttons Dean had whined for me to help him. When I refused he dashed into the garage so he could be first in the car and evidently he caught his clothes on the door. I almost believe he might have torn his pants on purpose. One time he deliberately left a sixty-five-dollar bicycle out in a rainstorm to pay me back for bathing his baby brother and telling him to bathe himself.

Dean is nearly eight and plenty old enough to be careful of his clothes; I'd dressed all three youngsters in their best outfits because I like my mother to be proud of her grandchildren. Dean behaves worse than either of the little boys and is twice as destructive and awkward. His clumsiness puts me in mind of myself at that age. I was overgrown, too.

My mother wouldn't let me discipline Dean. Among our three, he is her favorite. If I say no to Dean, she says yes, and he grins like a Cheshire cat and knows which of us is the boss. He tells everybody he loves his grandmother better than he loves me.

She offered to mend his pants and told Clark and me not to hurry back. She then remarked that the movie we'd chosen had received poor reviews. Aunt Ida, who is her youngest sister and boards there, had seen the film and chipped in to back up Mother. Clark never disagrees with my relatives, though they aren't always nice to him; he suggested we see the new Marilyn Monroe picture instead.

On the way to the shopping area I asked Clark to explain exactly what appealed to him in Marilyn Monroe's appearance—some people say the bone structure of my face resembles hers—and in the midst of our discussion I asked whether he thought Marilyn Monroe was better looking than me. Clark said I was better looking so far as his taste in girls was concerned and said he admired my figure, but I knew he was fibbing to cheer me up. The fact is he thinks I look awful. I have proof of his honest opinion.

Five nights a week Clark doesn't arrive home until 11 P.M., and by then I'm likely to be sound asleep. But even if I am awake he doesn't come in the bedroom. He heads for the hobby room he built for himself in a corner of the garage, and there he stays until midnight or later. Clark's hobbies would fill a book; he collects stamps and stones and coins, does leather work and bird-watching, is interested in magic and is learning to play the harmonica. I'm jealous of Clark's hobbies, I know. I have good reason.

Clark hasn't made love to me in more than a month. Not that I really blame him. How can a man feel warm toward a woman as big as the side of a mountain?

By the time we located a place in the parking area last night I was in tears, accusing Clark of preferring Marilyn Monroe to me, practically hating him for something that wasn't his fault. He went in the supermarket with the list, and I flounced off in the opposite direction. There was a penny scale on the sidewalk outside the drugstore. I'm ashamed to admit it, but I habitually lie to other people, my kinfolk included, about the amount of my weight and the size dress I wear. It's almost unheard of for me to weigh myself in public—I lock the door before using our bathroom scales—but nobody was in sight. I whipped out of my coat—I subtract 3 pounds for my shoes and other clothing—and stepped on the scales. Just as I discovered I hadn't lost an ounce and still weighed 195, I discovered Clark was standing right behind me staring at the arrow on the scales.

By then the evening was ruined for me. I was too heartsick to go to any movie. We picked up the boys early. Knowing something was wrong and suspecting poor Clark, my mother tongue-lashed him and did her best to comfort me. She had mended Dean's pants and tightened the buttons on the little boys' shirts and persuaded Aunt Ida to bake one of her cheese cakes. Both my aunt and my mother are inclined to be plump—I inherit my stoutness from that side of the family—and I can't recall a time the two of them weren't dieting. But they never diet on week ends, since my mother believes people deserve the pleasure of eating the food they want a part of the time.

Anyhow, my mother isn't sold on my latest diet. She pressed a piece of the cake on me. I didn't resist very strongly. I hated to hurt her feelings. And by then I was ravenously hungry, as achingly empty as though I hadn't touched a morsel for a week.

I started on the eating binge at my parents'. When we left there my mother gave me the half of Aunt Ida's cheese cake that hadn't been eaten. After Clark and the boys were in bed, I ate the cake to the last crumb and polished off nearly everything in the house that was edible. I used a quarter of a pound of butter on the four slices of bread I mentioned to you. Then I laid my head on the kitchen table and I cried. I was stuffed to the point I couldn't have swallowed another bite and miserably disgusted with myself.

Finally Clark came in the kitchen and talked me into coming to bed. By then I had washed the dishes, scoured my copper-bottomed pans, scrubbed the linoleum and woodwork. We both pretended I hadn't made a pig of myself, but had just been in the mood to scrub and clean in the middle of the night.

Clark professes to be satisfied with our marriage because he has the patience of an angel, but he can't conceal the truth from me. Two years ago, before our youngest was born, Clark had a nervous breakdown and spent six weeks in a Naval hospital while the older boys and I stayed with my parents. I'm quite sure my mother and father and I, all three of us, were responsible for his illness. The psychiatrist at the hospital as much as told me so.

My mother and father, my mother in particular, have never approved of Clark. He and I grew up in the same neighborhood back in Illinois and considered ourselves sweethearts from our early teens, something my parents refused to acknowledge for a long while. They had big ambitions for me; my mother and father both held jobs in order to provide me with the advantages other kids in our neighborhood lacked. I was given piano lessons, violin lessons, private dancing lessons. I didn't distinguish myself at the piano, at the violin, or at dancing.

I hardly knew how to behave among my contemporaries. I was shy and terribly afraid of boys. When I was in the fourth or fifth grade a boy tried to kiss me. I told my mother and what she said about the entire male sex frightened me; when I think about that conversation now it still makes me feel shivery and cold. But when I met Clark I realized here was a boy who respected girls. Except for Clark I would have had a thin time as a teen-ager. Everybody was crazy about him. I was invited to parties only because he and I were going steady.

I never gave any parties. My family had a large, nicely furnished apartment, but we lived in a poor section. I wasn't supposed to be friendly with anybody on our street. I wasn't permitted to join most of the clubs, attend the school picnics and such. For a short time, I *was* allowed to be a Girl Scout. Whenever there was a Saturday afternoon meeting and my mother was around, she would tell me I was the largest girl in the group and the loudest girl, too; that in the hub-bub she could always hear me shouting and yelling. I wonder . . . maybe the loudest ones are the loneliest.

I was the first girl in junior high school to be treated to a beauty-shop permanent wave. My hair has always been straight as a stick and the wave didn't take well. I was dressed in prettier, more expensive things than any of my schoolmates, but even in those days I was too fat. I began going on diets when I was ten years old, right along with Mother and Aunt Ida. Even so I was always the tallest, heaviest girl in my class at school. I hated my size but I hated dieting too.

I was a scholastic disappointment to my parents. I barely made college. When Clark went away to the Navy, my parents sent me to the state university in the hope I would break with him permanently. For several months I wore the fraternity pin of a college man, and my mother was in seventh heaven. But then somebody wrote Clark, and he got a furlough and flew back. When I saw him again, I knew there could never be anybody else for me. So my mother had to give in. I dropped out of college, took a job and Clark's ring. On my parents' account he and I did agree to delay our marriage until his discharge from the Navy.

I dislike to criticize anybody, especially my own mother. But one day we went shopping for my wedding gown and found a lovely, well-fitting dress priced at $45 in size twelve. "Don't buy now," my mother said. "In six months you will probably need a larger size." She was quite right! In the six months Clark was waiting for his discharge, I gained 20 pounds and could barely squeeze into a size sixteen.

I couldn't help blaming Mother for my tight-fitting size-sixteen wedding dress. I halfway convinced myself she had encouraged me to overeat because she disliked Clark. I'm sorry now that I had such thoughts. My parents have yet to spare expense on me and mine. They shower Clark and me with gifts. They buy practically all the boys' clothes; for Easter they bought suits, coats, and shoes for all three, although only Dean was in need of clothing.

If my parents had not stood by, there would have been many times Clark and I could not have managed financially. When I became pregnant with Dean in the first year of marriage I lost my job, and Clark was by no means solidly established in his work. I was just eighteen and terrified at the idea of having a baby. Dean was born in Illinois. I can still recall the sinking fear I experienced in the hospital at the moment Clark was herded into an elevator and I was left alone, lying on a stretcher in an empty hall.

Until the nurse put Dean in my arms I had never touched an infant in my life. I was scared to death I might make some terrible mistake. My mother got over being angry at my marriage in her pride at becoming a grandmother for the first time. She took complete charge of Dean from the beginning. Indeed Dean stayed in Illinois with her and my father when Clark and I came to California and located a home out here.

I have good parents, a fine husband, and wonderful children. I should consider myself the luckiest girl on earth. Instead I brood and feel wretched, scream at the boys, criticize my mother, snap at Clark, and go into a rage or a depression if he smiles at another woman. I eat until I can't bear to look in a mirror. Except for Clark's small shaving mirror there isn't a mirror in our house. Diets and pills haven't done a thing for me. I've read enough on the subject to realize an appetite like mine must have some psychological basis. That's why I came here to ask for your help.

* *

Clark Johnson was a year older than Abby. A man of medium height and normal weight, worry lines were carved on his forehead and around his sober gray eyes. What disturbed Clark was his wife's unhappiness:

* *

I wish Abby could understand I love her regardless of whether she is thin as a wand or has gained a little weight. But she subjects me to storms of baseless jealousy. So far I've been able to cope with that. What really gets under my skin is to hear Abby lament she is as big as a house and then pick on the kids—Dean is her favorite victim—because she has gone off a diet or has gone on one. Abby has a large frame and, in my opinion, can carry some extra poundage. I'd choose a woman with a sweet nature in preference to a woman with a perfect figure any day.

Long ago when Abby and I were growing up back in Illinois and she was a lonely, big-eyed kid, I decided her happiness would be my main objective in life. There was fun in my family, none in hers. My mother and father and all us kids—we were three boys, two girls—had less money, a smaller, shabbier apartment than Abby's family. But we lived in the present, so to speak. Abby's mother and father, her mother in particular, counted on a fortune in the future. While they attempted to get the fortune, Abby was left alone a lot.

Some of the others in our high-school crowd thought Abby was high-hat because her mother and father acted so stuck on themselves. I knew Abby was scared. Almost anybody would be scared of my mother-in-law. When she and her sister Ida team up together, there are few who can hold out against them. For years those two women have done the talking and deciding for my father-in-law, a nice enough guy but so henpecked he can no longer feel his scars.

My mother-in-law is generous with money but hell-bent to give you what *she* wants. Last Easter she bought clothes for our boys that Abby definitely didn't want the boys to have. Once in a while she would like the opportunity of choosing the suits and coats that please her own taste. Frequently she complains to me that her mother's taste is old-fashioned, but I notice she doesn't complain to her mother. I keep my mouth shut, too, although the truth is I would prefer to clothe my own family. There are other things in my setup I don't like.

On Dean's sixth birthday, his grandmother presented him with an English bicycle that would have been appropriate for a boy of twelve. Dean was not only too young to appreciate the value of the bicycle; it was too dangerous for him to use in a neighborhood as overrun with traffic as ours. Abby wouldn't allow him to ride the bike anywhere except in our handkerchief-size back yard, which was okay with me. However, she then nagged at the boy for being clumsy and slow in learning to ride the bike. Dean has grown too fast and is poorly coordinated, but I'm sure Abby's nagging isn't helpful to him.

Eventually the bicycle became such a bone of contention between Dean and his mother that the boy came to dislike it. Twice he pushed the bike out in the alley for the trash man to collect, but I managed to recover it without Abby knowing. When he left it in a rainstorm, she found out and there was a terrible row. Abby squabbles with Dean as though both of them were the same age. Sorry as I feel for him, there isn't much a father can do.

In my estimation, Abby sets impossibly high standards for our oldest son. She raises cain at Dean's awkwardness, his noisiness. She compares him unfavorably with his younger brothers, objects because he is too shy to make friends his own age, although she is so shy she won't call on a neighbor or visit Dean's school. I wish

Abby would realize she is too hard on an eight-year-old while her mother is too easy.

I think the primary cause of my breakdown two years ago was probably my mother-in-law. In the hospital I learned to live and let live. I now can take my mother-in-law's interference in our plans and her constant carping without too much pain. Neither she nor my father-in-law has ever accepted me as a son. The day after Abby and I were married the two of them and her Aunt Ida drove to the hotel where we were honeymooning. My mother-in-law invited my bride to drive home with them right then or to return at any time the marriage wasn't satisfactory. I moved to the West Coast in the hope of putting half a continent between Abby and her parents. I made a big mistake when I let Abby talk me into leaving Dean in their care. Instead of our going back for our baby, my in-laws brought Dean to the West, liked the climate, and stayed. The climate they liked best was in the neighborhood where Abby and I own a home. They bought a house only two blocks from ours.

My mother-in-law pops in on inspection tours at least once a day with the result that Abby wears herself out cleaning and dusting and vacuuming. She races for the mop and broom if her mother lifts an eyebrow. Even so, she can't measure up. A couple of weeks ago I walked in from the barber shop to find Abby tearful and angry. Her mother had found a few specks of dirt on our curtains and had washed, starched, ironed, and rehung the lot. For good measure she had also scrubbed the woodwork in our bathroom, although Abby scrubs it every second day.

Since Abby is nearly always on some kind of diet and hungry as a bear, she tires and flies off the handle easily. Her mother's peculiar eating habits—my mother-in-law starves all week and stuffs on Saturday and Sunday—seem to keep her weight close to normal. Those same eating habits don't suit Abby, but she is constantly exposed to them. We spend our week ends with my in-laws—all our week ends. For the past seven years I've played pinochle with my father-in-law every Saturday and Sunday afternoon—I dislike pinochle—and several hundred times I've watched my mother-in-law look at an overloaded dining table and heard her say, "Let's be sure and finish off everything, and then we can start dieting tomorrow."

My mother-in-law cooks enough to supply an army. The uneaten food is packed in the car for us to carry home. One Sunday several months ago, as we drove away, Abby began regretting she had accepted a coconut pie and a big chunk of cake. I pulled up at the curb and set the pie and cake on the sidewalk. Before I reached the end of the block I had to turn the car around, go back, and pick up the stuff we didn't want or need. Abby couldn't bear the slight risk of hurting her mother's feelings, and she wasn't willing to waste good food. She ate the pie and cake that night.

Abby and I have been married for nine years. Her parents' influence still surpasses mine. Although Abby hasn't said so, my guess is that she secretly disapproves of sex. Never in any way in nine years has she indicated that she wants my love. On the contrary, more than once, she has seemed to be shocked if I approach her in the mornings or afternoons. We haven't discussed the issue, but I'm convinced she believes sex should be confined to the night hours. I don't agree. I'm home in the daytime a good part of the week. I see nothing wrong with love in the sunlight and the morning.

I don't blame Abby for her beliefs. It's virtually impossible to escape the dominance of a woman like my mother-in-law. By hook or crook she contrives to even the score. Last summer I was determined to manage my two-weeks' vacation without her advice. I packed Abby and the three boys in the car, and we took off to Arizona. When we got back we discovered two new orange trees had been planted in our yard in places we didn't want orange trees, that our kitchen had been repainted in a color we didn't like, and that all five of us had been provided with brand-new bedspreads.

Abby thinks her weight is rough on our marriage, but I consider the weight of our other problems is more important.

✻   ✻

Abby and Clark Johnson were drifting toward trouble of a serious nature. Although Abby's inability to push away from the table brought her to the Institute, both she and Clark were aware that other disturbing elements existed in their marriage.

Our first prescription to Abby was the purchase of a full-length mirror. She bought the mirror and hung it in their hall so she would catch sight of herself every time she passed. It was a real effort, but each day she stood before the mirror for a full five minutes and studied her reflection from every angle. This practice in facing the facts about her figure was a useful adjunct to her counseling and helped her to avoid binges of compulsive eating. Previously she had overeaten whenever she was bored, lonesome, self-pitying, depressed, jealous of Clark and his outside interests, annoyed at her mother, or squabbling with small Dean.

Her physician prescribed a sensible diet for her which she followed conscientiously. Within six months she had dropped to 154 pounds and was well on the way to the 140 pounds suitable for a young woman of her height and build. Her desire to lose 80 pounds was unrealistic; Abby does bear a marked physical resemblance to Marilyn Monroe, but at 115, Abby would be a rack of bones.

At the end of three weeks, as a matter of fact, Abby walked jauntily into the counseling office and for the first time removed the loose, bulky coat she had worn to conceal a dress with popping seams. She had lost just 7 pounds, but her posture was vastly improved, the same dress fit nicely, and her spirits were high.

By then we had briefly surveyed the early days that had laid the foundation of her compulsive eating and emotional problems. In the first place, as a child Abby formed improper eating habits by imitating the eating habits of her elders. No physician would recommend living on grapefruit and coffee all week—as Abby's mother often does to this day—and then gorging over the week end.

In the second place, Abby's parents held before her the idea she was superior and at all times must turn in a superior performance. A girl of average intelligence, Abby always felt that nothing she accomplished was quite good enough. There is no question that her mother and father love her dearly, but she grew up in an atmosphere of parental possessiveness and overrated material possessions instead of true warmth. Because her mother worked in order to give her only child "the best of everything," Abby did not feel herself to be a part of a functioning family in the community. Her feelings of social uneasiness were strengthened by streams of advice from her elders: "Don't trust anyone but your family." On occasion, when Abby's parents were at odds, her mother would narrow the list of the acceptable to exclude the husband and father of the household and advise Abby to trust nobody except Mother.

Although Abby was left to herself more than the average child, her parents expected to choose her friends, clothes, activities, to make her decisions for her. At times she was subjected to sharp discipline, but for the most part she was coddled and petted; she was not trained to see an enterprise through if she tired of it and preferred to do something else.

This inconsistent upbringing laid the groundwork for her bouts with the knife and fork and for many of the unsatisfactory factors in her marriage. Since Abby had been taught to believe "Mother and Father know best," she felt guilty and uncertain about any independent opinion she reached. When Clark failed to win her parents' approval, she was incapable of standing up for him and defending her right to choose a husband. Her way of handling her divided and warring loyalties was to overeat and to brood. Her silence was interpreted by her mother and father *and* her husband as being an admission that she had made a poor marriage. In this fashion, she reinforced the domination of her parents and lessened Clark's confidence in himself and his ability to help her.

Abby needed to teach herself how to stick to a diet, not only to lose weight but to increase her own feelings of self-confidence and adequacy. Her paramount need, however, was to acknowledge and prove that Clark and her sons deserved first claim on her loyalty, emotional support, and energy.

Abby struck her first blow for mature independence in an amusingly domestic way. Clark brought home a glider for their terrace. His mother-in-law did not admire the glider, took it back to the store, and used the refund to buy two lawn chairs.

Abby returned the lawn chairs and came home with Clark's original purchase. Next afternoon when the inevitable drop-in occurred and this flouting of authority was discovered, Abby stood her ground and insisted that the glider remain. She carried her rebellion still further. Her sink was full of dishes, and she was helping Dean with a reading lesson. She refused to allow her mother to wash the dishes or to relieve Dean of his homework in favor of play.

Since then the Johnsons have changed their living conditions, and Abby has changed her appearance, and, more important, her personality almost beyond recognition. Los Angeles County covers a lot of space. Abby and Clark and their three children now live thirty-five miles from her parents; daily visiting back and forth has become impractical. Abby's mother and father, originally miffed by the move, are now resigned to the separation. Abby now understands the motivation for much of her irritation with her eldest son. To her mind and emotions, Dean was her mother's child, not hers. Further to complicate matters, the boy's awkwardness reminded her unpleasantly of her own awkwardness as a youngster. She held up to Dean the same overhigh standards that had confronted her in childhood and felt frustrated and a failure whenever Dean failed.

Dean is a bright youngster. He readily responded to love and praise where he had sullenly withstood criticism and resented the favoritism Abby showed the younger children. Dean's muscular coordination still lags—it is doubtful he will ever be a top-ranking athlete—but he quickly climbed scholastically. Dean's school in the new neighborhood, like many others in the nation, is understaffed and overcrowded. As her first conscious effort to end her self-imposed isolation, Abby offered herself as a room mother, a volunteer, part-time assistant to Dean's teacher. The offer was accepted. Naturally Dean was pleased and proud, and Abby met other young mothers and made friends.

Nowadays Abby and Clark spend perhaps a third of their weekend time with her parents (they no longer carry home rich cakes, puddings, pies); they spend the balance of their week ends with their own friends or pursuing hobbies they now share. Clark's working hours are abominable; during the work week he seldom arrives home before midnight. But Abby now understands his need for relaxing before sleep; at her request he wakes her when he comes in. She has a special easy chair in his new hobby room. She sits there in her negligee while Clark files his coins and stamps—he picked up many of his hobbies during his hospital stay—and they discuss the events of the day until finally they retire.

We don't know, to the pound, Abby's present weight. She is still sensitive on this subject. But the last time we saw her she was so radiant with happiness that it is doubtful if anybody's eyes could leave her glowing face long enough to study the dimensions of her waistline.

* *

Nearly always there are emotional problems behind obesity, and unless these problems are removed, we have discovered at the Institute that no amount of reducing is likely to be permanent. The personality study we make of every client indicates that women who seek our assistance in conquering excess weight are, like Abby Johnson, usually low in self-mastery. Many of them have masculine strivings—in other words, they are discontented with their own sex and wish they had been born male. As a general rule they have strong desires for satisfaction in many directions, and when the desires are unfulfilled, they eat to compensate.

Frequently in middle age, a woman feels that she is losing some of her attractiveness, that some of the romance is going out of her life, that her children no longer need her attention, and she turns to food as a substitute. Then as her waistline expands, she becomes even less attractive in her own eyes and increasingly dejected. When this happens, her husband often becomes disgusted and withdraws his affection at the very time the wife is most in need of affection. Whenever possible we talk to such men, explain the great value of encouragement and moral support to their wives, and in most instances we get cooperation.

Our practice is to attack obesity with all the weapons at our command. We always ask the client to obtain the proper, low-calorie diet from a physician. Then we try to help her to find new satisfactions by working for and with others in the community and by finding some creative outlet. Of course we also recommend outdoor exercise.

If it is possible we advise the dieter to participate in group counseling. Abby Johnson could not spare the time to join one of our groups. Each group is composed of ten women. All are struggling to lose weight and, guided by a counselor, give each other sympathy and reassurance. They keep a careful record of their weight, and at the weekly meetings each woman who has not lost a pound forfeits ten cents; if she has gained weight she forfeits twenty-five cents. Every three months they spend the accumulated forfeits to give themselves and their counselor a party (with very, very low-calorie refreshments). We have found group counseling very beneficial in helping those who need to lose weight, although solving the individual emotional problems of the afflicted person is, of course, of more importance.

❖   ❖   ❖

Kyra Hobart, two years older than Abby Johnson, looked even more unhappy when we saw her first. She was six months pregnant and the mother of a baby daughter, but she was planning to leave her husband. It was Brad Hobart's gambling, Kyra said, trying to keep back the tears, that was destroying their marriage:

❖   ❖

Last year Brad lost almost $2,000—nearly a third of his salary and commissions as a salesman. I haven't enough cash to buy a decent layette for the baby I'm expecting. Our two-year-old daughter is so poorly dressed the neighborhood youngsters laugh at her. After the new baby is born, I intend to return to teaching in order to support my children and myself. I don't know what will happen to Brad. I don't consider it my duty to pay the debts of a man who puts horses and cards ahead of the welfare of his wife and family. Even if I were willing to support Brad, and he was willing to let me, I couldn't earn enough to keep up with his gambling losses.

I still love the man I married six years ago. Brad used to be dependable, thoughtful, considerate. He has turned into an untrustworthy stranger. We once lived in harmony and peace. We now live in a financial nightmare. Our creditors hound me incessantly. Until our telephone was disconnected for nonpayment, it rang all the time. Bill collectors camp on our doorstep, trail me and little Sally to the market. Our creditors know that I still try to pay our bills. Brad doesn't even try. He just tosses the unopened envelopes on my desk. Then, as likely as not, he slips off to a race track or some bookie hangout and loses still more money.

On my wedding day, I thought I understood and knew my husband as well as I knew myself. Brad and I didn't rush into marriage. We fell in love practically on sight—Brad proposed the week we met—but he was in the Army at the time and I was a college sophomore. We waited until he completed his Army service, and I got my degree. The long engagement was my idea. I wanted to be very sure our love would last. Neither Brad nor I came from happy homes. His parents were divorced years ago, and my parents are hopelessly incompatible. An angel from heaven couldn't live in peace with my mother. Her bossiness has made my poor father's existence a misery.

I once shared Brad's hopes and ambitions, as he seemed to share mine. I taught school for three years after our marriage to help us get established. While both of us were earning, we bought and furnished a home. Brad built a guest cottage in the back yard to carry the mortgage payments. His father, a successful wholesale grocer, located a good job for him with a frozen food company. In those days, I thought Brad would advance fast. Together, we accumulated a sizable savings account.

For three years we got along fine. Brad is a sweet and gentle lover. Our honeymoon was wonderful. Our sexual adjustment was perfect. For three years I had no worries of any kind. However, Brad fretted about my working—despite his present behavior, he is extremely proud and sensitive—and he kept on begging me to stay at home and be just a wife. After we finally saved $1,000 I gave up my teaching, and soon Sally was on the way.

While I was pregnant that first time, all our troubles commenced. It took me quite a while to realize that something had happened to Brad, that he had changed. Possibly I should have sensed the difference. It still seems incredible to me he would choose the very time I was carrying his first child—the child he had begged for—to start on the road that is leading him to ruin.

During my pregnancy with Sally, he was far more tender and considerate than the average husband. I have never been especially interested in housework or cooking. Brad took charge of the marketing, helped with the meals and dishwashing, treated me as though I were a baby myself. I did notice there were evenings he arrived home very late. I assumed he was calling on prospective customers. I have always been ambitious for him. Consequently, I didn't object to his absences.

The week Sally was born, I found out how Brad had been spending his time and our savings. One morning my hospital bill—which I thought he had settled—was delivered to my room. A few minutes later Brad arrived with flowers, and I spoke to him about the bill. He seemed upset and embarrassed, but said he'd pay at the desk when he left. His manner was so strange I checked with the cashier during the afternoon, and sure enough Brad had paid. But then my father-in-law telephoned and told me Brad had borrowed $100 from him.

I was in a fever of nerves and anxiety until Brad's evening visit. When I asked for an explanation of the borrowing, he tried to evade my questions at first. Eventually he broke down and confessed he'd lost nearly all our savings gambling. His humiliation was a dreadful thing to see. He looked like a little boy I once caught cheating in my classroom. He begged me to forgive him. He promised to reform.

That was two years ago. Brad has been gambling ever since, gambling uncontrollably. Today he is as financially irresponsible as a child of six. He says he can't help it. His whole attitude is baffling to me. In my opinion, Brad doesn't actually *enjoy* gambling. With him, it seems to be almost a sickness. There are times he suffers such agonies of shame my heart aches for him. There are other times I almost hate him.

We go from one financial crisis to the next. I owe the milkman forty dollars, I owe my mother seventy-five dollars, I owe two years of back taxes, I'm behind on all our utility bills. Brad owes $600 to his father. I don't know the exact amounts he owes elsewhere; he tries to conceal his borrowing from me just as he tries to hide his gambling losses. In the early days of our marriage I kept a careful budget, paid our bills on the dot, and banked a regular amount each week. No budget is possible with a husband who gambles.

Our home and guest cottage are our sole remaining possessions of value, and recently Brad began clamoring for an increase in our mortgage. I do not intend to put our real estate at his disposal. We both know what would happen. Last January I learned I was pregnant again. I was desperate. One night Brad came in late and found me crying over a stack of unpaid bills. When he put his arms around me and asked what was wrong, I went to pieces. For the first time, I threatened to leave him. I don't make idle threats. He knew I meant it. He was terrified. He was filled with self-reproach. I made him sit down and go through the stack of household bills and add up the figures. There the story was—how much his gambling had cost us.

Brad acknowledged his future, our future, was at stake. We worked out a financial arrangement that seemed foolproof. Since he couldn't resist temptation—and admitted it—the two of us decided I would take charge of all our money. When he went to work next morning, Brad requested his company to mail his salary checks and commission checks straight to me. Every Saturday I divided up his earnings and paid a little to each of our creditors. I kept only enough money to buy food and give Brad a four-dollar weekly allowance. With an allowance that small, I didn't see how he could possibly get in trouble. Indeed he had so little spending money he was obliged either to cut out cigarettes or skip lunches. I didn't think a few sacrifices would hurt him. I, too, was sacrificing. I took no allowance for myself.

Within a few weeks Brad was right back at gambling. While I was paying old debts he ran up new debts. Brad is persuasive and charming. First, he borrowed from his friends. When he exhausted that list, he began to borrow from company customers. One of the customers is now pressing him for payment. Inevitably his boss will hear about that, and then he will be out of a job. Brad knows it, too. Strangely enough, this seems only to provide him with a further incentive to gamble. Now he feels he must win.

In trying to win back what he has lost, Brad gets in deeper and deeper. To his mind, he has had bad luck, and his luck is certain to turn. In our endless arguments he often tells me he is bound to hit a winning streak and that then he will quit gambling forever. I don't for a minute believe that good luck at cards and horses—even a long run of good luck—will cure him. He needs to change his thinking, his whole point of view. But apparently he has convinced himself he can't do it. And he has convinced me.

Brad does almost unbelievable things, sneaky, dishonest things, to finance his gambling sprees. Just last month he took the week's grocery money from my purse—intending, of course, to put it back. Somebody had given him a hot tip. The horse lost. We had a terrible scene. I cried, Brad cried, little Sally woke, and she cried. The old, tired promises of reform were trotted out. The very next day Brad wrote a fifty-dollar check that was no good, and he lost the fifty dollars in a poker game. The bank called me, and I had to phone his father who covered the check.

I cannot understand how Brad can bear to obligate himself that way. He loathes his father. My father-in-law is openhanded with money when he chooses to be but is intolerably patronizing. He is as free with orders and criticism and unwelcome advice as my mother. I am sure he treated Brad badly in his boyhood, and now he insults Brad at every opportunity.

If my father-in-law hadn't made me a personal loan—a loan I personally intend to return—I couldn't pay for my confinement. The money I borrowed is now in a safety deposit box so Brad can't get at it. My father-in-law insisted on the precaution, and I guess he was wise.

If I could help Brad I would stick by him even now. I can't help him so long as he refuses to help himself. My mother and my father-in-law both say I should get a divorce and go back to teaching. They say the children and I are entitled to live like normal human beings. Brad swears up and down he loves me and Sally and wants the new baby. Perhaps, in his strange, selfish way, he does love us. That isn't good enough for me. I cannot live with a man whom I pity a great deal, love at times, but for whom I have no respect.

❖   ❖

On twenty-eight-year-old Brad Hobart's handsome face there was an odd mixture of defensiveness and defiance as he confided to us:

❖   ❖

There's something about this business that Kyra doesn't know. When I was in the service I was lucky at cards. I left the Army with several thousand dollars in poker winnings. This may sound screwy, but in my mind that money stood for more than money. To me, my winnings went to prove I was just as smart as the other fellows, or even smarter.

I got a boot, a big boot, out of being good at something for once in my life. My father used to say I was the most brainless kid on earth. After my parents were divorced—I elected to live with my mother —he predicted I would wind up in the gutter. At the moment you are probably thinking my old man was quite a crystal-gazer. I don't blame you.

My best friends think I'm a heel. Everybody thinks so, up to and including me. I don't need to be told that I'm breaking Kyra's heart. I know I should never touch another card or bet another horse. I know I should reform. How to do it is the question. Three years of almost steady losing should be convincing evidence that my luck in the service was a fluke, but I ignore the evidence. My common sense tells me I was born a bad-luck guy. In the mornings when I wake up, I think of my losses and the spot I'm in, and I feel sick, physically sick. By nightfall my fine resolutions are forgotten. Invariably I break my promises to myself. Worse, I break my solemn promises to Kyra.

What's wrong with a guy like me? I have a little girl I love and another baby on the way. I have a nice home, thanks to Kyra. Why can't I count my blessings, quit gambling, and behave like other family men?

I have a good job, as sales jobs go. My income is adequate to support any family not in debt. By being careful, and with Kyra's help, I could even whittle down my debts. I particularly want to pay off my father and get him out of my marriage and out of my life. I'm not doing it.

It's easy for me to find ways to squander money. I have the use of a company car to make my calls on customers. My daily route leads me directly past the Santa Anita race track. In fifteen minutes you can drop a hundred dollars there if you've got the dough and are so inclined. Part of the year the track is closed. But Kyra and I live right next to a little town where gambling is legal, and the gambling houses operate a twelve-month season. Day or night you can drop in and match your poker wits against the next fellow's. My family isn't the only family that has suffered. You can look around the premises any time and see people who are taking a flyer with next week's grocery money.

When I sit down at a poker table, I never expect to lose. When I reach for my cards across the green felt a little inner voice, stronger than my conscience, stronger than my will, seems to whisper to me that this time I'm bound to hit. Life can be boring, frustrating. At least I find it so. When I'm at home Kyra looks at me with wounded eyes, with contemptuous eyes, and I feel like the worm I am. On my calls I'm pushed around by my customers; in the office I'm pushed around by my boss. In a poker game I can be a king—for a little while.

When I am winning I am flooded with a sense of power and of calm. I feel certain, absolutely certain, that my luck has come to stay. I imagine myself rushing home and pouring thousands of dollars in Kyra's lap, seeing her eyes open wide with surprise and admiration, as I tell her our financial troubles are over. So I stick with the game too long and lose my winnings and more, too. Now I am so far in the cellar I can't afford to quit. It's hard for me to concede bad luck can pursue a man forever.

When I married Kyra, I intended to be a good husband, a responsible citizen. Kyra is the only person, except my little girl, who has ever loved me. My mother was too busy fighting her own battles with my father to show much affection for us kids. She is dead now. She was a sweet woman but weak and lacking in will power—like me. I used to try to take her part. One time I recall my father jumped up from the supper table in a rage and told her before us kids that he was sick to death of his home and was spending the night with another woman. When he started for the garage my mother ran after him, crying, and he turned around and knocked her down. I made a jump for him. He grabbed up a carving knife and threw it at me. The knife grazed my cheek and then stuck, quivering, in the kitchen door. I reached for the knife, shouting I would kill him. But then I froze. When he hit her again, I broke out in tears and just stood there. My parents were divorced when I was twelve.

The first time Kyra ever smiled at me I wanted her to be my wife. When she finally married me, I knew the meaning of joy. Now I could have a real home. For a long while I did everything in my power to make Kyra happy. In some ways, she isn't exactly an easy girl to please. My picture of our marriage wasn't quite the same as hers. Before I joined the Army, I had two years of college, and it was my ambition to be an architect. I figured Kyra and I could rent a small apartment, and I could finish college, using my G.I. benefits.

Kyra thought one degree per family, her degree, represented plenty of education. She also thought architecture was a chancy profession. I wanted a house full of kids. Before we started our family, Kyra said I needed to be set with a well-paying job, and we needed to own a home. She made perfect sense. She always does. While I was hunting a job, Kyra and my father put their heads together and turned up a better job than I was able to locate. I found myself working as a salesman for a frozen food company. I don't like the food business, maybe because my father boasts so much about his brilliance as a wholesale grocer. I'm not the back-slapping salesman type. I prefer working with my hands or at a drawing board.

I had a chance to use my hands when Kyra bought a piece of land and decided the time had come for us to build a house. She also decided a back-yard cottage would yield extra income. I did most of the construction work, except for the plumbing and the wiring. There was no need for my drawing board. Kyra drew rough sketches of both our places, and I followed her directions. When we moved in our home, I thought she would resign her teaching job, and we would begin our family. But Kyra then decided we needed a $1,000 backlog to cover emergencies and that she should teach another year. In order to get the backlog, we cut our spending to the bone. Kyra gave up beauty parlors, went bare-legged, bought no clothes. It used to make me feel cheap to see her run around without stockings. When she suggested I cut down on my cigarette and lunch money, I did so. In the Army I never carried less than one hundred dollars in my pocket. I felt pinched and embarrassed in the company of the free-spending salesmen I met.

Sometimes, even in the early days of our marriage, there seemed to be no fun for me in the things we got by planning. Quite often I felt crowded and hemmed in, and caught myself looking back on my Army days as almost a period of freedom. I didn't complain to Kyra. I was ashamed to seem ungrateful, critical, quarrelsome. In those days I was determined she and I weren't ever going to quarrel as my parents had quarreled and that I would never raise my voice or bellow like my father.

After we finally got the $1,000, Kyra turned in her teaching contract. When she became pregnant with Sally, I walked on the clouds. I thought nothing was too good for her. At that time my company, a big wholesale concern, was offering a $500 prize to the salesman who peddled the most frozen chickens to his retail customers. Kyra was bound and determined I should get the $500 prize. So I went out to win it. For three months, with her cheering me on, I worked my tail off and blanketed the Los Angeles area with frozen poultry. Eventually I won top place and cinched the prize with a comfortable margin of 500 cases of chickens. Anyway, so I believed from the Friday night the contest closed until Monday morning. It then developed I had only won a moral victory. One of my customers, a big chain-store buyer with ten retail outlets, bought a thousand cases of chickens from me on Friday and put on weekend sales in the ten stores. The retail bargain sales flopped. On Monday morning the buyer returned 700 cases of unsold chickens to my company, a thing he had no right to do. But he claimed I had upped his order without authorization, that no contract existed. I had an order book in my pocket carrying his signature in black and white. I showed it to my boss. Afraid to risk offending the buyer and losing the chain's future business, my boss ran out on me. He tore up my order blank, took back 700 cases of chickens with profuse apologies, and then forced me to apologize to the buyer for a "mistake" all three of us knew I hadn't made.

Failing Kyra was worse than missing out on the $500. Her disappointment was hard to take. She doesn't understand the food business. She didn't say a great deal. But I could tell she blamed me for dropping from first to second place in the contest almost as much as I blamed that cut-throat buyer and my yellow-livered boss. I felt so sore about the whole affair I wanted to duck the convention where the prize—my prize—was to be awarded to somebody else. Kyra thought it wouldn't be sporting or manly for me to stay away. The company was meeting the travel and hotel expenses. She gave me twenty dollars spending money.

On the train, some of the fellows started a poker game. I hadn't played a hand of poker since my Army days. For a while I watched. Then suddenly I asked to be dealt in the game. Maybe, like a fool, I figured I would win $500 to take home to Kyra. My twenty dollars were gone in nothing flat. I got hot under the collar, excited. Almost before I knew it, I turned to a kibitzer and borrowed fifty dollars. The fifty dollars went too.

I couldn't go home to Kyra and admit that in addition to losing the contest I'd whopped off seventy dollars. I thought I would win back the seventy dollars on the return trip and clear the slate without her knowing it. On the return trip, I lost one hundred dollars. Then and there I was hooked. Since I took that convention trip, I have lost nearly $5,000 trying to get back $170 and be even with the board. The way I feel is the poker tables and the tracks *owe* me the money I have invested there. If I ever once get even, I can quit.

Anyway, that's what I think some of the time. Other times I decide I'm kidding myself and that I will never quit, that I can't quit. Often I am convinced I was fated to be a rotten human being and a rotten husband like my old man. His vices are women and whisky. Me—I'm stuck with gambling. To raise a gambling stake I will stoop to anything. The urge is irresistible. The only time I feel really good, really wide-awake and alive, is when I'm gambling. How I wish I knew a way to break loose from the spell, the fascination! Unless you can help me, my wife and kids will leave me, my job will leave me, and I will be done for.

✿   ✿

Kyra and Brad Hobart were both agreed that all the faults in the marriage were on Brad's side, that she was blameless. While professing his desire to reform, Brad was eluding the discomfort of reform by pleading lack of will power. This dodge, a favorite with gamblers and drinkers, is hard to get around. It is not possible to set a man in a chair, serve him a portion of will power, and make him swallow it.

Excessive gambling, like excessive drinking, is nearly always rooted in a hidden psychological dilemma. Brad proclaimed his love for Kyra, but it was curious he had begun to gamble during her first pregnancy and had been gambling heavily during her second pregnancy. His failure in the company contest readily explained the first poker game, but did not explain the years of reckless gambling that followed. Some emotionally immature men consider a wife's pregnancy as a rejection of themselves, and some gamblers substitute the thrill of the pari-mutuel machine and the roulette wheel for sexuality. This was not the case with Brad. His sexual relationship with Kyra was good. He desired children. Then why would he gamble away the family money at a time Kyra had most need of his emotional and financial support? Some gamblers, guided by obscure and difficult-to-explain motivations, subconsciously want to lose their money, wind up penniless, and thereby punish themselves. Although Brad told us there were occasions when he was relieved to lose the last dollar in his pocket so he could leave the gambling house and go home to bed, we did not think he wanted to punish himself.

It seemed to us that Brad's gambling represented a subconscious attack on Kyra. It appeared that he subconsciously wanted to punish and hurt his wife. The question was: why?

We had further interviews with Kyra and Brad. Slowly, a different picture of their marriage emerged. On the surface Kyra was not bossy. Nevertheless she was a clever, soft-spoken version of the critical, pushy, domineering mother she very much disliked. In marrying Brad, Kyra got a husband whose self-confidence was already badly shaken by his abusive, domineering father. Brad needed to be built up by his wife. Instead, Kyra did the exact opposite. She began by placing him in a sales job he disliked—a type of work, incidentally, to which he was temperamentally unfitted—and furthermore she got his father's assistance in doing so. Before the honeymoon was over, Brad's love (his wife) and his enemy (his father) were, in his mind and feelings, conspiring together against him. Easygoing Brad did not protest and scarcely acknowledged his resentments.

Next Kyra maneuvered herself into a position where she made the decisions, did all the planning, managed the family budget. It is hardly surprising that Brad was not interested in household bills. Until his gambling produced a crisis, he was never shown any of the bills. Kyra paid them. Brad was impulsive, generous. Kyra was cautious and—adamant. From the first week of his job, she decided the amount of Brad's personal spending money. It was all very well for thrifty Kyra to save on beauty parlors, but she had no right to inquire into the sums Brad spent in the barber shop.

Kyra treated her husband like one of her adolescent students. Without either of the two realizing it, she created for Brad an emotional atmosphere very similar to the detested atmosphere of his childhood. He felt stifled and thwarted in his work, stifled and thwarted in his home. Guiltily, he suppressed the feelings. By his code, criticisms of Kyra were *verboten*. Too often he had heard his father shout abuses at his mother. Imprisoned in an emotional trap set and sprung by his wife, Brad simmered inwardly.

He was virtually compelled to find a release from the boredom, frustration, and tensions of a life where he had so little choice of action. In some fashion he had to assert the manhood his wife had subtly stolen away. Liquor and infidelity—his father's vices—had no appeal for him. Gambling provided a perfect escape hatch, a perfect means of punishing Kyra, who robbed him of gaiety and fun and freedom and who thwarted him emotionally as he had been thwarted in his childhood.

Before Brad could break the chains that bound him—he was a real slave to gambling—he needed to understand the psychological reasons for his plight. Kyra also needed to acquire an understanding of her husband and herself. Then the conditions of their life together needed to be changed.

Kyra was appalled when she came to recognize her resemblance to her mother. By reflecting each night on her suggestions of the day to Brad, her little hints, her maneuvers to triumph over him and get her own way, she perceived the truth. Almost immediately, she dropped her habit of command. She began to seek Brad's opinions, ask his advice, lean on him whenever possible. She also stopped requesting his assistance with the housework. Kyra was inclined to take advantage of pregnancy, and she had been imposing on her husband. Among the males of Brad's acquaintance housework was not customary. Drying dishes and washing diapers made Brad feel servile; he was a man who already felt too servile, too pushed around and put upon. Only when he was gambling did he feel a sense of mastery, a confidence that he stood equal with his fellows. He felt a failure in his marriage, a failure in his business, a failure in his personality and character, but he felt he could beat the wheel, the pari-mutuel machine, the cards. For always there was a chance. Kyra set out to make Brad *feel* like a success. She gave him many proofs of her love and trust and awakened his slumbering self-respect.

Kyra requested no promise, but once again Brad promised to stop gambling. This promise, unlike his promises in the past, was real to him. He now understood his gambling was a symptom of an emotional dissatisfaction and frustration for which he was not wholly responsible. He realized there were mature ways of asserting the manliness to which he was entitled. He forced himself to become a more dominant partner in the marriage. He did not bottle up his resentments. If Kyra forgot to ask his advice in a household matter, he pressed his ideas on her. If she showed signs of brushing his wishes aside, he resisted.

Boredom, being at loose ends, can be fatal to a person who has the habit of gambling. In order to fortify his promise to himself and steel his resolution, Brad took another concrete step. He found an evening job—a physically exhausting job—at a drive-in restaurant. He earned an extra sixty dollars a week. The long hours filled the time when otherwise he might have been tempted to gamble. The hard work helped to alleviate his deep feelings of guilt. Brad was the kind of man who had a definite emotional need to expiate past sins.

On the practical side, the extra money he earned assisted materially in reducing the size of his debts. His nighttime income was directly applied to past-due loans and bills. Brad collected his own earnings and made the payments in person. He now was handling the family finances. It took him eighteen months of hard work to climb to solvency. During this period, Brad's taste—his craze—for gambling left him. Assisted by Kyra's encouragement, the change in her and in their emotional environment, he cured himself of gambling fever.

Brad and Kyra are now the parents of three, two girls and a boy, of whom they are very proud. They are buying insurance policies which will put all three children through college, although the payments are stiff for them to meet. Brad gave up selling frozen food a year ago and went into the construction business. Kyra applauded the decision. It seems unlikely Brad will ever be able to complete his architectural studies, but he enjoys his present work.

The last time we saw Kyra and Brad, he said: "In many cases similar to mine I am sure the trouble is never resolved because many gamblers feel too degraded to seek help. Kyra and I and our children were saved from ruin because of the counseling we received. Now that Kyra and I understand what was behind my gambling, I have no further need of it. Gambling just bores me. Kyra and I are free and we are happy."

Section V: Summing Up

Luckily, not all marriages are as seriously threatened as were the marriages of the couples we have discussed. However, many people who never have seen and never will see a marriage counselor might solve some of their day-by-day domestic problems with more ease if they had a clearer comprehension of the ingredients that make a happy marriage.

According to scores of studies conducted at the Institute through the years, the majority of successful marriages depend in great measure upon the similarities between a man and wife. The couples who get along best in wedlock usually share similar backgrounds, tastes, habits, attitudes. In choosing a husband or wife it is a sound idea to select someone with whom you have a great deal in common. If your marriage is in trouble, the chances are that your difficulties stem from a lack of similarity between you and your spouse at some important point. Locate the dissimilarity, not always a simple process, modify or compromise it, cherish your similarities, and you are launched on the road to success.

In our experience the major differences between the average husband and wife fall into a few broad categories. In-laws, as has been previously pointed out, regularly touch off explosive battles in many households. Another great troublemaker is recreation or, rather, lack of recreation. Time and again our counselors can bolster a faltering marriage by helping the husband and wife find some wholesome, inexpensive, satisfying social or creative activities to pursue which break the monotony of daily life and provide them with something to think and talk about together. Arguments in this field are quite natural; usually the husband's work lies outside the home while the wife's lies inside. By definition, recreation means doing something different from what you have been doing. Something different for the wife is to go out in the evening; something different for the husband is to stay at home!

Leisure time should be budgeted just as intelligently and conscientiously as finances. It is up to the husband to make some concessions, even some sacrifices of his own comfort, to give his wife a fair share of social life. On the other hand, the wife should take pains to see that this social life is of a kind that her husband also enjoys. She should not attempt to drag a rabid baseball fan to a Bach festival.

Judging by our records, family finances seem to cause less dissension among our clients than in the past. Nevertheless, arguments over spending, with accusations of extravagance hurled from both sides, still mar many marriages. Few young people have adequate training in money management. Even in this day and age a young husband sometimes automatically assumes that he will handle all the finances and dole out to his wife the amount he thinks she needs. Although he may be liberal and freehanded, his bride is almost certain to feel put upon and defrauded. One of our students, a mature matron, remarked in a thesis, "Many men are generous financially with their wives but very few men are financially *just* with their wives." Her point was well taken. An intelligent young woman, who has probably earned her own living and handled her salary competently before marriage, is seldom content to exist on handouts after the wedding ceremony. A simple but businesslike budget should be part of the first equipment in any new home, and it should include a separate allowance, in proportion to the total income, for both husband and wife.

Disagreement as to how the children should be reared is a highly damaging form of conflict in the home, and our recent statistics show the conflict to be very common among our clients, particularly among the better educated. Sometimes the trouble arises from what the textbooks call "the cultural lag of the male." In plain English, the husband is a generation behind his wife in understanding the nature of children. As a rule she has taken courses in child guidance in high school or college. She has attended child study groups, talked with other mothers, gained a few modern ideas. Her husband, who has missed these opportunities, is inclined to cling to the dubious proposition that the way he was raised is the best way, that what was good enough for him is good enough for junior.

In these cases, our recommendation is that the husband increase his knowledge of present-day educational trends and theories. There are scores of inexpensive and excellent books readily available which any father can read. A fairly high percentage of classes for parents is conducted by women, even by unmarried women, and the average male is resistant to such a source of knowledge. But our experience indicates that most men are willing, and indeed eager, to attend evening lectures or discussions led by masculine educators. In any case, it is imperative for the well-being of the children and the marriage that the husband and wife agree upon the way to bring up their youngsters.

Sexual disharmony has long been recognized as a leading cause of unhappiness in marriage. In most instances, no anatomical or physiological peculiarity is to blame, and the trouble can be explained by a dissimilarity of attitudes on the subject. Successful sexual adjustment depends more on feelings of love, companionship, and mutual consideration than on any technique. If sexual intercourse is based on self-love rather than on love for another, the relationship neither brings nor begets true intimacy and warmth.

Unfortunately, many young couples are so poorly prepared by their parents they are obliged to work out their sexual problems after marriage. Sex should be a powerful force in drawing two persons together. Obviously, this can hardly be true when a girl has been taught from infancy that sex is evil, nasty, or dangerous. Nor is it true when a man has grown up with the belief that sex is a matter of self-gratification, useful for the exploitation of females. Often we find that a good deal of intensive re-education is necessary before a husband and wife are able to regard the subject of sex with that similarity of views which is so essential.

We always try to help our clients acquire an understanding of the general differences between the sexes. Not only do men and women differ in their bodies and physiques, but they are also likely to behave differently in many situations merely because they are male and female. In large and important areas of life men and women have different standards of value. Acceptance and comprehension of this fact could transform many marriages from failure to success.

Men need to understand the feelings of insecurity that exist in most women, their deep need to be loved and to be continuously assured of love. The strong, silent man who never tells his wife that he loves her because, he says, "I told her that when I asked her to marry me and it holds good until revoked," is a menace not only to his wife and to his marriage but also to his children. On the other hand, no wife wants the kind of husband described by the woman who complained, "When I say to my husband, 'Do you love me?' he thinks I'm asking for information!" It is widely acknowledged that the couples who marry most successfully and make the best sexual adjustment nearly always come from homes where fathers and mothers loved each other and displayed their affection openly. Anthropologist Ashley Montagu has even argued that children may be damaged if their parents sleep in separate beds. The use of the common bed is a symbol and evidence to children of the unity of the parental partnership. Our advice is: leave twin beds to the twins.

Intelligent men are observant and alert to the fluctuations in a woman's moods during the various phases of her monthly cycle. They understand and are sympathetic with a woman's greater sensitiveness to outside incidents and disturbances during love-making. Surveys indicate that at least one-fourth, possibly one-third, of all wives fail frequently, if not invariably, to reach a climax in sexual intercourse. This is a problem in which competent counseling is helpful, but an understanding husband can sometimes do more for his wife than anybody else.

Wives need to understand the more direct and more easily aroused sex drive of the male. In one sense, sexual intercourse might be said to represent an act of aggression on the part of the husband, an act of submission on the part of the wife. Although she may participate actively in the love-making, generally speaking the young wife's role is to be seductive and alluring while her husband's role is to lead. The male is expected to possess a greater degree of aggressiveness than the female in our society, and herein lies another important difference between the two sexes.

Out of this difference there often arises a situation which has perplexed and distressed many women. Husband and wife engage in a violent quarrel. At the conclusion of the angry scene, the husband desires intercourse. To him love-making would wipe out the memory of the quarrel. To his wife such a solution is unthinkable. The memory of the quarrel must be expiated, perhaps over a period of days, before she is in a loving mood. She interprets her husband's reaction as crude, vulgar, almost insulting, as was illustrated in several of the cases previously mentioned.

The explanation of the two sharply contrasted attitudes is quite simple. The increase in male aggressiveness produced by the quarrel has made him more ready for sexual intercourse, while the increase in her aggressiveness occurring in the same conflict has effected the opposite result, making her less ready. Awareness of this biological difference should lead to concessions on both sides.

Just as wives should understand the more direct, easily aroused masculine sex drive, men should remember that most women need to be wooed and won whenever they come together for intercourse. Too many husbands skip preliminary overtures and rush through to the final act only to wonder why their wives are unresponsive to them. Other men, who pride themselves on being good sexual partners and are eager to make sure their wives enjoy intercourse as much as they themselves do, need to learn there are occasions when a woman takes pleasure in giving herself to her husband without wishing to reach a climax herself. Husbands whose egos suffer because they cannot "satisfy" their wives in every union put a strain on their marriages and sometimes drive their wives into pretending satisfactions they do not feel, a pretense that can lead to nervousness and frustration for both.

In many marriages a pronounced slump sets in after fifteen or twenty years. Sexual relations become infrequent, monotonous, uninspiring. With the passage of time some slackening of sexual interest and activity is inevitable, but most marriages, after ten, twenty, or thirty years, would benefit by more frequent intercourse than usually occurs.

A middle-aged wife should keep herself as physically attractive as possible, and beyond this, it would often be advisable for her to take a more active and aggressive part in love-making than she took in her youth. She should make every attempt to be more seductive and stimulating than in earlier years. As a young wife perhaps her problem was to avoid stimulating her husband too much. In middle age her problem well may be to give him additional stimulation, and she should feel entirely free to use her imagination and experiment in this direction. Many men are oversensitive about their gradual decline in virility; a wise wife endeavors to protect her husband's vanity by praising and reassuring him on this point—the best reassurance she can offer is to make him feel she cannot resist him.

Even if a wife does not feel the desire for intercourse very strongly, for the sake of her marriage and her husband we advise that she try to arouse him sexually once or twice a week. If she hesitates because she regards such action as unfeminine or thinks her husband should take the initiative, she is damaging the relationship. By exerting herself to be appealing to her husband she probably will find her own interest in sex reviving; if neither he nor she reaches a climax, there is still great value in the closeness attained at a time of love-making. Too often the sexual side of marriage is allowed to wither away merely for lack of use.

Sometimes a wife's desire increases with the years, while her husband's amorous interests wane. It is important that both realize this fact so they can cooperate to maintain a solid sexual foundation in the marriage for their mutual benefit. It should be recognized that the menopause does not result in a lessening of sexual desire or capacity in a woman, except in unusual cases. Many women report that intercourse is more desired, more enjoyable, after the menopause than it was before. No woman should allow the sexual side of her marriage to deteriorate in the mistaken belief that the menopause is responsible.

A man's sexual drive is strongest, biologically, even before he is old enough to vote. It slows down steadily, though very slowly, all the rest of his life. Normally, a happily married husband is still having intercourse with his wife at least once or twice a month, well into his seventies, sometimes his eighties. If a man begins to misbehave in his middle years, it may be because his wife does not understand him (or herself) and is not doing her share in the marriage. In other cases the man in his forties and fifties has more leisure time but does not know how to employ the time; perhaps he and his wife have never built up a real partnership of interests and friendships, and boredom nudges him into drifting off alone and into trouble.

Every wife is entitled to some definite means of self-expression beyond fulfilling her functions as a wife and mother. She has the right to feel that she not only deserves recognition for success in her family circle but that independent of any relationship she is also a person on her own. In short, every wife needs an absorbing interest outside of the home—not absorbing enough to tempt her to neglect her duties, but absorbing enough to endow her with the feeling of completeness of personality that identifies her to herself and others as a unique individual. Many wives slide into a rut of cooking, cleaning, baby tending, diaper washing, and become dull to themselves, their husbands, and their youngsters.

Early in their lives women should learn to plan for sufficient time to cultivate outside, community interests. Their husbands should be willing to cooperate in this purpose, allotting money for baby sitters or expending some of their own time so their wives can escape from the house for a few hours. Many a wife is miserable in marriage simply because she has no variety, no change of interests at any time.

As cannot be too strongly emphasized, the way to make a failing marriage succeed is to play down the dissimilarities between a husband and wife and play up their similarities. The two can read together, study together, attend lectures together, but they seldom achieve closeness, companionship, similarity, unless they talk over with each other the many things they have learned, felt, and thought in common. Failure to communicate is almost universal in unhappy marriages. Even very intelligent married people admit to us that they find it almost impossible to discuss their sex life frankly with each other.

In talking things over, particularly where a difference of opinion exists, it is vital for a couple to focus on the real point at issue and not get off into personalities. To avoid introducing an unwelcome bit of personal truth at the wrong moment is to learn lesson A in the technique of side-stepping unnecessary and profitless marital unpleasantness. Without differences of opinion in a household there could be no improvement. But if these differences are to be managed in a constructive rather than a destructive way, the discussion should be limited to "the question before the house." Usually a domestic discussion is immediately diverted into a rehashing of other irrelevant disputes and thence into a name-calling contest. As soon as a quarrel starts, stop and ask yourself, "Wait a minute, what's the shouting about? What are we actually quarreling about?" Fix upon the point at issue, take action to deal constructively with that point, and leave your other grievances for some other time.

In some families it is worthwhile to hold a monthly, fact-finding session to clear the air. These couples set aside the "mensiversary" (not anniversary) of their wedding for the purpose. On the evening of the twenty-third of each month, say, they go out to dinner and after a pleasant meal in a quiet place they bring forth the topics they want to discuss. They keep a list during the month, probably eliminating a few items every time they add new ones. Over the dinner table, calmly and cooperatively (it is to be hoped), they talk out and agree on how to settle the various unsettled matters in their minds.

The attitudes husbands and wives have toward marriage outweigh every other factor in helping them achieve happiness. The men and women who regard marriage merely as an episode, a gamble, an opportunity to have their own way while the other fellow carries the load, are headed for the divorce court. If you look on marriage as the most important job you will ever tackle, if you determine you will invest all your resources in the job, if you decide you will let nothing short of a catastrophe interfere with your doing your level best, you will make a success of your marriage, and in marriage you will find the greatest happiness that human nature knows.

Index